The Search for Excellence

The Christian College in an Age of Educational Competition

THE SEARCH FOR EXCELLENCE

The Christian College in an Age of Educational Competition

ROBERT T. SANDIN

ISBN 0-86554-037-3

All books published by Mercer University Press are produced on acid-free paper which exceeds the minimum standards set by the National Historical Publications and Records Commission.

Library of Congress Cataloging in Publication Data

Sandin, Robert T.
The search for excellence.

Includes bibliographical references and index.
1. Education, Higher—1965- 2. Education, Humanistic. 3. Education (Christian theology) 4. Church and college. I. Title.
LB2322.S27 1982 377 82-12482
ISBN 0-86554-037-3

TABLE OF CONTENTS

Introduction **1**
Bench Marks of Quality 2
The Challenge of Excellence 6
New Vistas for Christian Colleges 10

Chapter 1 Faith and Learning **15**
Obstacles to Integration 17
The Rule of Faith 21
Fundamentals of Christian Belief 25
The Rule of Faith and Academic Freedom 35

Chapter 2 The Aims of Education **43**
John Henry Newman 45
John Dewey 48
Alfred North Whitehead 57
The Essence of Liberal Education 61

Chapter 3 The Task of the Christian College **63**
Cognitive Goals 64
Affective Goals 67
The Cultivation of Maturity 72

Chapter 4 General Education in the Christian College **79**
The Christian College and Liberal Education 82
Outcomes of General Education 85

Chapter 5 Structure in the Curriculum **105**
Specialized Education 105
The Principle of Parsimony 110
Education in Values 115

Chapter 6 The Christian Teacher **123**
Education without Instruction 123
Functions of the College Teacher 130
The Vocation of the Christian Teacher 143

Chapter 7 The Student Culture **147**
Institutional Aims and the Student Subculture 148
Admissions Policies and the Student Culture 153
Student Personnel Administration 160
Rights and Responsibilities of Students 163

Chapter 8 The Organization of Learning **171**
Signs of Administrative Malfunction 172
The Functions of Administration 177
The Cult of Efficiency 181
The College as Institution and Idea 184

Chapter 9 The Christian College and Public Support **191**
The Federal Interest in Higher Education 192
Sectarianism and Tax Support 196
A Guide for the Sectarian Conscience 202

Chapter 10 Ideology in an Age of Pluralism **217**
The Instability of Pluralism 219
The Recovery of Confidence 222
The Faith of a Christian Scholar 229

Bibliography **231**

Index **237**

INTRODUCTION

This book presents an analysis of the situation of the Christian colleges in an age of heightened educational competition, economic stress, and cultural pluralism. The analysis focuses on the problematic aspects of the situation. The book is written, however, out of a profound belief in the viability and worth of the distinctively Christian college. The discussion of weaknesses in these institutions is intended as the point of departure for reconstruction and development.

Judged by a general standard of excellence, many of the religiously oriented colleges (some observers would say "most") are weak in institutional resources, academic quality, and theological coherence. Little is to be gained by seeking to establish the reputation of these institutions by special pleading or by comparing them with even weaker systems. The recognition of the facts of their situation is the beginning of edification.

It is obvious that the circumstances in which American colleges and universities now find themselves are vastly different from those of even a generation ago. The increased complexity and diversity of scholarship, the prevalence of religious pluralism and ethical relativism, the physical and economic magnitude of an educational enterprise, and the growing public concern about the quality of education are all part of the new milieu which is presenting the colleges of the church with an assignment of unprecedented difficulty.

Many of these colleges, with their traditional emphasis on the liberal arts, will find it increasingly difficult to maintain a competitive position in the next twenty or thirty years. Yet the survival of the liberal arts is not the heart of the issue. As writers like Earl McGrath have long observed, the American liberal arts college has been perhaps the most adaptable and resourceful of educational institutions in surviving through periods of rapid social and economic change. The issue concerns rather the quality of education in these colleges. Survival as second-rate institutions without a distinctive educational mission would be only another form of death for the ideology which has inspired the Christian colleges in their past century of struggle and sacrifice.

The present crisis concerns the ability of the religiously oriented colleges to maintain that level of educational effectiveness which the competitiveness of the times demands. Some will compromise the theological dimensions of their mission in an effort to compete with secular institutions for students and support. Others will maintain their religious distinctiveness but will be too weak academically to exert a decisive influence. The question is how many of them will succeed in combining religious distinctiveness and academic excellence in a manner which will fulfill the promise of Christian higher education.

BENCH MARKS OF QUALITY

Studies of those institutions loosely characterized as Christian colleges and universities have been greatly hampered by the absence of precise definitions. Yet it is clear that until some basic distinctions are drawn, meaningful and useful generalizations about Christian higher education cannot be obtained. The Christian college movement is not monolithic and it is not possible to offer descriptions or recommendations which will apply equally to all church-related colleges and universities. Yet most studies have sought to treat Christian higher education as a composite and have failed to take note of major variations of institutional types within the movement.

One of the most systematic efforts at analysis was sustained recently by the Danforth Commission on Church Colleges and Universities.[1] The Commission sought a basis for a classification of types of church relationship in six different factors which it considered important: board composition, ownership, financial support, acceptance of denominational standards or use of denominational name, educational aims, and selection of faculty and administrative personnel. Using these criteria the Commission identified three major institutional types: The "defender of the faith" college, the "free Christian college," and the "nominally church related (nonaffirming though church-related) college."

The Commission's procedure is indicative of the kind of taxonomy which is needed, but its work requires further refinement and extension. Consideration should also be given to the taxonomical significance of factors of a more functional nature: for example, the degree of sectarianism in the controlling denomination or rule of faith, the manner in which a theological criterion is applied in faculty selection, the use of a religious or ethical test in student admission, the curricular requirement in religion, the frequency and character of the chapel services, and the nature of institutional controls over student behaviour. Factors like these are at least as important as the more formal ones used by the Danforth Commission.

Most informed observers will recognize something approximating the Danforth classifications as appropriate groupings for American colleges with religious origins or orientations. Of roughly 3,000 postsecondary institutions in the United States, about 800 maintain some form of religious orientation or were founded under a religious sponsorship. This number is about equally divided between Protestant and Catholic institutions, with only a scattering of institutions associated with other religious groups. About a hundred institutions originally founded under religious sponsorship have abandoned any such sponsorship and have explicitly disavowed any religious purpose. (I call these colleges "nonconfessing.") Another 400 or so fall into the Danforth category of nominally church-related colleges. There may be 300 colleges or universities, therefore, which are decisively controlled by a religious purpose or ideology, the precise form of this religious orienta-

[1]Manning M. Pattillo, Jr., and Donald M. Mackenzie, *Church-Sponsored Higher Education in the United States* (Washington DC: American Council on Education, 1966).

tion varying considerably, of course. It is safe to estimate that such colleges account for perhaps five percent of the total enrollment of American higher education.

Statistical analysis will show that, of these types of Christian college, the colleges of a more pronounced and conservative religious orientation tend to be weaker institutionally and academically than those of a less marked or more liberal religious orientation. Of course, the quality of an educational program does not always submit to quantitative measurement, and there are always individual institutions which diverge significantly from the average. Yet it cannot be denied that the sectarian and free-Christian colleges as a group do not compare favorably with the nominally church-related colleges, and especially with the nonconfessing colleges, when measured by the customary bench marks of educational quality. Their financial, library, instructional, and physical resources are significantly weaker, and they are accordingly less prepared to meet the educational and economic competition of our times.

A similar mix of quality and effectiveness can be found, of course, within the public sector. I am by no means saying that private or church-related colleges are generally weaker than state-supported institutions. On the contrary, the resources of many private institutions, including many of strong religious orientation, compare very favorably with those of public institutions of comparable size and scope. The point of this anlysis is rather that, within the group of colleges which recognize some form or degree of religious orientation, the colleges of more pronounced and more theologically conservative orientation tend to be weaker in institutional resources and academic quality than those which are only nominally church related or have effectively abandoned their church relationship. It is this circumstance that poses the challenge to the Christian colleges in the present period of heightened educational competition.

The sectarian colleges are generally of more recent founding, while the colleges in the other groups tend to become progressively older as one moves towards the non-confessing group. Of course, the age of a college is not in itself a measure of its effectiveness, but there is a significant correlation between the age of an educational institution and its reputation for quality. It takes many years for an institution to develop resources for excellence in educational service and a reputation as a superior institution ordinarily is established only over a long period of time. The sectarian colleges tend to be of more recent regional accreditation, and many of them are still seeking to become fully accredited.

Strongly religious colleges also tend to be somewhat smaller, on the average, than nominally church-related and non-confessing colleges. Of course, the size of a college is not a necessary indication of its strength. Some colleges of very small student bodies maintain instructional programs of the highest quality. But such colleges are the exception rather than the rule. There are positive advantages in smallness, indeed, but they relate more to the personal and social development of students and less to their scholastic development. Generally, the colleges with very small enrollments are forced to reduce the range of the curriculum or the level of instruction or both. It is only rarely that a very small college achieves excellence. Hence it is significant that the sectarian and free-Christian colleges tend to have considerably smaller enrollments than do the nominally church-related and non-confessing colleges. Almost half of the strongly religious colleges in the United States have enrollments of fewer than 600 students.

Tuition charges at the sectarian and free-Christian colleges tend to be considerably lower than at the nominally church-related and non-confessing colleges. This fact reflects the socioeconomic constituencies of the colleges in question, but it also means that the sectarian colleges generally lack the reputation which would allow them to command a higher tuition. The pattern of tuition charges is reflected, in turn, in the pattern of educational expenditures per full-time student. Colleges which are able to command a higher tuition can afford to spend more money per student in providing educational services of higher quality.

Again, library holdings tend to be smaller in the sectarian colleges and larger in the non-confessing colleges. About a third of the sectarian and free-Christian colleges satisfy minimal standards for a library collection as defined by the American Library Association, as compared with over half of the nominally church-related colleges and nine-tenths of the nonconfessing colleges. The average collection in the sectarian colleges runs in the neighborhood of 75,000 volumes.

The competence of the faculty, as measured by the percentage of the faculty holding the doctorate, tends to be considerably lower at the sectarian and free-Christian colleges than at the nominally church-related and nonconfessing colleges. The proportion is about one-third at the average sectarian college, well over one-half at the average nonconfessing college. A related progression in the levels of faculty compensation can also be observed. Average faculty salaries are lowest at the sectarian colleges and increase progressively as one moves towards the nonconfessing group. The difference is most conspicuous at the upper ranks. Admittedly, there are always some highly gifted, well-trained, and experienced teachers whose idealism may lead them to serve out their careers at institutions which pay them salaries much lower than their professional competence might command elsewhere, but by and large greater competence and higher compensation are correlative.

Finally, the value of the physical plant at the average sectarian or free-Christian college is about two-thirds of what it is at the nominally church-related colleges and about a third of what it is at the nonconfessing colleges. To some extent this difference reflects the difference in size already noted. But the data also exhibit the superiority and greater diversity of physical resources at the colleges of less marked religious orientation.

By all the quantifiable bench marks of quality, therefore, the colleges of more marked religious orientation tend to be measurably weaker than similar colleges of less sectarian orientation. Christian college representatives will, of course, continue to speak in glowing terms of the high quality of their programs and of the excellence to which they aspire. But their speech merely bears out the relativity of all such terms. An objective comparison using such quantifiable bench marks of quality as the foregoing has only limited validity, of course, but the facts of the comparison are undeniable. The Christian colleges are not as strong as they need to be to do well in the present period of heightened educational competition.

THE CHALLENGE OF EXCELLENCE

The difficulties under which the smaller liberal arts colleges have been laboring in recent years have been elaborated in many discussions.[2] The colleges for whom these difficulties are the most painful are

---

[2]See, for example, Lewis B. Mayhew, *The Smaller Liberal Arts College* (Washington, DC: Center for Applied Research in Education, 1962); Andrew Greeley, *From Backwater to Mainstream: A Profile of Catholic Higher Education* (New York: McGraw Hill, 1969); C. Robert Pace, *Education and Evangelism: A Profile of Protestant Colleges* (McGraw Hill, 1972); Alexander W. Astin and Calvin T. Lee, *The Invisible Colleges: A Profile of Small Private Colleges With Limited*

often those of the most pronounced and most conservative religious orientation. It is becoming increasingly clear that, from the standpoint of educational competition, the religious colleges of America are going to face a growing challenge in the coming decades.

Even in a condition of open competition these colleges would be hard pressed at the moment. But a number of societal factors are disrupting the openness of educational competition and are serving to tip the competitive balance further in the direction of the larger and less sectarian institutions. The private sector is feeling the competitive pinch, and the weaker private institutions are going to suffer from it the most.

The question is how the Christian colleges will meet the competitive challenge, not merely for the purpose of surviving, but also for the purpose of exercising a vital influence in American life and in the life of the church. This volume is written in the conviction that the challenge can be met through sacrificial effort to achieve efficiency and excellence and through faithful dedication to the religious and moral ideology which serves to give the Christian college its distinctive character.

The volume takes its stand on the Biblical principle that success in an hour of test is to be attained not through institutional accommodation to the forces of opposition, nor through reliance on material resources and economic strength, but through the faithfulness of the remnant. The prophetic faith warned against the temptation to look to Egypt for help in times of testing. So we warn that the viability of the Christian college as an instrument of the Church's witness and nurture depends not on the material help of Washington, but on the clarity and firmness of the church's own faith in the enterprise of Christian higher education.

What is at stake is the form in which the Christian faith will manifest itself in the academic world. For many years the Christian college has been one of the most effective forms in which the church has mobilized its educational ministries. Certainly there are other forms in which the church might serve in the academic community, but the Christian college is an institution which is irreplaceable in several respects. The decline of these colleges would result in a serious weakening of the church's witness in contemporary society. The crisis at the

---

Resources (McGraw Hill, 1972); Morris Keeton, *Liberal Arts Colleges* (McGraw Hill, 1971); Morris Keeton and Conrad Hilberry, *Struggle and Promise: A Future for Colleges* (McGraw Hill, 1969).

moment, however, is whether the Christian colleges can be maintained as an educational force of significance under present competitive conditions.

The test will be passed only if the leaders of the Christian churches in general and of the Christian colleges in particular have a clear concept of the place of religion in the life of scholarship, a strong sense of vocation about the ministry of Christian higher education, and the organizational capacity to achieve peak efficiency in the institutional pursuit of their objectives. There is a divine redemptive power which exceeds economic or material strength, but a condition of its efficacy is the existence of a remnant possessed of a vital and creative faith. The question is whether or not the Christian college movement will prove to constitute such a remnant.

As Nels Ferré has pointed out, God "educates the many through the few."[3] In matters of the spirit—in religion, in morality, in education—a creative and dedicated minority can exercise the control of a majority. Religion can be a decisive force in the community of learning. Religion can inform both the aims, the methods, and the content of higher education. But it is only a dynamic faith that can accomplish this control. Hence the crisis of the Christian colleges concerns the quality of their religiosity. Even if it comes in the form of an economic crisis, the test which these institutions face is a test of their faith.

In 1958 Jerald Brauer wrote that "the next quarter century might well determine whether the Christian college can or should continue to exist in American higher education." The Christian college movement, he declared, is reaching the point of no return.

> Either the Christian college should play the creative and distinctive role in American higher education it once played, or it should cease to exist. By "cease to exist" it is not implied that such institutions go out of existence, only that they become transformed into institutions that do not pretend to be what they are not.[4]

There are many Christian colleges which will manage to demonstrate, in the next quarter century, that they *can* continue to exist; the question may remain, however, whether these colleges *should* continue to exist.

---

[3]Nels F. S. Ferré, *Christian Faith and Higher Education* (New York: Harper, 1954), p. 93.

[4]Jerald C. Brauer, "The Christian College and American Higher Education," in *The Christian Scholar* 41: Special Issue (Autumn 1958): 234.

Civilization needs religion, and scholarship requires a religious understanding. But in society religious participation is too often imitative and perfunctory, and in scholarship the propositions of religious faith are too often indistinct and inconsistent. From the standpoint of an educator the requirement of our time is, therefore, as Bernard Loomer has put it, a presentation of religion which meets the requirements of intellectual respectability. This requirement

> places a heavy burden upon religious intellectuals. They must not only know their own subject matter as competently as other faculty members know theirs; they must also know their subject matter in relation and as relevant to other disciplines. But the fulfillment of this obligation will become a real possibility only to the extent that the academic representatives of the religious enterprise believe in the value of intellectual disciplines as such. They cannot compromise their devotion and vitiate their contribution by wondering whether they are really serving the church in their intellectual labors. They cannot afford to be swayed from their singleness of purpose by appeals from ministers and misguided laymen to make their work relevant to the so-called practical needs of the church. In one sense the fundamental intellectual issues of our time are the pressing practical problems of the church. The attempt to find adequate answers to these issues demands the devotion of men who regard the intellectual life as a calling. It is not an escape. It is not less real. And it is not a luxury for the church.[5]

In short, the task confronting the Christian colleges today is the achievement of excellence in both piety, learning, and educational service. These institutions must find ways of getting beyond the first plateau—the status of educational acceptability—to the higher level of educational excellence. For without excellence these institutions will not be qualified to meet the competitive test which they can expect to face. The dimensions of the assignment are stupendous, including at least the following tasks. The Christian colleges must

- articulate a comprehensive theory of the relationship between faith and learning and a coherent philosophy of education.
- realistically define their distinctive objectives and commit themselves unhesitatingly and sacrificially to the pursuit of those objectives.
- organize a curricular program suited to the effective realization of their distinctive educational objectives.
- recruit a corps of Christian teacher-scholars whose professional

[5]Bernard Loomer, "Religion and the Mind of the University," in Amos N. Wilder, ed., *Liberal Learning and Religion* (New York: Harper, 1951), pp. 165, 166.

skill and Christian personalities combine to make for superior teaching.

- successfully exploit the opportunities for personal growth which are afforded by a Christian campus culture.
- secure the highest level of organizational coherence and efficiency through effective college-wide planning and enlightened administration and assemble the physical resources needed to conduct their programs.
- honestly solicit public support of their programs on the basis of acceptance of their controlling purposes.

Will the successful performance of these tasks guarantee a significant role for the Christian colleges in the future? Nothing like that can be guaranteed. But these tasks are inherent in the responsibility of the faithful remnant in the world of education. Certainly an institution which discharges its responsibilities in each of the above respects will have good reason to exist. It will serve a unique role in American higher education. Whether or not it does survive, at least it can be said that it should survive. In many ways such a college will afford the finest opportunity for higher education to be obtained anywhere.

This book is written in the hope that conservative Christian colleges may be helped to become clearer about their task and that the Christian churches may be helped to become more concerned about the future of the system of Christian higher education. It is written in Ferré's conviction that "higher education, in order to climb in the direction of its own summit, needs to become resolutely Christian. To make it as Christian as possible is as profound a task as has ever been offered to man by God."[6]

NEW VISTAS FOR CHRISTIAN COLLEGES

It is undeniable that the Christian colleges face mounting pressures today. Yet it is not the chain of refractory circumstances which is the real problem of Christian higher education. It is what Denis Baly has called the failure of nerve. The real problem of the Christian colleges is the loss of poise, the break-down of self-confidence, the erosion of faith. They are often too vague about their distinctive aims, too diffident about their real strengths while being at the same time too

---

[6]Ferré, *Christian Faith and Higher Education*, p. 245.

oblivious of their real weaknesses. Lacking adequate operational models of their own design, they have often resorted to imitation of educational patterns which serve them badly. In short, they lack a functional ideology which will equip them for meeting the current challenge with courage and conviction.

The Christian church in America had an opportunity in the twentieth century to realize the promise of Christian higher education on a grand scale. That opportunity has been missed, and it has probably been missed for a long time to come. It may have been missed for all history. Rarely have the political, social, and economic forces at work in a society combined to afford the opportunity to establish a network of Christian colleges on the scale that was possible in the United States in the first half of the twentieth century. The environment of political freedom, wealth, cultural and social pluralism, the frontier, and expanding technology created for the American church a unique and perhaps unrepeatable opportunity to fulfill the promise of a program of higher education that is both intellectually rigorous and Christian. All that remains now, however, is the opportunity to establish here and there an institutional example of what was once possible as a wide-ranging system of institutions.

Yet the opportunity that remains can be missed, too. The implementation of the idea of a Christian college on even a limited scale requires talent, dedication, and resources which this generation, too, may be unable to commit to the task. For the next two decades or so, the opportunity to establish strong Christian colleges remains a practical and real one. Before long, however, the church will find it extremely difficult to broaden the institutional base of its educational ministries. I am predicting that the church's performance in the next two decades will establish the level of its operations in the field of higher education for the greater part of the twenty-first century.

The idea of a Christian college as developed by the forerunners in the Christian college movement needs to be adapted to the changed educational and social circumstances of our own times. One of the lessons of history, Will and Ariel Durant have remarked, is the discovery that, "Civilization is not inherited; it has to be learned and earned by each generation anew." Thomas Carlyle once said that each generation must write history in its own idiom. Culture, as the accumulated wisdom and art which the human race has developed to deal with the problems of living, is not something given to us for the taking; it is something which we must create for ourselves out of materials which we are able to draw from the past.

The idea of a Christian college is one of the unique contributions of America to educational history. During the last century the Christian college movement in America has produced an educational theory and a system of institutions that are without precedent in any other time or place. The Christian college was the creation of a generation of churchmen and educators who needed an institutional model for addressing a shared set of educational and spiritual concerns. Our generation shares many of those same concerns, and the traditional idea of the Christian college holds a number of suggestions for useful ways in which we might approach our own task. But we shall have to go over the issues again, in our own particular way and in relation to our own unique circumstances, and we shall need to create an institutional model which meets our peculiar needs. If, instead, we insist on the authority of an anachronistic model, we shall only succeed in making ourselves and the traditions we value irrelevant.

The advocates of Christian higher education in the present generation must recognize that the educational situation in which they must implement their educational idea is radically different from the one which confronted preceding generations of Christian educators. The Christian college of 1980 cannot be modeled after the church colleges of the nineteenth century or of the 1920's or even of the 1950's. Our generation needs a variant of the traditional model, true to the ideal which inspired the founders of the Christian college movement, but applied in radically different social circumstances.

Secular culture is now more important than the church in determining the character of American higher education. Once the church colleges thought it their aim to judge secular culture in the name of Christ. Now a church association causes embarrassment to many academicians, and when the church does acknowledge its function in the field of education it is often to stress its role as the agent and ally of society. The colleges have come to be viewed not merely as places for the nurture and discipline of intelligence, but also as instruments for social reconstruction and reform. Young people have come to look upon education primarily as a tool of economic advancement and vocational and professional development; and law-makers have come to regard the colleges and universities, in Clark Kerr's phrase, as "a prime instrument of national policy."

These are times which call for an education which equips an individual to deal with the unexpected. What is needed, Robert Theobald has said, is an education which deals not only with the actual, or even with the possible, but also with the impossible—that is, an education which prepares an individual to deal with what is now the unknown. In times of revolutionary change (such as our times *are*) static educational programs produce only obsolescence and irrelevance.

In the present environment, a Christian college must resort to approaches which could not have been contemplated in an earlier generation. The Christian college today has an assignment which is, in many ways, infinitely more difficult and complex than the one which was given to its forbears. At the same time the Christian college has the same task, namely to design, organize and conduct educational programs for the purpose of enabling students to approach scholarship, career preparation, and living from the perspective of Christian ideals of faith and conduct.

A new model is needed for the Christian college, adapted to the requirements of a new time. In meeting the new challenge the Christian college needs

- to adapt its programs to serve a wider range of career-preparation needs of students.
- to implement a pragmatic approach to teaching, adapted to the requirements of student development.
- to find ways to preserve its distinctive qualities of piety and faith while accomodating a greater degree of diversity in the makeup of the campus population.
- to find ways to work cooperatively with secular organizations and governmental agencies in the pursuit of shared goals.

The mission of a Christian college is to exhibit the integration of faith and learning, to cultivate the development of the young in the direction of Christian maturity, and to equip the church of Jesus Christ for its ministry in the world. The need for such colleges in both society and the church has never been greater. This book is dedicated to fostering a new sense of vocation about the enterprise of Christian education and a new understanding of what such an enterprise requires in a changing time.

Chapter 1

FAITH AND LEARNING

The fundamental issue facing Christian higher education today is a theological one. Financial problems are mounting, and the development of adequate resources calls for strenuous exertion, yet these are not the fundamental problems. The fundamental problem for the Christian colleges is that of actually achieving their professed aim of integrating faith with learning, since if they fail to perform this function, they have no principle by which to justify their continued existence in an age of heightened educational competition.

An educational institution is a Christian college if and only if it is designed, organized, and conducted to integrate a Christian understanding with scholarship and to equip persons for Christian vocation. This idea of the Christian college should be a familiar one to those who know the literature of Christian higher education. Howard Lowry has expressed it by arguing that in the Christian college religion is viewed not as "a fragment or phase of the educational process, but its permeating factor and its inner unity. Christian education is thus a study of all of life for the discovery of divine truth."[1] D. Elton Trueblood has expressed it in his contention that what distinguishes a Christian college from other types of educational institution is "the penetration

[1]Howard Lowry, *The Mind's Adventure* (Philadelphia: Westminster Press, 1950), p. 104.

of the total college life by the central Christian convictions."[2] And Nels Ferré has expressed it by saying that a Christian college is one in which "theology is avowedly the center of the curriculum," one in which "academic life centers in the total life of the Christian community. . . . The vocation of the (Christian) college is to find for the world, and to help the world to do, the will of God. . . . A college is Christian only if it is a fellowship of inquiry under God."[3]

Such definitions express an educational ideal which is by no means universally endorsed, either in circles of American higher education generally or in circles of Christian higher education in particular. The celebrated Harvard report on general education, for example, tended to look upon this collegiate ideal as anachronistic and scarcely practicable under modern conditions. A century ago, the Harvard committee recognized, colleges might have hoped to find in Christian theology the principles which would give meaning and unity to the various parts of the curriculum, but "religion is not now for most colleges a practicable source of intellectual unity."[4]

The Harvard committee based its judgment on an assessment of the tension between sectarianism and democracy in America. What made it impracticable for the colleges to seek a sectarian principle for unifying their educational endeavors was the growth of public support of higher education. But it has become apparent that the problem also has a deeper intellectual root. Newman's claims about the integrative function of theology with respect to the sciences inspires little conviction in academic circles today. Even among the faculty and administration of church-related colleges there are many who neither understand nor endorse the claim that the aim of the Christian college is to exhibit the integration of Christianity with all of learning. Ferré said that the college which fulfilled his description of a fully Christian college did not exist, but we may add that there are also fewer and fewer colleges which even aspire to his ideal.

---

[2]D. Elton Trueblood, "The Marks of a Christian College," in John Paul von Grueningen, ed., *Toward a Christian Philosophy of Higher Education* (Philadelphia: Westminster Press, 1957), p. 163. Cf. his *The Idea of a College* (New York: Harper, 1959).

[3]Ferré, *Christian Faith and Higher Education*, pp. 121-35.

[4]Report of the Harvard Committee, *General Education in a Free Society* (Cambridge, MA.: Harvard University Press, 1945), p. 39.

Those who hope for the progress of Ferré's concept in American education are offered but little encouragement by the picture of church-supported higher education drawn by the Danforth Commission on Church Colleges and Universities. The Commission sought to measure the degree to which church-related colleges were succeeding in enabling their students to develop a vital religious perspective from which to view learning, and concluded:

> A few church colleges are engaged in significant demonstrations, but, on the whole, church-related higher education is not doing much better in helping students face fundamental questions than are other institutions. Much of the confusion and uncertainty regarding this responsibility which one finds in public and independent colleges and universities, and indeed in the world at large, is also present in church-related institutions of higher learning.[5]

Two patterns are all too typical. On the one hand, there are colleges which have allowed their distinctive religious character to be eroded until they have been assimilated, for all practical purposes, into the secular culture. On the other hand, there are colleges which have given place to dogmatism or anti-intellectualism and have become the scene of inner tension and sometimes open conflict between the adherents of an unbending theological dogma and liberal scholars of independent mind. What is generally lacking in both groups is the sense of the essential unity of faith and learning, derived from a combination of clear theological understanding and free inquiry.

OBSTACLES TO INTEGRATION

In 1951 Bernard M. Loomer, then dean of the Divinity School of the University of Chicago, wrote: "The nature of religion today and the nature of education today are such that the problem of 'religion in higher education' is surrounded with almost insurmountable obstacles."[6] Loomer expressed doubt that any fundamental solution would be forthcoming in a short time. His judgment has proved an accurate one, for if anything the difficulties have only increased with the passage of time. The problem is rooted in a cultural and social context which has been long in developing and which is unlikely to change in the immediate future.

---

[5]Pattillo and MacKenzie, *Church-Sponsored Higher Education*, p. 100.

[6]Loomer, "Religion and the Mind of the University," p. 147.

The Situation in the Church

There is mounting evidence that the Christian churches are losing their influence in American life. For almost two decades following World War II the churches felt the flush of success. Now the churches are experiencing a reversal of that trend. "Probably no major institution in American life," say Patillo and Mackenzie, "faces greater uncertainty than the church as to its function and the validity of its premises in a changing society."[7]

Harsh criticisms are being directed at the churches both from without and from within. The unchurched are becoming increasingly vocal in scorning what they regard as the irrelevance of the church's preoccupations. But there is also lamentation among the devout. The triviality of much religious activity is bemoaned by clergy and laity alike. Even churchmen and seminary students harbor deep reservations about the work of the churches which they serve.

The problem of religion in higher education is, in large part, the problem of religion in the modern age. This generation seems to be in a period of reappraisal, doubtful about the relevance of religion in its traditional forms but unable to identify new forms which will be found more suitable. The problem of the church college is the same as that of the church itself. Religion must be more than pious sentiment, more than devout feeling, more than churchly activity, and more than blind faith if it is to become a controlling force in the lives of thinking people.

In the present condition of religion and of culture, however, religion is, as Albert Schweitzer once put it, without the power to command. Religion, said Schweitzer, is not a force in the spiritual life of our age.

> There is still religion in the world, there is much religion in the church, there are many pious people among us. Christianity can still point to works of love and to social works of which it can be proud. There is a longing for religion among many who no longer belong to the churches. I rejoice to concede this. *And yet we must hold fast to the fact that religion is not a force.*[8]

---

[7]Pattillo and Mackenzie, *Eight Hundred Colleges Face the Future*, p. 49. Cf. ch. 8, "Religion in America," in the final report of the commission, Pattillo and Mackenzie, *Church-Sponsored Higher Education,* pp. 124ff.

[8]Albert Schweitzer, "Religion and Modern Civilization," *The Christian Century* (21 November 1934): 1483.

The Situation in Education

The integration of faith and learning is made doubly difficult by certain conditions in the system of higher education, which obstruct intellectual unity irrespective of religion.

The Fragmentization of Scholarship. One of these conditions is the growing fragmentization of scholarship and the decentralization of educational planning. The emerging pattern is the price which has to be paid for specialization in a complex society. The life of society has become so complex and scholarship has become so diversified that competence now can be conceived only within a relatively narrow scope. College and university administrators, seeking to recruit what are sometimes called "generalists," whose training will be suited to the demands of undergraduate teaching, sometimes complain about the influence of the graduate schools, which, they say, produce only narrowly specialized scholars. The nature of research in our time, however, is such that the established pattern of advanced study is inevitable. If nothing else, the sheer volume of scholarly publication guarantees the continuation of the restricted focus of research. Advanced scholars are required to concentrate their attentions narrowly; yet it is on such scholars that undergraduate education must depend for the conduct of instructional programs.

If integration is actually to occur in learning, those who teach will have to possess not only a full mastery of the subject-matter of their special interest, but also a knowledge of that subject-matter in relation to other disciplines. But the chances are not great that an American scholar will emerge from graduate study with even the disposition to seek such a correlated understanding. Even in small colleges, faculty members are finding it difficult even to communicate with one another unless they share a common area of specialized study, and the tendency toward departmental isolation is magnified on larger campuses.

If integration is to take place on the foundation of a common religious faith, those who teach will need to be able to correlate the subject-matter of their special interest not only with other liberal disciplines but also with religious ideologies. But there is a tendency for scholars to think of religious thought as another specialized function. Scholars who have not engaged in special studies in the field of religion tend to withdraw from the discussion of the relevance of religion in education on the ground that they are not theological specialists.

Religious education tends to be consigned to departments of religion.

Currently there is much talk about the integration of learning in higher education, but what is most often in evidence on college campuses is a composite of fragmentary learning experiences. Scarcely anywhere is there an organic unity in education; usually an education is a collection of isolated experiences drawn from disparate contexts. Nor is the situation likely to change fundamentally in the foreseeable future. These patterns are also in evidence in Christian colleges, although sometimes to a lesser degree, and they constitute a major obstacle to the actual achievement of the aims of Christian higher education.

Authority in Education. Another obstacle to integration is the concept of authority which pervades most educational institutions. In educational theory authority can be justified only on the basis of competence. With the fragmentization of scholarship it has become all but impossible, however, to achieve the breadth of understanding which would justify the exercise of educational authority in a comprehensive scope. The exercise of authority over a college as a whole presents the appearance of arbitrariness, for it is assumed that no one can know enough to decide the larger institutional questions on the basis of reliable understanding. This assumption is one root of the typical hostility towards college administrators among scholars—this together with resentment over the administrator's presumed role in determining the scholar's salary and destiny. Most faculty members assume that administrative authority, outside of a very narrow province, will inevitably be arbitrary and biased.

In the nature of American higher education, however, institutions depend heavily on administrative initiative for the coordination of the various parts of the educational program. Yet if that initiative is thought to be arbitrary, one cannot expect much of the result. Most college faculty members resign themselves to the situation and are content to care as well as they can for the welfare of the activities of their own departments. The nature of the exercise of educational authority seems to them to make it idle for a scholar to be occupied to any significant degree with extra-departmental and interdisciplinary concerns.

Current trends in both religion and education, therefore, pose substantial obstacles to the realization of the ideals of Christian higher education. The integration of faith and learning is becoming an increasingly difficult undertaking. Faith is not a controlling force in the total life of our society, and it is therefore not surprising that it should not be a controlling force in our educational centers. There are many ambiguities in the religious situation, and the impression is often created that theological definitions are hopelessly vague and contradictory. It is not clear what is meant by saying that faith may be the point of integration for learning. And furthermore, the trend toward fragmentization and decentralization in higher education makes integration difficult on any basis.

THE RULE OF FAITH

The first step towards integration of the educational program at a Christian college is the achievement of a clear theological consensus. If the fundamental issue facing the Christian colleges today is a theological one, then the first task presented to their faculties and administrations is the task of theological clarification. What is needed for this purpose is not so much a comprehensive and technically adequate theological exposition as a set of working theological definitions, an articulation of Christian doctrine which exhibits its applicability in the educational enterprise. A Christian college cannot depend upon professional theologians alone to produce such a formula; the theological analysis which is demanded is incumbent upon the entire intellectual community.

The study of the theological basis of Christian higher education must begin with a consideration of the nature and content of the rule of Christian faith, that is, the criterion by reference to which the Christian faith is to be distinguished from alternative belief systems. The character and practice of a Christian college will be significantly influenced by its understanding of the content of the rule of faith, of the method by which that rule is defined, and of the manner in which the rule is applied in the governance of the institution. Clarity on these matters is the foundation of everything in Christian higher education.

The dominant opinion in church-related institutions of higher education, and in contemporary theology, is that it is not possible to define a rule of Christian faith. We must therefore begin by seeking to establish the possibility of a rule of Christian faith against two kinds of doubt: the doubt which is based on a theological concept of the nature of Christianity and the doubt which is based on an educational concept of the nature of academic freedom.

Biblicism

Despite their other differences, theological Biblicists and theological subjectivists are in agreement that there can be no rule of Christian faith. Biblicism contends that no rule of faith is possible or necessary except the Bible itself. The genius of Protestantism, it is often said, is its insight concerning the use of Scripture as the sufficient guide for Christian faith and practice.

But no segment of Protestantism and no school or system of theology has ever actually succeeded in making the whole Bible authoritative as the Word of God. As soon as the biblicist principle concerning the authority of Scripture is enunciated, interpretation proceeds to prescribe a hermeneutical principle which limits the range of permissible biblical understanding. Of course, it may be claimed that the hermeneutical principle is itself derived by an inductive analysis of the biblical materials, but whatever its source the doctrinal emphasis of that principle becomes a criterion for judging between conflicting biblical interpretations.

Within biblical scholarship, therefore, a rule of faith has always operated. As W. P. Paterson put it in an earlier generation, "It appears as matter of historical fact that for Protestantism the actual norm of doctrine has never been the Scriptures in their entirety, but has ever been a scheme of saving truth extracted from Scripture."[9]

The present theological crisis in Protestantism is not the discredit into which the doctrines of plenary inspiration and verbal inerrancy have fallen. The crisis is a much deeper one. It lies in the understanding of what is the essential content of the biblical message. It is at this level that the faithful church should take up its polemic. Contending for a certain doctrine *about* the Bible is of secondary importance at best; what is of primary importance is contending for the system of saving truth expressed *in* the Bible.

The Reformers' principle that the Bible is the touchstone of orthodoxy may have been highly relevant in a time when the Scriptures were regarded as an insufficient and incomplete record of revelation, requiring supplementation by an allegedly coordinate ecclesiastical tradition or philosophical scheme. But outside of that kind of apologetic context, the declaration that "the Bible is our creed" tends to be an evasion.

---

[9]W. P. Paterson, *The Rule of Faith* (London: Hodder and Stoughton, 1933), p. 170.

The claim is analogous to the rule, "Truth is the standard by which opinions should be judged." I do not wish to take issue with either statement, but neither is illuminating as a criterion. Truth is no norm until it has been possessed, and the Bible is no norm until it has been understood. We may say with Paterson, therefore, "It is now a legitimate, and even a necessary demand, that any system of theology should give an account of the conception of Christianity which governs its dogmatic use of Scripture."[10]

Subjectivism

But if biblicists have reservations about the possibility of a rule of Christian faith, so do those theologians who may be described, for want of a better label, as subjectivists. There can be no rule of Christian faith, it is said by these theologians, because there is no set of dogma which is essential to a religious consciousness.

The fountainhead of this sort of theological perspective in recent times is Schleiermacher, who based his polemical defense of religion to its cultured despisers on the contention that a true belief is not the summit of religion, nor is it to a set of beliefs that one is converted when one becomes religious. "It matters not," said Schleiermacher, "what conceptions a man adheres to, he can still be pious. His piety, the divine in his feeling, may be better than his conception, and his desire to place the essence of piety in conception only makes him misunderstand himself." Religion, Schleiermacher argues, is not to be confused with the knowledge which belongs to theology as a science. Indeed, religious faith in its essence has nothing essentially to do with the knowledge of theological propositions. "If ideas and principles are to be anything," Schleiermacher says, "they must belong to knowledge, which is a different department of life from religion."[11]

Schleiermacher's claim that faith cannot be conceptualized has exerted a profound influence upon contemporary theology. His understanding of the nature of religious faith has commended itself to a great many religious intellectuals, who have been distressed to discover what they regard as contradictions between the traditional dogma of religion, as literally interpreted, and modern secular scholarship. The

---

[10]Ibid., p. 171.

[11]Friedrich Schleiermacher, *On Religion*, tr. John Oman (New York: Harper Torchbooks, 1958), p. 46.

supposed conflict between religion and science may be resolved, they have suggested, if it can be agreed that religion, properly understood, involves no propositions of science.

Paul Tillich, for example, has contended that religion and science *cannot* be in conflict, for the reason that they belong to essentially different orders of experience and of meaning. One order is cognitive, he seems to imply, the other non-cognitive. "Science can conflict only with science, and faith only with faith; science which remains science cannot conflict with faith which remains faith. One dimension of meaning is not able to interfere with another dimension."[12] Tillich's theological method assumes that the authenticity of faith is never to be judged from the point of reference of a theological symbol. Strong doubts about provisions of the church's doctrinal formulations are, in his view, entirely compatible with an authentic faith.[13] It is in the psychological dimension, rather, that the authenticity of faith is finally vindicated. Faith is the state of being ultimately concerned.

The assessment of these pronouncements on the nature of faith requires some distinctions. In one sense Tillich's analysis is entirely correct, but in another sense it is entirely wrong. We must distinguish, for example, between dogmatics and symbolics, between the rule of faith and the creeds. It should be agreed on every hand that no creedal formulation may be regarded as finally authoritative and ultimate and that the revision of the church's doctrinal articles is a continuing necessity. But to deny that the creeds are authoritative is one thing; to deny that there is a rule of Christian faith is another. Understood in the first context, Tillich's denial of the possibility of stating the propositional content of Christian faith is entirely correct; understood in the second context, it is entirely wrong.

Similarly, we must distinguish between the propositions which *are* essential to the Christian teaching and those which are *thought*, in a given time and place, to be essential. The history of Christian apologetics has been marred by misplaced polemics, by opposition to scientific findings in the name of what has been mistakenly presumed to be an article of faith. Tillich's warning about the tendency of Protestantism to "elevate its concrete symbols to absolute validity" is certainly well

---

[12]Paul Tillich, *Dynamics of Faith* (London: George Allen & Unwin Ltd., 1957), p. 82.

[13]Ibid., p. 22.

taken. But it is something else to declare that the authenticity of Christian piety has nothing at all to do with what one believes about God or the world.

Again, we must distinguish between the declaration that Christian faith is not merely assent to the truth of certain theological propositions and the declaration that there are no theological propositions assent to which is necessary to Christian faith. To the first declaration practically everyone, on all sides of the theological spectrum, would agree. Faith is more than credence, more than mere assurance concerning the truth of certain propositions. But it is one thing to say that to be a Christian is not simply to believe something; it is another thing to say that there are no propositions which one must believe to be a Christian. The first statement is certainly true, the second is certainly false.

Whether or not Christianity and science are in conflict cannot be decided a priori. It may be the case that there is not, *in point of fact*, any conflict between any properly derived proposition of Christian theology and any empirically confirmed proposition of natural science, but this is not to say that there *could* not be a conflict. As long as there are theological propositions, there remains the theoretical possibility that such propositions might be inconsistent with the propositions of the sciences. Hence it is only by denying that there are any religious propositions—and thus by declaring that religious faith has nothing whatever to do with assenting to theological propositions—that one can maintain (with Tillich) the *impossibility* of a conflict between religion and science. But to deny propositional content to Christian faith is the end of Christianity as a system of belief.

FUNDAMENTALS OF CHRISTIAN BELIEF

Against both biblicism and subjectivism, therefore, we maintain the indispensability of the rule of faith in Christian theology. Neither biblicism nor subjectivism is an acceptable account of the criterion for theological belief. Biblicism is unacceptable because we cannot dispense with a concept of Christianity by reference to which biblical interpretations are to be criticized. Subjectivism is unacceptable because we cannot dispense with the propositional character of Christian doctrine as a system of belief. Contrary to both biblicism and subjectivism, Christian theology must operate with the assumption of a rule of faith as the point of reference for theological criticism.

The fundamental problem for Christian theology then becomes that of articulating such a rule. Serious questions remain, however, about the possibility of a rule of faith which will be determinative for educational policy and practice. What is the content of the rule of Christian faith? What is the theological method which permits acceptance of a rule of faith without dogmatism? How can a rule of faith be reconciled with the spirit of freedom and openness which is essential not only in scholarship but also in all true religion? The answers to such questions are to be found in a proper understanding of the methodology for defining the rule of faith. Lack of clarity concerning this methodology is responsible for most of the confusion which exists in circles of higher education concerning the place of theology in the life of learning.

"The real goal of theological quest," W. P. Paterson says, "is a material norm consisting of the central and guaranteed body of Christian truth."[14] In order to define a rule of faith which can be applied in the practical life of the church, theology must determine a criterion for distinguishing between those articles of faith which are fundamental for Christianity and those which are not. The distinction between fundamental and non-fundamental doctrines is a historic one for Protestantism. It is central to the theologies of Calvin, Luther, and even Wesley. Theological analysis in the Christian colleges today needs to be based on a recovery of this historic insight.

For Calvin the distinction between necessary and nonessential doctrines is the foundation of the unity of the church.

> Not all the articles of true doctrine are of the same sort. Some are so necessary to know that they should be certain and unquestioned by all men as the proper principle of religion. Such are: God is one; Christ is God and the Son of God; our salvation rests on God's mercy; and the like. Among the churches there are other articles of doctrine disputed which still do not break the unity of faith. . . . A difference of opinion over these nonessential matters should in no wise be the basis of schism among Christians.[15]

Agreement on all points of doctrine would be desirable, of course, but Calvin sees no real prospect of such agreement. He is prepared to accept error and delusion in matters where lack of true knowledge may

[14]Paterson, *The Rule of Faith*, p. 26.

[15]*Institutes of the Christian Religion*, IV, 1, 12.

be "without harm to the sum of religion and without loss of salvation." The unity and ministry of the church, he says, are based on agreement concerning those matters which are essential to the gospel.

Wesley is sometimes regarded as having a low regard for the importance of theology, on the grounds, as he himself put it, that Christianity is "not so much a way of believing as it is of acting." Orthodoxy, he said, "is, at best, but a very slender part of religion, if it can be allowed to be any part of it at all."[16] But such statements must be viewed against the background of Wesley's distinction—so important for his ecumenism—between what he calls "opinions" and what he calls "essential doctrines." In matters of opinion—that is, concerning church government, modes of worship, and many details of doctrine—"which do not strike at the root of Christianity," he says, "we think and let think." Schilling explains, in his commentary on Wesley's distinction:

> The Christian is free to accept or reject any belief which does not hamper the grace of God or the human love which this grace calls forth. But by the same token there are beliefs which are central and necessary. . . .
>
> Even the "right heart" turns out on definition to include doctrinal elements. It involves not only love toward God and neighbor and other deeply personal aspects of the Christian life, but also belief in God "and his perfections"—"his eternity, immensity, wisdom, power; his justice, mercy, and truth"—belief in Jesus Christ and submission to the righteousness of God through faith in Christ, with renunciation of all one's own goodness.[17]

In matters of "essential doctrine" Wesley draws a clear line separating those who are in the faith from those who are not. The distinction allows Wesley to preserve a keen concern about purity of Christian doctrine, while remaining aloof from controversy over details and nonessentials. Quarreling about details, he warns, will only create schism in the church and will hinder the work of Christ. The church includes all those who are Christ's, even though they may hold different theological and ecclesiastical views at many points.

This same distinction explains Wesley's opposition to theological exclusivism in all its forms, while he preserves an unreserved commit-

---

[16]In an address in 1859, quoted by S. Paul Schilling, *Methodism and Society in Theological Perspective* (New York: Abingdon Press, 1960), pp. 25, 26.

[17]Ibid., pp. 32, 33.

ment to what he regards as the central affirmations of the Christian faith. His point of view is expressed in the ecumenical motto: "In essentials, unity; in non-essentials, liberty; in all things, love."

For Luther the distinction between fundamental and non-fundamental doctrines is important not so much for purposes of theological exposition as for ecclesiastical administration. His terminology grows out of his debate with the papists, whom he accuses of adding to the gospel (the Word of God) the "doctrines of men" (human tradition). The authority of the Word of God he never questions; he rejects the authority of the "doctrines of men" until they have been shown to be in conformity with the Word of God.

The distinction is developed more systematically, however, by Luthardt, working within the tradition of Lutheranism. The assumption which controls Luthardt's definition of this distinction serves, indeed, to indicate the methodology by which the content of the rule of Christian faith should be construed. The distinction between what is fundamental and what is non-fundamental in Christian doctrine must be made in the light of an understanding of what Christianity is. Luthardt begins by assuming that Christianity is essentially a gospel of redemption, and he identifies as "fundamental" whatever must be believed for the gospel to be efficacious for the redemption of an individual. "Christianity," he says, "is, on the one side, the salvation of sinners in Christ Jesus; on the other, the faith which assures us hereof."[18] The fundamental articles of Christian faith, then, are those, without the knowledge of which no one can be saved (the "primary fundamental" articles) and those the resolute denial of which involves the forfeiture of salvation (the "secondary fundamental" articles), while the non-fundamental articles are those which one may be ignorant of or deny and still be saved.

Paterson's conception of the rule of faith is based on a similar assumption concerning the essential character of Christianity as a message of redemption:

> Our conception of the authentic content of recorded truth would be that it is the knowledge of God and man, and of the acts of God, which was needed to ensure the efficacy of the Christian religion. On the other hand, for all religious doctrine which merely serves a specula-

---

[18]Christopher Ernest Luthardt, *Apologetic Lectures on the Saving Truths of Christianity*, tr. Sophia Taylor (Edinburgh: T. & T. Clark, 1868), p. 29.

> tive interest no higher claim will be made than that at most it represents sound reasoning upon data of revelation, or probable opinion upon various problems that start up on the circumference of the religious sphere. In other words, the intellectual content of the revelation attested in Scripture consists in such knowledge as "maketh wise unto salvation"; and no provision can be depended on for the satisfaction of intellectual curiosity in regard to problems of which, without detriment to our religious standing and our spiritual life, we can afford to be ignorant.[19]

The methodology for defining the intellectual content of the Christian faith is determined by our concept of the nature of Christianity. If, as Schleiermacher says, what differentiates Christianity from other religions is that it has reference to the redemption wrought in Jesus of Nazareth,[20] then the fundamental content of the Christian message consists of that series of propositions without which there is no gospel of redemption. Included in the summary of the fundamentals of the Christian gospel would be propositions about man and about God which are implied in the possibility and necessity of redemption.

Man

In the first place, evangelical theology declares, the possibility and necessity of redemption imply certain assumptions regarding the condition of man. On the one hand, redemption is possible because man is a being of extraordinary dignity, made to bear the likeness of God, a being capable of fellowship with God. But on the other hand, redemption is necessary because God's image in man has been effaced through man's free choice. Indeed, the needy condition is a universal one, affecting all men. It is also a desperate one, allowing no hope of restoration apart from God's act.

Evangelical theology holds that once God acts redemptively it is possible for any person to appropriate the benefits of his grace. What the Christian message emphasizes is that man is redeemable. The gospel declares the availability of a divine power which enables anyone to become obedient to God's righteous will.

God

The gospel also declares that God is both able and willing to redeem

[19]Paterson, *The Rule of Faith*, pp. 27, 28.

[20]Friedrich Schleiermacher, *The Christian Faith* (Edinburgh: T. & T. Clark, 1928), p. 52.

man. Evangelical theology therefore presupposes some convictions about God—that he exists in a transcendent mode, that he controls the world, that he has a loving nature which disposes him to act in the interest of men's welfare.

Evangelical theology is, above all, Christocentric. The gospel declares that it is in the person and work of Jesus Christ that God reveals himself to men. More is implied in this declaration than that a faithful and trustworthy communication about God is conveyed in the life and teaching of Jesus. Christianity makes the further declaration that Jesus Christ is the Word who became flesh and dwelt among us (John 1:14). The characteristic form of Christian doctrine is determined by the assumption that what we know of God is mediated by the event, the Incarnation of his Son.

Evangelical theology is based on the assumption that the revelation of God is given in the gospel. The gospel, of course, comes to us through the pages of Holy Scripture. Thus evangelical theology must be first and foremost biblical theology, and the content of evangelical doctrine must be induced from a rigorous analysis of the Scriptures. Evangelical theology assumes that the Bible is an effective and satisfactory instrument, indeed the only instrument, for conveying the revelation of God to men. The Bible, however, must be interpreted both inductively and Christocentrically and must be regarded not as a book of mysteries, which has to be de-coded through the use of an authoritatively promulgated doctrinal key, but as the means of knowing Jesus Christ. Scripture is the cradle in which Christ lies, as Luther said, adding that Christ is King and Lord also of Scripture. Christ is the center and truth of all Scripture, its essential content and meaning. "In the whole of Scripture," Luther says, "there is nothing else but Christ."

Redemption

The fundamentals of Christian belief, as understood by evangelical theology, also include some convictions about the effects of the divine redemption in the life of man. These effects are three-fold: (1) the forgiveness of sin and the restoration of God's paternal relationship to man through the atonement; (2) the creation of a new disposition towards righteousness and godliness and the guarantee of the possibility, by the power of the risen Christ, of persistent progress in the direction of spiritual perfection; and (3) the bestowal of eternal life, which means both a life of a divine quality and a life of endless duration.

The condition under which these effects may be conveyed to individual men is, according to evangelical theology, men's repentance and faith toward God in Jesus Christ. It is through Christ that God's nature is revealed to man, that God's will is disclosed to man, and God's power is conveyed to man.

The fundamental intellectual content of Christianity, understood as a message of reconciliation through Jesus Christ, is therefore the set of convictions about man and God which are implied in the possibility and necessity of redemption. The foregoing summary illustrates how such convictions might be articulated. The fundamental articles of Christian faith are those which cannot be denied without jeopardizing the efficacy of the gospel. And the rule of faith which is required in the practical life of the church, and in the witness of Christian higher education, is a summary of those beliefs in the absence of which Christianity as the gospel of redemption does not exist.

The Christian gospel is, as Paul says, "the power of God unto salvation to anyone who has faith" (Romans 1:16). The Christian scholar seeks, as a Christian witness, to communicate this gospel to men. The essential problem for him, from the intellectual side, is to express the intellectual content which must be believed in order for the message to become effectual. But in accomplishing this purpose it is not necessary for him to defend every detail of a particularized articulation of the message. Nor are the categories in which the message is enunciated as important as the message itself. Any categories and language may be employed as long as they are effective in communicating the essential elements of Christian belief. On the other hand, Christianity is destroyed when the Christian witness seeks to make the Christian gospel credible by translating it into something which it is not, for example, existential philosophy or psychiatry.

A college is possible only under conditions of freedom of inquiry, and a Christian college is possible only if commitment to the truth of the Christian faith can be combined with free inquiry. Two tendencies within evangelical theology, however, have made the achievement of this synthesis unnecessarily difficult. Both tendencies can be shown to be mistaken from the standpoint of theological method.

(1) In the first place, evangelical theology has tended to identify the

rule of Christian faith with determinate doctrinal formulations which are not, in fact, essential to the gospel as a message of redemption, but are actually the subject of controversy within the Christian church. For example, the gospel implies that men are made in the image of God, but some theologians proceed to make it essential to orthodoxy to declare that man has a tripartite nature. The gospel declares that men need to be saved, but some theologians proceed to make some particular interpretation of original sin or total depravity a touchstone of orthodoxy.

Dogmaticians have sometimes interpreted the doctrine of total depravity to mean that even man's mental processes are totally corrupted by sin, and some Christian colleges have been led to endorse this interpretation. It is then explained that scientific research (for example, mathematical analysis) is possible only because of "common grace." It is simply a mistake to make this kind of explanation a fundamental theological assumption for Christian higher education. A Christian scholar might consider that such an account involves an unnecessary metaphysical fiction, or that it is simply false, and still accept the fundamental thesis that men are in need of being saved. In other words, the doctrine of man's sinful nature does not need to be expounded in Augustinian terms to be authentically Christian.

Again, the Christian gospel implies the transcendence of God. But some evangelical theologians have proceeded to make acceptance of the validity of certain metaphysical demonstrations of the existence of God essential to Christian orthodoxy. It would be a tragic mistake, however, for the church to insist on metaphysical-theological articulations which might subsequently prove to be philosophically or scientifically untenable, when these are not essential to its message. Determinate positions on the validity of the classical proofs of the existence of God may be left the subject of debate among philosophers of religion; evangelical theology has no stake in maintaining the philosophical demonstrability of any of its propositions about God.

Similarly, that God has power to intervene in human experience is implied in the possibility of divine redemption. The gospel is the message that this is God's world, that he is sovereign over its history and destiny, and that he acts redemptively in man's behalf. Doubtless there are cosmologies which are incompatible with such a declaration and which cannot be reconciled with the Christian faith. But on the other hand, there are details in the explanation of the doctrines of creation and of providence which may be left indeterminate without jeopardizing the fundamental assumption about God's sovereignty over the world. The specific method of creation, the time-span during which creation occurred, and the process of creation may be matters concerning which one may be without dogmatic opinions or matters where one's opinions run contrary to popular persuasions; one may still believe firmly in creation for all that. Acceptance of God's providential care for the world does not entail any particular belief about the nature of miracles nor does it need to encourage disregard of known laws of nature or of the freedom and responsibility of man. What is fundamental in Christianity is only the belief that God is able to intervene in the experience of man.

Or, to take one final example, evangelical theology takes the biblical revelation as the point of departure for its doctrinal exposition. But the debate as to the inerrancy of Scripture in every detail is of no essential importance in the attempt to establish the authority of the Bible as the Word of God. The faith of the Christian church is centered in Jesus Christ, God's Son, and from the standpoint of analyzing the essentials of this faith, the debate over the accuracy (in every detail) of the biblical descriptions is beside the point. Luther's respect for the Word of God was not diminished in the least by his admission that there might be a gradation in the quality of the various parts of the Bible. Whether there are factual errors in the Bible was to him a debate concerning which Christian theologians might disagree without compromising any essential article of Christian faith. The true direction of evangelical theology was indicated by Luther, who was prepared to allow, if the evidence proved to be decisive, that there might be confusions and inconsistencies, for example, in the chronological narratives (within certain limits) and in the factual observations of the gospel writers who report to us the death of Christ. "Let it pass," said Luther, "it does not endanger the article of the Christian faith, because all the evangelists agree in this that Christ died for our sins." It is on the article of faith, rather than on a more determinate and technical viewpoint of theological science, that the church should be prepared to take its final stand.

(2) The second tendency in evangelical theology which has made the work of the Christian college unnecessarily difficult is its tendency to assign finality and authority to the creeds of the Christian church. This, too, is a serious error from the standpoint of theological method.

The Christian faith is something objectively given. It is possible, both Catholic and Reformation doctrine assure us, to discriminate on an objective basis between persons whose beliefs are distinctively Christian and persons whose beliefs are not. The same kind of discrimination is also essential for identifying and preserving the distinctive character of a Christian college. But although the Christian faith is something objectively given, it must never be identified with any particular doctrinal or creedal formula. Tillich is undoubtedly right in maintaining that Christian faith is dynamic and that to make a creedal formulation the object of faith causes faith to become static and dead.[21] Creedalism is a form of idolatry. Doctrinal formulae may play a vital role in the experience of the church, and the creeds of Christendom deserve to be treated always with respect. But the content of the Christian faith, though an objective datum, is not identical with any creed. It is the message which the creedal statements variously express.

Language and philosophical perspectives change in the course of history, and viewpoints which make a given doctrinal emphasis or articulation relevant and comprehensible in one generation may not be present in another. The task of theology is therefore never finished, and this means that the propositions which definitively and finally express the content of the Christian faith will never be stated. Christian theology is always in the process of historical development, as is every other scholarly discipline. Hence the methodology which is appropriate for theological analysis is entirely compatible with the freedom of inquiry which responsible scholarship demands.

From the church's side, the theology which our times demand must be distinctively Christian and yet properly ecumenical. The result of theological analysis has too often been schism; what is needed is a delineation of the fundamentals of Christian belief which will be inclusive rather than exclusive. The rule of faith is not any particular confession, which is presumed to represent authoritatively and finally what is distinctively Christian, but what we may call with Aulén "the ecumencial Christian faith."

> "Ecumenical" is the watchword against any kind of closed and self-sufficient confessionalism. This does not mean that theology should produce a kind of extract of doctrines which would be common to all Christians. Such an endeavor would be of very little value. We

[21]Tillich, *Dynamics of Faith*, pp. 28, 29.

> are not dealing with a kind of common conception which would represent a Christianity stripped of all denominational expressions. Such a common Christianity has never existed, just as there has never been a common religion. Christianity has from the very beginning appeared in different forms, each of which has its own peculiar character. But the central theological problem posed by these denominational forms must always be whether or not and to what extent they express that which is genuinely Christian.[22]

It is through such an understanding of the nature of the rule of faith that the faculties of the Christian colleges should undertake their analysis of the theological assumptions underlying their work, not necessarily with the technical or pedantic concerns of the professional theologians—and not without reference to the denominational context in which they serve—but with sufficient rigor and ecumenicity to successfully focus thought on what is distinctive in Christian belief. A Christian college, worthy of the name, cannot be based on a static creedalism or dogmatic confessionalism, nor can it serve a narrow denominational purpose; still it must operate with a clear analytical understanding of what is essential in the Christian faith and it must allow that faith to define its distinctive intellectual task.

THE RULE OF FAITH AND ACADEMIC FREEDOM

Christian theology can provide a firm foundation for a program of higher education in a manner which is entirely consistent with the nature of scholarship. But it is only by guaranteeing a measure of flexibility in the delineation of the essential content of the Christian faith that theology can be integrated into the life of learning. Education is not possible without freedom, and any restriction on freedom will result in an impoverishment of education. When inquiry is prohibited, the work of intellect is frustrated and its growth is stunted. Hence it is only as theology qualifies as an inquiry of the free spirit that it can be allowed to dwell in "the house of intellect." "The mind," Ferré says, "finds satisfaction in the service of a flexible faith."[23] The flexibility of faith is the condition under which faith may provide a point of intergration for learning.

---

[22]Gustaf Aulén, *The Faith of the Christian Church* (Philadelphia: The Muhlenberg Press, 1948), p. 18.

[23]Nels F. S. Ferré, *The Finality of Faith* (New York: Harper, 1963), p. 64.

It is an inadequate concept of the flexibility of the rule of Christian faith which lies at the bottom of the present theological crisis in Christian higher education. To some the theological quest is arbitrary and doctrinaire, unworthy of the scholar. To others the work of theological research is a closed system and its conclusions set the bounds of inquiry. Neither view is an adequate basis for the integration of faith and learning. What is needed is the combination of open inquiry and responsible discrimination of what is essential to Christian belief.

Christian colleges often sense the need for some kind of creedal formula for carrying on their work. If the formula is viewed as dynamic, and if the interpretation of its provisions allows for some flexibility, the provisions of a creed can be a helpful and powerful instrument of guidance and evaluation. But if a creedal provision becomes static or loses its relevance, its use is inappropriate and may be injurious in a community of critical scholarship.

Many of the creedal formulae currently in use among the Christian colleges include provisions of detail which are the subject of controversy within the church and which therefore cannot be enforced—or which, if enforced, would be unduly restrictive. Usually the formulae have been carried over from a previous generation, and many of the provisions are no longer crucial or relevant. Rigid insistence on an anachronistic letter of the doctrinal law has resulted in the suppression of intellect in some of these institutions.

Freedom is an indispensable requirement of all intellectual activity, including theological research. Not only must the content of a controlling statement of faith allow for a measure of flexibility in the definition of what is fundamental in Christianity, but the manner in which any theological norm is applied in institutional affairs must also express the freedom and trustfulness of a responsible and mature academic community. Doubtless there are conscientious and self-respecting scholars who feel at ease at fundamentalist colleges, in spite of institutionally imposed restrictions on independent thought. But most scholars, regardless of their theological persuasions, would agree with Ferré:

> At whatever point the mind is forbidden to probe any subject, precisely there it loses its confidence in its own usefulness or in its being needed, and develops fears and frustrations in relation to the fenced-off area. . . . Intellectual no-trespassing signs frustrate and give us

> basic insecurities. When men are not allowed to interpret revelation for themselves on account of its absolute authority but must accept it as it is, the mind, by thus being fenced out and deprived of its rightful function, feels frustrated.[24]

Education is possible only under conditions of freedom. Institutional definitions and provisions for the protection of academic freedom vary greatly throughout American education, but at the very least academic freedom means freedom of inquiry. For the scholar it means a full opportunity to responsibly determine the content of instruction; for the student it means the opportunity to learn through questioning. If a college operates on a theological base, the method by which its integrating theological assumptions are applied must preserve the condition of freedom, without which education is nothing but indoctrination.

The freedom which is indispensable in education is sometimes misrepresented, however. There are those who contend, for example, that academic freedom at a Christian college means open advocacy of conflicting ideologies by persons who individually represent them and insist that an employment policy which is designed to create an ideologically homogeneous faculty would entail a curtailment of academic freedom. The American political system makes much of freedom in this forensic sense, and American education shows a related tendency to think of freedom in terms of the opportunity to advocate opinions and represent interests. But this concept of freedom does not go to the heart of the matter when it comes to education. A college where there is open advocacy of conflicting opinions by persons who individually espouse them is not necessarily a place of freedom, nor is a student guaranteed the opportunity of inquiry in such a climate.

Freedom is not the state of affairs in which a welter of prejudices tumbles about heedlessly. Freedom is founded on seriousness of inquiry, and inquiry, in a classroom, is founded on a dialectical method of instruction. A college in which there is nothing but advocacy may never provide students with genuine dialogue and so may lack freedom. On the other hand, freedom in the sense of seriousness of inquiry is often most feasible for students in an academic community which is socially and religiously homogeneous, provided that the faculty understand and implement a dialectical method of instruction. Sometimes

[24]Ibid., p. 61.

the clash of ideas is more explosive at a sectarian Christian college with selective employment and admissions policies than at an ideologically heterogeneous public university.

Nor is freedom to be understood in terms of indifference to social necessities, disregard for the requirements of politeness, or tactlessness. Academic freedom is not the right of a teacher to ignore the social realities in which he conducts his work. Teaching is a social act, and tact imposes limitations on freedom of action in all social situations. Every teacher, no matter where he teaches, must adjust the content and style of his teaching to the aptitudes, backgrounds, preconceptions, and prejudices of the students whom he serves. The predispositions of students set real or operational limits on the freedom of instruction, irrespective of institutional guarantees of academic freedom or the lack of them. A teacher cannot demand freedom in the sense of independence of action without regard for the limitations of the student clientele. The character of that clientele always operates to restrict the options which are open to the teacher.

What the teacher can demand—at the Christian college as well as at the secular college—is protection against arbitrarily imposed control, exerted from without, which deprives him of the opportunity to exercise his own conscientious, professional judgment. Academic freedom consists simply of this system of protection, by which the choice of the academic conscience is guaranteed. No college is free without these guarantees, whether formally or informally defined. A college which provides them is free, whether or not it is operated from the point of view of a common religious persuasion and valuational commitment.

Again, academic freedom is widely conceived in terms of detachment and lack of commitment to a controlling belief. But an individual is not free simply by virtue of the fact that he has suspended his judgment, nor is an educational institution free simply by virtue of the fact that it has no controlling purpose. What differentiates between those who are free and those who are not free is the quality or object of their respective commitments. A person who is committed without reservation to the truth is free; a person who is committed to error is not free. It is the truth that sets one free.

A Christian college dares to operate in the conviction that the gospel is true, that it is "God's power unto salvation to everyone who has faith." It holds no brief for particular human formulations of that gospel, but as far as the gospel itself is concerned, the Christian college is not ashamed of it. Unrestrained commitment to the gospel truth is no compromise of freedom. It looks like a compromise of freedom only to the person who does not think of the gospel as true.

To the academic mind it seems patently obvious that, as Robert M. MacIver has put it, "Any theological commitments postulated by an academy of learning must constitute a limitation on academic freedom."[25] The American Association of University Professors (AAUP) statement of Principles on Academic Freedom and Tenure asks only that "limitations of academic freedom because of religious or other aims of the institution should be clearly stated in writing at the time of the appointment." The AAUP statement recognizes that a given set of theological definitions may be an inevitable and, in some educational contexts, entirely proper restriction on academic freedom. It asks only that the restrictions be made as explicit as possible in order that the teacher-scholar may be fully aware of them when he begins his association with the institution. All the AAUP asks is that the "intellectual no-trespassing signs" should be posted conspicuously at those points where the inquiring mind is not permitted to enter.

The AAUP gesture to the sectarian institution is generous enough, but it is not based on an adequate theological understanding. Following the AAUP principle would actually turn the rule of faith into a creed and would reduce the range of free inquiry. But it is the merit of the Christian faith that it conceives itself as having a character of flexibility in propositional articulation which makes it possible always to guarantee freedom in the effort to analyze its meaning and content. There can be no "intellectual no-trespassing signs" in the Christian college, either inside or outside the theological tradition in which the institution operates. There should be nothing but a resolution to pursue truth by means of honest inquiry. Scholarship is based on the assumption that no dogma are justifiable a priori, that, as MacIver puts it, "fundamental doubt is the father of knowledge."

> This doubt, this readiness to question accepted things, is a heuristic principle and not a goal. By doubting and questioning, within any area of study in which we have some competence, we may arrive at tested and retested knowledge, and in view of the endless evidence history affords us of the errors to which human beings are prone when they

[25]Robert M. MacIver, *Academic Freedom in Our Time* (New York: Columbia University Press, 1955), p. 287.

> make proclamations of eternal truths, the caution to 'prove all things' has particular significance for the scholar.[26]

If "fundamental doubt" is a viable heuristic principle in any field of scholarship, it is no less viable in theology, in man's endeavor to uncover that additional truth which God has yet to break forth out of his Word. The maxim to prove all things was proposed, of course, by a theologian. From the Christian standpoint faith, like learning, demands the flexibility which permits "fundamental doubt" to operate as a heuristic principle. This is why faith and learning can be unified in a single, coherent consciousness.

The declaration that the Christian faith is flexible is readily misinterpreted. So is the declaration that there is a rule of faith by which individual belief is to be judged. Yet both declarations are indispensable in theology. Theological perspectives in Christian higher education have tended to alternate between two extremes, neither of which is acceptable. On the one hand, scholars of liberal inclination have given insufficient recognition to the determinacy and distinctiveness of the Christian faith in contrast to other forms of religiosity. On the other hand, thinkers of conservative persuasion have allowed the forms of faith to grow rigid, static, and inflexible and have created frustration for Christians of scholarship and intellect. The middle ground between relativism and absolutism, between inclusivism and exclusivism, between subjectivism and dogmatism is the only ground on which a program of Christian higher education can be built.

There is today widespread doubt that an educational program based on commitment to the historic Christian faith is compatible with academic freedom in its fullest meaning. The success with which Christian higher education meets the challenge posed by these doubts will determine the role it will play in our society in the future. Freedom is indispensable in education. The Christian colleges must therefore succeed in maintaining their integrity as institutions of Christian faith with the same guarantee of academic freedom as can be expected of educational institutions generally. The basis for accomplishing this synthesis of faith and freedom is a proper understanding of the nature of the Christian faith. It is the inadequacy of that understanding in many of the Christian colleges that poses the fundamental crisis facing the movement.

---

[26]Ibid., p. 289.

Jacobi once said that he was in heart a Christian but in head a heathen. American education is full of people like Jacobi, whose sentiment is influenced by devoutness but whose reflection is determined by logicality and scientific necessity. But Jacobi's state of mind is not an adequate basis for Christian higher education. The Christian college and the Christian scholar must operate rather with the outlook of a man like Luthardt, who argued that a true faith is fully reconcilable with enlightened thought.

> Faith is not merely an unenlightened feeling, nor religion merely a matter for the sentimental. Faith is the firm and joyful certainty of the heart which knows what it believes. Faith is not the opposite of knowledge, but the highest kind of knowledge, which is more worth knowing than any other. Those who believe and those who know, are not so opposed that the former belong to one, the latter to another party, or that they must be abandoning the world of faith who are advancing towards knowledge. A man does not cease to be a scholar because he becomes a believer.[27]

---

[27]Luthardt, *Apologetic Lectures on the Saving Truths of Christianity*, p. 37.

Chapter 2

THE AIMS OF EDUCATION

The concept of purpose is central to the idea of education. Both etymologically and substantively, the process of education involves the exercise of leadership. Furthermore, the measurement of educational progress presupposes the specification of an expectation of performance derived from a concept of educational aims. Education is possible only where there is a sense of purpose. Conversely, the vagueness and ambivalence of the sense of purpose are the cause of a tragic reduction of educational effectiveness in a great many institutions.

In all its phases and at any level the work of a college must be purposeful if it is to be effective. Effective teaching requires a clear delineation of the objectives of the instructional program. Effective college-wide planning requires a workable understanding of the nature and mission of the college as a whole. Satisfactory budgetary administration involves the determination of priorities in accordance with a firm commitment to the ideals of the institution. What is needed throughout the college is a consciousness of objectives which is concrete and definite enough to allow for responsible planning, for deliberate implementation, and for dependable measurement. More than in any other human activity, a workable definition of objectives is indispensable in educational work.

What is urgently needed in the movement of Christian higher education is a more analytical delineation of the idea of a Christian college and a wider distribution of that concept among those who work in Christian colleges. Of course, there is already a very substantial literature devoted to the refinement of this idea. Generalized formulations of this sort certainly have their place. But the ideological base of operations for Christian colleges is more than an abstract and theoretical analysis of what some sociologists speak of as an "ideal type." It is also a realistic and pragmatic outline of the task of this, that, and the other particular Christian college, as seen from within an understanding of its own heritage and resources. Such an outline can be produced only by the staff of the college at which the definition will be put into effect.

The delineation of the task of the Christian college involves the coordination of the two sets of objectives, the educational and the religious. Perhaps, as David Riesman has observed, it is a peculiarly American tendency to add rather than to integrate. Thus the "American" way to run a Christian college might be to construe the college's objectives as an educational institution and then add on the objectives of the church. To integrate the two objectives effectively, however, may give one greater pause. To accomplish integration one is required to have an extraordinary analytical grasp of both poles of the relation. One needs to have penetrated to the heart of both education and Christianity if one is to establish an essential unity between them.

The point of departure for integration should be an understanding of the great educational traditions. The preservation of a sense of purpose requires a firm grasp of basic principles of perennial application and relevance. Currently there is much doubt that there are any such principles to guide educational planning in the new age. Indeed, there are those who say that our age as a whole is faced with such unprecedented circumstances that we have no hope of obtaining guidance from any outside source.

In the development of civilization the continuity of culture has always been the basis of progress. Yet some contemporary writers advise that ours is an age which is discontinuous with history and that the traditions of earlier generations are not suited to our present needs. Hannah Arendt, for example, has recently argued (in *Between Past and Future* and in *Men in Dark Times*) that no tradition can claim validity today. Arendt distinguishes carefully between the past, in the sense of some preceding historical stage, and tradition, which is an attempt to interpret the past in terms of a system of beliefs. She thinks not that history (in the sense of the past) is dead, but that we have no reliable guide through it anymore. We may be able to study traditions as part of the past, but what the study of history has served to accomplish, she contends, is the destruction of traditions. The study of history shows only that our age has no past to guide it.

Such a reading of the relevance of historical traditions for modern culture grossly exaggerates the uniqueness of our times. Amid the admitted novelty and unprecedented complexity of contemporary society, there remain important points of continuity between our present task and the principles and precedents which have been functional in the past. Specifically, the mainstream of educational literature contains a number of important formulations of that perennial philosophy by which responsible educators in every generation must be guided.

JOHN HENRY NEWMAN

Newman, for example, views the aims of education primarily in terms of the acquisition of general knowledge, which he distinguishes from the "useful arts." Newman's view is often associated with an anti-vocational understanding of liberal education. Actually, however, his concept of the aims of education can be made the basis for the integration of liberal and professional concerns. It is true that he rejects a narrowly utilitarian or vocational approach to education as training for the performance of very specific functions. But this is not to deny that the liberal arts, too, are useful in their own way, nor that professional education, too, rejects a narrow training which fails to stimulate the imagination or to prepare the student for dealing with the unpredictable.

A liberal education, according to Newman, is one which encourages the acquisition of knowledge as a good in itself; its aim is the "accurate vision and comprehension of all things," interpreted in the context of the whole of experience, the apprehension of the meaning of phenomena as explained by reference to general principles. The antithesis of liberal education is a narrowly utilitarian training, a fact-gathering or information-collecting study which assimilates data without regard for their meaning, a cumulative piling up of subjects, which constitute the presumed materials of learning, without selectivity or interpretation. In sum, says Newman, liberal education is "the process of training by which the intellect, instead of being formed or sacrificed to some particular or accidental purpose, some specific trade or profession, or study or science, is disciplined for its own sake, for the perception of its own proper object, and for its highest culture."[1] A liberal education

> is the education which gives a man a clear conscious view of his own opinions and judgments, a truth in developing them, an eloquence in expressing them, and a force in urging them. It teaches him to see things as they are, to go right to the point, to disentangle a skein of thought, to detect what is sophistical, and to discard what is irrelevant. It prepares him to fill any post with credit and to master any subject with facility.[2]

The aim of university education, as Newman understood it, is "the culture of the intellect." The objective of liberal education is "the force, the steadiness, the comprehensiveness, and the versatility of intellect, the command over our powers, the instinctive just estimate of things as they pass before us." It is the cultivation of the powers of the mind that education should be designed to accomplish—"to open the mind, to correct it, to refine it, to enable it to know, and to digest, master, rule, and use its knowledge, to give it power over its own faculties, application, flexibility, method, critical exactness, sagacity, resource, address, eloquent expression."[3]

The aim of education is to correct certain patterns of thought and action which run counter to the steadiness and discipline of intellect—to remove the flippancy and inconsistency of men's thought, to control random and arbitrary thinking and acting, to curb obstinacy and prejudice, impetuousness and instability, intractability and intemperance—to replace such intellectual infirmities with the intellectual virtues, such as good sense, sobriety of thought, reasonableness, candor, self-control, steadiness of view—and to cultivate in individuals a capacity to enter into any subject with ease.

Viewed negatively, the liberal arts are those whose value is not contingent on their being immediately useful as means to some ulterior end. We should observe, however, that this character of self-sufficiency and completeness which Newman ascribes to liberal studies is not

---

[1]John Henry Newman, *Discourse on University Teaching*, 7: 1.

[2]Ibid., 7: 10.

[3]Ibid., 5: 9.

necessarily associated with or reserved to any particular set of academic subjects. It would be quite possible for theology, to use Newman's example, to be studied in a narrowly utilitarian, and therefore illiberal, manner, and it would be quite possible for a technical or professional subject to be studied in a liberal manner. The definition of the liberal arts, therefore, is not primarily a matter of classifying certain subjects of study, some of which should be labeled "liberal" and others merely "useful." It is a question of the end which guides and motivates study. Liberal knowledge is knowledge which is viewed as an end in itself; it may, incidentally, be good also as a means, yet this utilitarian value is not the primary reason it is pursued.

Newman stresses that liberal education is to be distinguished from the mere acquisition of facts regarding some subject. Even a life-time of study in subjects which humanists like to class as liberal—for example, literature or philosophy or history—may leave one without a liberal education. What liberal education requires, says Newman, is more than a "passive reception into the mind of a number of ideas hitherto unknown to it." It involves an enlargement of the mind through "the mind's energetic and simultaneous action upon and towards those new ideas, which are rushing in upon it." Liberal education

> is the action of a formative power, reducing to order and meaning the matter of our acquirements; it is a making the objects of our knowledge subjectively our own. . . . And therefore a truly great intellect . . . is one which takes a connected view of old and new, past and present, far and near, and which has an insight into the influence of all these one on another; without which there is no whole, and no center. It possesses the knowledge not only of things, but also of their natural and true relations; knowledge not merely considered as acquirement, but as philosophy.[4]

Liberal education, says Newman, "makes everything in some sort lead to everything else; it would communicate the image of the whole to every separate portion, till that whole becomes in imagination like a spirit, everywhere pervading and penetrating its component parts, and giving them one definite meaning." The vision of this whole is the goal of liberal education. The aim of education, as Newman sees it, is "the accurate vision and comprehension of all things . . . each in its place." Hence the teacher must master the art of generalization—"he must

---

[4]Ibid., 5: 9.

reduce to method, he must have a group of principles and be able to group and shape his cognitive acquisition by means of general principles."[5]

A perennial defect of education is the multiplicity and disparity of subjects. Education has too often been a potpourri of disconnected and fragmented experiences whose relevance for a unified interpretation is never made clear. Newman, in his own day, accused the university of

> distracting and enfeebling the mind by an unmeaning profusion of subjects; of implying that a smattering in a dozen branches of study is not shallowness, which it really is, but enlargement, which it is not; of considering an acquaintance with the learned names of things and persons, and the possession of clever duodecimos, and attendance at eloquent lecturers, membership with scientific institutions, and the sight of experiments on a platform and the specimens of a museum, that all this was not dissipation of mind, but progress. All things are now to be learned at once, not first one thing, then another, not one well, but many badly. Learning is to be without exertion, without attention, without toil; without grounding, without advance, without finishing. There is to be nothing individual in it; and this, forsooth, is the wonder of the age.[6]

After a century of progress the university curriculum has succeeded only in creating new institutional forms of the same basic educational malfunctions which distressed a perceptive observer such as Newman.

JOHN DEWEY

Dewey has acquired a reputation for being an opponent of liberal education, but that reputation is due to the unfortunate way in which his name has figured in controversies with people like Robert Maynard Hutchins. Any sensitive reader, however, will perceive the continuity of Dewey's thought with the tradition we have been tracing in Newman.

Education, Dewey says, is essential to the self-renewing process of life and of civilization. But life is developmental. Life means growth. Dewey sees two implications in the relation between education and developing life.

(1) The first is that education must always recognize the developmental stage which the student as an individual has currently attained.

---

[5]Ibid., 6: 7.

[6]Ibid., 6: 8.

The basic weakness of much formal education is that it imposes adult standards on the immature. It fails to take realistic account of the powers of the young; it substitutes drill for the creation of conditions which will allow the learner as a person to perceive the significance of what is to be learned; and it focuses planning on static patterns, previously determined, rather than on a novelty yet to emerge. In educational circles, as in society generally, youth is regarded as the lack of desired (that is, adult) traits. Dewey contends that if education is to be developmental, it must be based on respect for youth, that is, a respect for the potential for development, and on the capacity to recognize the signs of possible growth.

(2) The second implication which Dewey sees in the idea of education as essential to the self-renewing process of life is that education has no end beyond itself. Education aims at growth. But, says Dewey, "there is nothing to which growth is relative except more growth."[7] Hence formal education must be conducted in the light of the expectation that the student's learning and growth will continue after he has left school. (The appearance of the term "terminal education" in recent educational discussion symptomatizes the tendency of educators to exaggerate the importance of the period of formal education in personal development.) "The purpose of school education," Dewey says, propounding a principle which can be collated with Newman's emphasis on the principle of mental training, "is to insure the continuance of education by organizing the powers that insure growth. The inclination to learn from life itself and to make the conditions of life such that all will learn in the process of living is the finest product of schooling."[8]

Education means the creation of conditions which are conducive to growth in a desired direction. The general function of education is the direction, control, or guidance of growth. The tendency for adults, of course, is to want to direct the young to grow toward an ideal which they associate with their own adulthood. Defining maturity by reference to adult accomplishments, they think of education in terms of escape from immaturity. Liberal education, however, must be based on recognition of the distinct potentiality latent within the student as a person, and it should guide him as a growing organism towards the

---

[7]John Dewey, *Democracy and Education* (New York: Macmillan, 1916), p. 60.

[8]Ibid.

realization of those potentialities.

It is misleading to think of education as a preparation for something, for example, adulthood, a career, or some eventual productivity. Education should be viewed, by both teachers and learners, rather as an activity aimed at facilitating, in Dewey's language, "a continuous process of growth, having as its aim at every stage an added capacity for growth."[9] The notion of education as preparation suggests that growth is an escape from some kind of second-class status. The concept of education as preparation actually suggests a condescending view of youth. In any case, a futuristic approach to education is almost guaranteed to result in a loss of momentum. The learner lives in the present, but the motivational appeals of the educator require the youth to place himself in some remote or possible future. It should not be surprising that procrastination is the result. To maintain attention and discipline the educator then has to resort to adventitious motives of pleasure and pain, and the result is—the grading system. Dewey says:

> The future having no stimulating and directing power when severed from the possibilities of the present, something must be hitched to it to make it work. Promises of reward and threats of pain are employed. Healthy work, done for present reasons and as a factor in living, is largely unconscious. The stimulus resides in the situation with which one is actually confronted. But when this situation is ignored, pupils have to be told that if they do not follow the prescribed course penalties will accrue; while if they do, they may expect, some time in the future, rewards for their present sacrifices.[10]

The anomaly of the higher learning, particularly in America, is that it continues to pursue the idea of liberal education within a system of sanctions which is both cause and result of educational artificiality. The curricular structure, the credit system, and the academic requirements which academia employs in the attempt to organize a program of liberal education make it highly unlikely that a learner will recognize in his course of studies an occasion for personal growth. What the learner sees is the opportunity to eventually qualify for something which he deems desirable. The fundamental mistake is in the educator's divorce of futuristic planning from present concerns.

Of course, growth is always from stage to stage, and education must always anticipate a new stage of development. In that sense, all

---

[9]Ibid., p. 63.

[10]Ibid., pp. 64, 65.

education is preparatory. Growth is, as Dewey says, "a continuous leading into the future." But the continuity of the future with the present must be patently clear before the future can have any bearing on the motivation of conduct. The mistake which Dewey attributes to the schools is not that of attaching importance to preparation for some future need, but that of making the future the mainspring of present efforts. It is the mistake of failing to show the student how he might see himself, with his present interests and at his present stage of development, in relation to the activity of learning.

Dewey is generally known for his insistence on the relationship between education and experience. "Education," he insisted, "in order to accomplish its ends must be based upon experience—which is always the experience of some individual . . . [Education is] intelligently directed development of the possibilities in ordinary experience."[11] That concept of the nature of education implies: (a) that the primary point of reference in an educational program should be the student and his life; (b) that the relevance of education is dependent upon its being correlated with life experience and that an idea must be assimilated into experience in order to be mastered; and (c) that educational activity needs to be organized so as to contribute optimally to the formation and accomplishment of purposes in the individual. Such principles form the basis of a perennial philosophy of liberal education.

Education is the constant "reconstruction or reorganization of experience which adds to the meaning of experience, and which increases ability to direct the course of subsequent experience."[12] Neither past experience nor future experience, however, have any meaning for the learner when they are isolated from his present. Correlation of both past and future with the student's present is the way education becomes an instrument of culture and of personal growth.

The reconstruction or reorganization of experience results in an improved perception of the connections and continuities of experience and enables us to act intentionally through anticipation of consequences. Education makes the individual aware of connections in expe-

---

[11]John Dewey, *Experience and Education* (New York: Macmillan, 1938), p. 89.

[12]Dewey, *Democracy and Education*, p. 89.

rience which had previously been imperceptible to him. The result of education is an increased power of subsequent direction or control and an enhanced capacity for problem solving through the utilization of intelligence.

The key concept in Dewey's theory of education is the concept of thinking. Thinking is what gives meaning to experience. Thinking, Dewey says, is "an explicit rendering of the intelligent element in our experience." Through thinking we apprehend a connection in experience which enables us to *expect* something to occur and to act *intentionally*. Thinking is the basis of responsible action, as contrasted with capricious behaviour (which accepts things as they happen to fall out) or routinized behaviour (which accepts things as they have always been). Education aims at enhancing the powers of reflection, in this broad sense of the acceptance of responsibility.

All thinking is problem solving; all thinking is instrumental, Dewey believes. "The starting point of any process of thinking is something going on, something which just as it stands is incomplete or unfulfilled. Its point, its meaning, lies literally in what it is going to be, in how it is going to turn out."[13] To fill one's head with facts about what is going on is not to think, but to function as a registering apparatus. Thinking means considering the *bearing* of what is going on upon what may be, but is not yet. It is applying what is known about the structure of experience to the task of projecting a plan of action for an unknown which lies beyond experience.

Thinking is what leads to intentional doing. Thinking is the method of intelligent learning. Thinking aims at the increase of efficiency in action, the application of skill in purposive conduct. And the fundamental aim of liberal education is the enhancement of thinking. Skill obtained apart from thinking has nothing to do with education; and information severed from thoughtful action is dead (though it may resemble knowledge) and is a mind-crushing load. "The sole direct path to enduring improvement in the methods of instruction and learning consists," Dewey declares, "in centering upon the conditions which exact, promote, and test thinking."

Education, as centered on thinking, involves the following stages, all of which are indispensable for any process of education: experience, data, ideas, and applications.

---

[13] Ibid., p. 171.

(1) Learning, Dewey always insists, begins with *experience*; it begins, that is, with recognition of a situation which calls for some sort of doing. The starting point of learning is a problem. Education, however, is dominated by that tendency to separate thinking and doing which, as Dewey has argued in *The Quest for Certainity*, is the most conspicuous characteristic of modern philosophy. Even when they follow a problem-posing approach, teachers easily succumb to the artificiality of academic life. They pose a contrived problem; they bring before the student a situation in which there is nothing but a problem and they assign to the student the task of solving a problem for its own sake. Or they pose a problem which is their own problem and not the student's problem—or a problem which is made the student's problem not through being related to his ordinary life, but through being made a hurdle which the student must surmount in order to gain the desired grade or be promoted.

Many teachers who say that they begin with experience fail to do so. For they, too, fail to connect up the activity of learning with the student's actual experience in common life. They begin not with an experience which directs the individual's attention to the connections of things, but with an experience to which the individual can relate only through the medium of an external requirement. Formal instruction does not characteristically supply a context of experience in which problems naturally suggest themselves. The difficulty here is not with the technique of the teacher. The difficulty is with the irrelevance of the stimuli for learning which the educational system employs—that is, the absence of materials and occupations which generate real problems, which identify the student's real problems. Indeed, in our system the student's problem is not even that of meeting these conventional and formal requirements of his school-masters, but of merely seeming to meet them, or of meeting them with the least possible inconvenience.

(2) We begin with a problem posed by experience. We must then gain command of *data* which will help us to deal with the difficulty which has been presented. Some "progressive" teachers make the mistake of thinking that solutions to problems emerge almost magically or fortuitously from imagination or from discussion with others. But solutions are seldom spun out of our own heads, and the "sharing" of ideas or of experiences is often nothing more than a pooling of ignorance. To think effectively one must be able to command data which bear on the problem at hand.

Data may be supplied by direct observation, by reading and other forms of communication, by memory, and so forth. No one source is primary or indispensable. For much of the data which we require for thinking we must, of course, depend on others. It is important, however, to distinguish between depending on others for the data which provide the materials of thinking and depending on others for the solution of our problems in a way that eliminates the necessity of thinking. The latter is a form of dependency which is incompatible with the notion of education.

The schools, says Dewey, provide both too little and too much data—too little that the student can use, too much disorganized and miscellaneous clutter. The communication of information is, practically speaking, often an end in itself, the goal of the student being merely to heap up his store of data and display it. The tragedy, says Dewey, is that "pupils who have stored their 'minds' with all kinds of material which they never put to intellectual uses are sure to be hampered when they try to think."[14] On the other hand, if thinking were actually going on there would probably be a greater demand for information, drawn from a variety of sources, than the schools are now able to supply.

(3) The assimilation of data in relation to an experienced difficulty generates suppositions, tentative explanations—what Dewey calls *ideas*. The data arouse suggestions which extend beyond what has been previously given in experience. The data are facts; the ideas (suggestions) which spring from them forecast possible results. Thinking involves an act of inference which, Dewey suggests, always involves an invasion of the unknown, a leap out beyond what is known.

Thinking is an incursion into the novel and always demands some measure of inventiveness. The new suggestion arises, of course, out of what is familiar; the novelty attaches to the different use to which what is familiar is now put. All ordinary thinking is creative, and it is fatuous to identify creativity with the extraordinary and fanciful. Creativity means putting everyday things to uses which had not yet occurred to other people—and that is precisely what thinking means.

Liberal education is the attempt to mobilize the creativity of individuals in the activity of thinking. Ideas, as Dewey uses the term in this context, must be generated out of the originality of the thinker. No

[14] Ibid., p. 185.

idea, he says, can ever be conveyed from one person to another. All that can be communicated from one person to another are data, on the basis of which an idea may be created.

> No thought, no idea can possibly be conveyed as an idea from one person to another. When it is told, it is, to the one to whom it is told, another given fact, not an idea. The communication may stimulate the other person to realize the question for himself and to think out a like idea, or it may smother his intellectual interest and suppress his dawning effort at thought. But what he *directly* gets cannot be an idea. Only by wrestling with the conditions of the problem at first hand, seeking and finding his way out, does he think. When the parent or teacher has provided the conditions which stimulate thinking and has taken a sympathetic attitude toward the activities of the learner by entering into a common or conjoint experience, all has been done which a second party can do to instigate learning. The rest lies with the one directly concerned. If he cannot devise his own solution . . . and find his own way out he will not learn, even if he can recite some correct answer with one hundred per cent accuracy.[15]

Socrates thought of the teacher as a mid-wife, who is important in assisting the birth of the child whom the mid-wife herself is unable to produce. Similarly, teaching for Dewey involves participation in the activity of thinking, but not a vicarious substitution for the thinking of the learner. In shared activity the teacher, too, is a learner and the learner is a teacher—and "the less consciousness there is, on either side," says Dewey, "of either giving or receiving instruction, the better."

(4) Ideas are anticipations of possible solutions, of a possible connection between activity and desired consequences. The testing of an idea, of course, is acting upon it and seeing what results. Ideas are not the final end of learning; they are intermediate goals, significant only in so far as they guide and organize further observations, recollections, and experiments. The getting of an idea simply poses a new challenge for thought, in that the idea must now be tested and used as a basis for action.

Many academic attempts to apply an idea, and to fix the idea through *application*, are misplaced. Too often, the application is contrived and remote from common life. And the practice which "fixes" the idea becomes routine and loses the intellectual quality which would make it effective in causing the idea to be assimilated into the real

[15]Ibid., p. 188.

experience of the individual.

The schools need to make provision for the application of ideas in active pursuits related to the vital concerns of life, both individual and social. A major institutional reorganization and re-tooling of curriculum and facilities are probably entailed. While the institutional realignment is taking place, however, every teacher may make his own provision for establishing the connections between the subject-matter of the classroom and the wider experience of ordinary life.

The essentials of educational method are therefore identical with the essentials of reflection. These elements are as follows:

- The student must have a genuine situation of experience—there must be a continuous activity in which he is interested for its own sake.
- A genuine problem must develop within the situation as a stimulus to thought.
- The student must have access to relevant information and must make the observations needed to acquire it.
- Suggested solutions must occur to the student which he can develop in an orderly way.
- The student must have opportunity and occasion to test his ideas by application, to make their meaning clear and to discern their validity.

Thus the basic problem in educational planning is that of designing a program of instruction out of regard for the individuality of the learner. It is easy to become confused, however, about the way in which the individuality of the learner should be made primary in instruction. Two common mistakes are to be avoided. (1) The first is a mistake which arises from being overly enthusiastic about the relationship between education and freedom. It is true that education without freedom is a contradiction in terms. But freedom is not the end of education. Freedom, as Dewey saw, is a means, not an end. After freedom has been achieved, the question remains what end is going to be served by this freedom. Freedom, says Dewey, is "power to frame purposes and to execute or carry into effect purposes so framed."[16] Freedom is to be prized, but only as the power to act wisely, to evaluate impulses and desires in light of knowledge of the consequences which will result from acting upon them.

---

[16]Dewey, *Experience and Education*, chapter 5.

(2) The second mistake, which is closely related to the first, arises out of a failure to recognize the distinction between desire and purpose. Education is of value not, as the Sophists would have it, as a means for enabling individuals to express their impulses, to get what they want, and to satisfy their desires. Education involves the evaluation of desire by intelligence. Intellectual growth, which is what education seeks, involves a reconstruction of impulses and desires which will inhibit some impulses out of regard for the perceived consequences of following them. A person who is guided by impulse is, as Plato saw, only a slave; freedom consists in reaching decisions on the basis of intelligence. It is the direction of life by intelligence that liberal education seeks, and the ideal of liberal education is therefore diametrically opposed to the current perversion of education by sophistry.

ALFRED NORTH WHITEHEAD

Whitehead's understanding of the aims of education centers on his distinction between inert ideas and vital ideas. Inert ideas, he says, are those which are "merely received into the mind without being utilized, or tested, or thrown into fresh combinations."[17] But the aim of education is to generate vital ideas—ideas which are appropriated in a manner which makes them usable in new contexts and combinations, ideas which have been tested by the individual so that he is personally assured of their reliability, ideas whose meaning and significance are clear and whose relevance is apparent. Passive reception of the materials of learning produces only inert ideas. What is essential in all education is the active involvement of the learner in utilizing and testing the ideas presented. Any program of instruction must therefore be dominated by a methodology which places the burden of testing and use upon the student. Education at any stage, Whitehead says, must permit each individual student to experience the joy of discovery—that is, to discover that ideas can provide an understanding of the significance of events and a basis for practical decision.

Scientific criticism is, of course, the fundamental methodology of the scholar; Whitehead insists that it must also infuse the higher learning. The use of evidence by an educator, however, requires a

---

[17]Alfred North Whitehead, *The Aims of Education* (New York: Macmillan, 1929; Mentor, 1949), p. 13.

carefully laid strategy, aimed at obliging the student to actively apply the available evidence in the testing of ideas. First, the teacher must avoid providing a proof in such a way that there is nothing left for the student to do but to receive the fruits of the teacher's research. Second, the teacher must always assume that the proof of the validity of a given conclusion is accompanied by a demonstration of its significance. Whitehead recognizes that scientific training has to do primarily with the proof of ideas; only he calls for an extension of the idea of "proof." He thinks that the teacher-scholar who is interested in proving an idea should also seek to prove its worth.

An idea is not worth much, of course, unless it is *true*; but it must also be *important*. And there is room for debate as to whether it is the proof of the *truth* of an idea or the proof of the *importance* of an idea which should come first in the education of the young. Whitehead notes that in ordinary experience—by contrast to the artificial and contrived experience of the schools—it is the question of the *importance* of an idea which is primary. Only after we recognize the importance of an idea do we become concerned to enter into inquiry and debate concerning its truth.

A teacher kills education if he is forever occupying his and his students' minds with abstractions. The teacher needs, says Whitehead, to

> choose some important applications of his theoretical subject; and study them concurrently with the systematic theoretical exposition. . . . The consequences of a plethora of half-digested theoretical knowledge are deplorable. Also the theory should not be muddled up with the practice. The child should have no doubt when it is proving and when it is utilizing. My point is that what is proved should be utilized, and that what is utilized should—so far as is practicable—be proved.[18]

Whitehead thinks that the awareness of the utility of ideas is a function of the recognition of the relationships in which the ideas stand. Education, he thinks, must "eradicate the fatal disconnection of subjects which kills the vitality of our modern curriculum. There is only one subject-matter for education, and that is Life in all its manifestations."[19]

---

[18]Ibid., pp. 15, 16.

[19]Ibid., p. 18.

The idea of liberal education is generally dominated by a desire to give the student a balanced schedule of subjects. But Whitehead thinks that general education, too, must begin with the recognition that "mankind is naturally specialist." Educational artificiality results from the failure to recognize this fact. "In education whenever you exclude specialism," Whitehead affirms, "you destroy life."

Long experience with the higher learning has shown us that it is specialized study which is normally of particular interest to students. We have been able to maintain the program of general studies only through a system of requirements and sanctions. The specialized studies interest the student because he *wants* to know them, sees the use of them. About the general studies he knows only that someone thinks he ought to know them, thinks he will find them useful, and therefore requires them of him. But education is, as Whitehead says, nothing but the communication of inert ideas unless the student sees the utility, the importance, the functionality of what he is learning. No program of education, no matter how purely theoretical its content, can be liberal if it succeeds only in communicating inert ideas.

All vital education is specialized.

> There is not one course of study which gives general culture, and another which gives special knowledge. The subjects pursued for the sake of a general education are special subjects specially studied; and, on the other hand, one of the ways of encouraging general mental activity is to foster a special devotion. You may not divide the seamless coat of learning. What education has to impart is an intimate sense for the power of ideas, for the beauty of ideas, and for the structure of ideas, together with a particular body of knowledge which has peculiar reference to the life of the being possessing it.[20]

This statement is another of those classic formulations of that perennial idea of liberal education by which present collegiate policy should be guided. Whitehead's view of education overcomes the dichotomies which seem so important to lesser people. Those who think superficially about education frequently assume that the theoretical is incompatible with the practical, that the general cannot be combined with the particular and specialized, that value is discontinuous with fact. They believe that we cannot have both freedom and discipline, both liberal learning and professional preparation, both mastery of principles and memorization of data. But the merit of

[20]Ibid., p. 23.

Whitehead is that he has undercut all such dichotomies.

> The antithesis between a technical and a liberal education is fallacious. There can be no adequate technical education which is not liberal, and no liberal education which is not technical; that is, no education which does not impart both technique and intellectual vision. In simpler language, education should turn out the pupil with something he knows well and something he can do well.[21]

Education is learning for Life. And what is needed for Life are ideas which provide a basis for determining through foresight what actions are appropriate. "Education," says Whitehead, "is the acquisition of the art of the utilization of knowledge."[22] It is "a preparation by which to qualify each immediate moment with relevant ideas and appropriate actions."[23]

> The primary reason (for the existence of universities) is not to be found either in the mere knowledge conveyed to the students or in the mere opportunities for research afforded to the members of the faculty. . . . The justification for a university is that it preserves the connection between knowledge and the zest of life, by uniting the young and the old in the imaginative consideration of learning. . . . A university which fails in this respect has no reason for existence. . . . Fools act on imagination without knowledge; pedants act on knowledge without imagination. The task of a university is to weld together imagination and experience.[24]

For the achievement of such a goal, Whitehead argues, education must follow a characteristic rhythm or dialectic. The imaginative pursuit of learning requires a combination of discipline and freedom. The rhythm of educational growth involves the following stages: the development of interest and the general apprehension of the subject in its vaguest details; the acquisition of specific knowledge and mastery of the relevant details through the pursuit of an objective method; the comprehensive ordering of the subject as a whole in the light of all relevant knowledge; and the understanding of the general principle for purposes of creative application in new situations. Ideas acquired through this process will be vital, not inert; comprehended, not merely memorized; applied, not forgotten.

---

[21]Ibid.

[22]Ibid., p. 16.

[23]Ibid., p. 46.

[24]Ibid., p. 13.

Education demands freedom as well as discipline. The motive of learning must come within the learner. The first task of the teacher is to elicit desire and enthusiasm in the learner. Education cannot take place unless the learner is involved, through his own recognition of the importance of the inquiry and his own sense of wonder, curiosity, and reverence. The second task is to provide the environment of rigorous study and purposiveness which will permit the learner to accept the discipline of truth and enable him to learn without the waste of a trial-and-error method.

THE ESSENCE OF LIBERAL EDUCATION

Such formulations of the aim of education display an extraordinary depth of agreement. The differences which can be detected among them turn out on close analysis to be largely heuristic, stylistic, and terminological. Each in its own way promulgates essential elements of that perennial philosophy by which educators of all generations must be guided. The definition of the essence of education is proferred not in terms of the subjects to be covered, but in terms of personal development. What matters is not the external form of the curriculum as defined by the interrelationships of subject matter, but the formation and discipline of intelligence and of imagination.

Yet in institutional life there is always a tendency for means to become more important than ends. Once a program of education is created as a means for achieving a set of objectives understood in terms of the development of the student as a person, the curriculum tends to become an end in itself, tends to become more significant from the operational standpoint than the student whose needs it is supposed to serve.

The tradition of liberal education is actually compromised today in the purely dogmatic way in which it is being defended and applied in the liberal arts colleges. We dogmatize that it is only certain subjects that are liberal, that it is only individuals who meet certain admissions criteria that can be educated in a liberal fashion, that it is only through a certain distribution of courses or types of courses that a liberal mind can be formed. By contrast, when Whitehead viewed the introduction of professional curriculums into the university, he suggested that, based on its own liberal education, the university should be expected to welcome the newcomer with the only gift it had to give, namely, the gift of imagination. Anti-professional dogmatism, being the very opposite of the liberal and adaptive mind at which education is ostensibly aimed, cannot serve the purposes of liberal education.

Our present need is for a fresh adaptation of the traditional concept of liberal education in a new circumstance. Our former dogmatic conceptions about the means for achieving the ends of liberal education will not serve us any longer. We need to devise new strategies, new curricula, new instructional approaches—while maintaining essentially the same course, aiming at the same ends. It is a new tack that is needed, since the wind has changed. But we have the same destination. The task is to help students to achieve freedom and autonomy as persons, to realize the potential within them, to exploit the power of thought as an instrument for practical decision. It is to develop the capacity to explain phenomena in a way which enables us to control them. It is to clarify the general principles which give unity and meaning to our cognitive experience and then to exhibit how our knowledge may be applied in problem solving. Our task is not to treat subjects, save as these are the appropriate means for achieving our ultimate objective. Knowledge, however admirable in itself, is not a self-sufficient aim of education. It is sought in liberal education only as an instrument through which individuals may realize themselves and become more effective in their world.

The task of liberal education today is, in the words of Charles Frankel, to help people to secure the means to find meaning in an age of meaninglessness. The task is not merely that of transmitting cultural or intellectual traditions which have been found meaningful by other generations, but also that of guiding individuals in the use of these traditions as data for their own interpretations. The development and refinement of the capacity to see one's actual and potential life-experience in its wholeness are what a modern liberal education should seek to offer to the undergraduate. The task is to prepare the young for life, which is to be understood, as Justice Holmes put it, as "action, the use of one's powers. As to use them to their height," he said, "is our joy and duty, so it is the one end that justifies itself."

Chapter 3

THE TASK OF THE CHRISTIAN COLLEGE

Such is the nature of education and such the task of the college. If, now, a religious institution assumes for itself the label "college," it must be prepared to accept this concept of education as a criterion for self-assessment. A college without freedom is a contradiction in terms. Fortunately, as Whitehead so perceptively noted, religious education, too, requires the rhythm of freedom and discipline. "No part of education has more to gain," he says, "from attention to the rhythmic law of growth than has moral and religious education."[1] Yet Christian colleges, and especially those which attach the greatest importance to moral and religious nurture, often insist prematurely on a rigidity and precision in the articulation of religious beliefs which are likely to make ideas inert and to deaden the religious sense. The ground on which education and Christian faith may be integrated, however, is the circumstance that neither of them is conceivable without freedom.

A college which is Christian must first be a college. But the institution assumes additional responsibilities when it aligns itself also with the purposes of the Christian church. It will not do to construe these other responsibilities merely additively. The college which would be

---

[1]Whitehead, *The Aims of Education*, p. 48.

Christian assumes responsibility for *integrating* the functions of the university (conceived in a manner such as Newman, Dewey, and Whitehead suggest) with the functions of the church. In accepting a religious purpose the Christian college is not merely declaring its willingness to accept *more* concerns than are typically accepted by colleges and universities. It is declaring its intention to construe its educational objectives by reference to a religious orientation as the principle of unity and integration. How, then, shall the task of the Christian college be understood?

COGNITIVE GOALS

The aims of education may be classified under two main headings, cognitive goals and affective goals. The Christian college has distinctive objectives in both respects. The primary concern of an educational institution, of course, is with the enlargement and dissemination of knowledge. What distinguishes a college from a mere reformatory institution is precisely its emphasis on objectives in the cognitive domain. But although knowledge is the primary concern of a college, it cannot be its only concern. Both cognitive and affective objectives must be considered in a complete concept of the task of a college.

The cognitive goals of education are always construed in the light of assumptions about the nature and grounds of knowledge. When a Christian college defines its goals in the cognitive domain, it must bring into play a theory of knowledge which expresses its understanding of the nature of religious faith. As a foundation for an understanding of its cognitive goals, the Christian college has, it would appear, two distinct alternatives from which to choose. The one, which we may call an "ontological" method, is illustrated in the classical traditions of metaphysical religiosity; the other, which we may call an "analytical" method, is illustrated in the main stream of Reformation theology.

According to the first type of theory, ontological knowledge in the religious sphere is, at least in part, deducible by rational procedures either a priori or a posteriori. Knowledge of God is, to some extent at least, continuous with knowledge of the world. The canons of evidence, either deductive or inductive, lead objective thought to the recognition of certain truths about God and about the relation of God to the world. The supreme systematic formulation of this theory of religious knowledge is seen in scholasticism and owes its major outlines to the genius of St. Thomas Aquinas. Fundamentalist apologetics is a

Protestant version of the same method, although the level of scholarship and the clarity of understanding of the basic philosophical issues are generally inferior among the Protestant representatives. From this point of view, the Christian college accepts it as its aim not only to convey those orders of knowledge which relate to the world and its processes, but also to establish the evidential grounds of certain beliefs about the nature of ultimate reality and about God. Learning is taken to include appropriation of the data on the basis of which one may certify, for example, belief in the existence of God. The cognitive goal of education, then, is to convey religious knowledge along with, and as an outgrowth of, other knowledge.

The "ontological" method leads to a conception of Christian education as apologetic and demonstrative in purpose. Since scholarship is thought to issue in demonstrations of the truth of Christian dogma, the theory understands scholarship itself as Christian. There are a Christian philosophy, a Christian psychology, a Christian archaeology, a Christian view of history, a Christian biological understanding, and so forth. The Christian college is distinguished, on the cognitive side, as being a center for the preservation and distribution of this body of scholarship.

To expose the inadequacy of what we have called the "ontological" theory would require an elaborate philosophical and scientific argument. That the theory is inadequate is, however, the inevitable conclusion of criticism. There are no demonstrations of the truth value of religious propositions. Atheistic and fundamentalistic apologists are alike mistaken in believing that religious belief is arguable. The role of reason in religion is not in the demonstration of the truth of religious opinions about the nature of reality.

Is the alternative to scholasticism, then, some form of anti-intellectualism or existentialism? Contemporary religious thought is, unfortunately, preoccupied with these polarities. But there can be no question of a nonrational or antirational religious faith. No one can suspend his essential rationality, unless he is willing to settle for thoughtlessness or absurdity. The question is not *whether* or not reason plays a role in religion, but *what* role it will play.

The "analytical" method suggests that the role of reason in religion is not the demonstration of the *truth* of religious propositions but the achievement of conceptual clarity, of precision, and of coherence in religious belief. It is the analysis of fundamental concepts and the removal of ambiguity and self-contradiction in religious discourse that scholarship can bring to religion. On this view, however, there is no objective scientific or philosophical basis for establishing or confirming a religious (or antireligious) world view. And there is no such thing as Christian scholarship; there are only Christian scholars.

There is much more at issue here than a technical debate among professional philosophers and theologians. The choice between an "ontological" and an "analytical" approach is of tremendous importance for the entire witness of the church in Christian education. A proper understanding of the whole character and value of science is at stake. The Christian who values scholarship only as an aid to faith has not comprehended the essential character of either. The idea that scientific study should vindicate Christian belief is contrary to the nature of both science and faith. Systems of Christian apologetics, mobilized through educational programs, will be repudiated by both scientific criticism and theological analysis.

If there were a fully rationalized Christian philosophy, then it would be possible for an educational institution to devote itself to the promulgation of that philosophy as part of its dedication to rationality and intellectual freedom. A university exists to discover and declare the truth as it is disclosed to rational inquiry, and if the truth of Christianity were disclosed to reason, a university could quite properly include Christian truth within the scope of university research and teaching—as long as freedom of a heuristic sort was preserved, so that inquiring minds could satisfy themselves concerning the reliability of the evidence.

But a Christian philosophy, in the sense of a fully rationalized system of Christian belief, has not yet been articulated. Christianity itself declares that it is not a philosophy, in the sense of a demonstrable body of doctrine. Hence a Christian college will never discover an adequate apologetic basis for pursuing its cognitive goals under the control of an "ontological" method. If, on the other hand, the only alternatives to the formulation of a fully rationalized Christian philosophy were dogmatism or subjectivism, then there could be no Christian college, since dogmatism and subjectivism are incompatible with the idea of education. An "analytical" method, however, offers an alternative to the dilemma of religious knowledge and establishes a basis for a consistent construction of the aims of Christian education in the cognitive domain.

All the cognitive goals of higher education, whether the general goals which all colleges share or those which are unique to Christian colleges, must be comprehended in the light of a broad understanding of the nature and limits of human knowledge. Undergraduate education must be characterized not by the indiscipline and forensic license of a debating society, but by the rigor and seriousness of the pursuit of truth; not by timorous respect for an unchallenged and unsubstantiated authority, but by fearless criticism and appraisal of all knowledge claims, as the context demands; not by pedantic preoccupation with factual detail or narrow specialization, but by concentration on principles of general application and meaning. The Christian college, too, must take such an understanding of the nature of knowledge as the point of departure for construing its objectives in the cognitive domain.

AFFECTIVE GOALS

The primary task of the college is to contribute to the enlargement of knowledge. But this is far from its only task. What justifies the fantastic labor and expense of maintaining a college is, finally, not the necessities of the community of learning, but the service which can be rendered to personal growth. One element in the maturation of personality, certainly, is the acquisition of knowledge, and colleges quite properly place the greatest stress on their cognitive goals. But there is also an affective dimension to personal maturity. A college whose aim is to promote the maturation of human personality cannot, therefore, confine itself to the cognitive domain alone.

In some quarters in higher education there is doubt that aims outside the cognitive domain are a proper concern of an educational institution. Some teachers, anxious about preserving the ethical neutrality of the sciences, insist that concern about the emotions and values of individuals is not within the competence of scholarship—and it is merely with scholarship that education is concerned. Others are led by the division of labor in our society to assign responsibility for emotional and moral culture to other institutions, like the family or the church. The majority of the American public seems to be in such a state of mind. Once families chose a college in the light of what the college might do for the personalities of their sons or daughters; now they decide largely on the basis of the college's resources for imparting the special knowledge which seems to be vocationally demanded. If educators are in doubt as to whether or not the university should concern itself with the values of students, most of the American public seem to be plagued by no such uncertainty. The university is not really expected to play a decisive role in the development of the total personality, but is expected to confine itself largely to the communication of knowledge and the development of skill.

Such a view of the function of the university involves a compartmentalization of human personality which is unthinkable, both for those who understand the nature of personality and for those who have experience in teaching. It is *irresponsible* for an educator to say that he is concerned only about imparting knowledge to his students. Furthermore, it is *impossible* for him to really achieve even that limited objective in detachment from the life of feeling and willing.

In the first place, cognitive pursuits are, at certain points, inevitably influenced by the affective life. Emotions can be either a block to learning or an aid to learning. Interest often determines success. Ferré expresses what every experienced teacher could also report: "No community of seeing can become effective without right relation to the community of feeling and the community of doing. Thought without emotion and will is stillborn; thought driven by emotion and directed by the will has incalculable power."[2] It is, therefore, impossible for colleges to confine their concerns to the cognitive domain. "The endeavor to develop a bare intellectuality," as Whitehead said, "is bound to issue in a large crop of failure."[3]

Vision is often dependent on emotion and will. Nowhere is this principle more important than in religious education. The vision of God is conditional upon purity of heart. The acceptance of religious truth is occasioned not by incontrovertible rational demonstrations through which belief is commanded but by the disposition of believing obedience. This is the cardinal principle of Christian education. An affective stance of sobriety, earnestness, and repentance is, therefore, the foundation of any program of learning in the things of God.

But in the second place, education must be concerned with values as well as with knowledge because knowledge plays an important role in practical decision. If one says, with Whitehead, that "education is

---

[2]Ferré, *Christian Faith and Higher Education*, p. 115.

[3]Whitehead, *The Aims of Education*, p. 50.

the acquisition of the art of utilization of knowledge," then the educator must accept responsibility for guiding his students in putting their knowledge to use. Immediately he enters the realm of values and moral decision. The goal of education is to enable individuals to qualify their decisions and actions by knowledge and reflection. But this means that the relevance of knowledge must be shown through an illustration of its application. The Whiteheadian concept of education assumes that valuational decisions can be influenced by cognitive experiences. It assumes that the person who possesses the relevant knowledge and an attitude of critical objectivity will be able to decide responsibly, provided that he is also able to establish a valuational perspective and context in which to decide. The educator cannot show the practical relevance of knowledge, however, unless he helps the student to define that context. Part of the task of education, in other words, is to teach the decision-making skills.

But a third reason for making concern about values appropriate for the college is found in a realistic assessment of the present social situation. A sufficient reason for assuming a task is that no one else is doing it adequately or that no one else seems likely to muster sufficient resources for doing it. If there is a valuational gap in our society, the colleges seem to be in the best position for mounting an effective program to fill it. The churches are limited by their conservatism, their tendency towards social isolation, and their waning influence. Families too often lack the spiritual resources and the coherence for performing this function, and although one may continue to labor to increase their effectiveness in moral education, it is too much to hope for a reversal of what is by now a well-established social trend. Of all American institutions, the colleges, and especially the Christian colleges, appear to be our best hope for moral education.

Knowledge is a good, but it is not the whole of goodness. Knowledge does not necessarily bring virtue with it. Knowledge can be put to the service of immoral purposes. It can destroy life as well as preserve it; it can lead to the exploitation of humanity as well as to the service of humanity; it can be used persuasively for evil purposes as well as good. Erudition is not a guarantee of honor. Learned men who tower as giants in some field of scholarship may turn out to be moral midgets. Enmity and stinginess may appear in their ugliest form in learned departments of great universities. The basis of goodness is not simply learning. Knowledge is *not* enough.

Yet there are few colleges which have engaged in adequate planning for systematic efforts in the field of aesthetic and moral education. Pressures for institutional economy tend to squeeze out all that is peripheral to a narrowly conceived vocational productivity. Professional preoccupation with the enterprise of scholarship erodes concern about the personalities of students. The Christian colleges could achieve a real breakthrough in regard to one of the most critical problems of our times if they could successfully define and exploit the interrelationship between intellectual training, religious education, and personal nurture. Herein lies their great opportunity.

Education, properly understood, cannot avoid concern about the life of feeling and willing. This is so because education, at all levels, exists for the sake of human personality and human society. In a Christian college concern about the nurture of personality will have both an intensity and a direction which reflect its connection with the Christian church. The Christian church is embarked on a mission of personal redemption. The educational arm of the church must therefore inspire young men and women in the pursuit not only of truth but also of goodness and holiness.

The goals of education for personal Christian growth might be expressed in the words of Paul: "Whatever is true, whatever is honorable, whatever is just, whatever is pure, whatever is lovely, whatever is gracious, if there is any excellence, if there is anything worthy of praise, think about these things" (Philippians 4:8). Emotional self-control and stability, moral integrity, discipline, courage, endurance, patience, meekness, tolerance, honesty, consistency, justice, reliability, purity, temperance, love, graciousness, reverence—such are the elements of Christian honor, the qualities which the Christian educator hopes to see arise in the lives of those whom he serves.

Mere conformity to some institutional norm of conduct or belief is not what is sought, however. It is a gross misunderstanding to think of the Christian life as a pattern of conformity. The only conformity of which the New Testament speaks is conformity to Christ himself. The individualism of the Christian faith makes it impossible to obtain faith by proxy or goodness by imitation. The mission of the church is to participate in the redemption of individual personalities. And this means that the church, and all its agencies, must aim to help each person to realize his own potential as an individual. Individuality, of course, presupposes freedom, not only in the sense of the absence of slavish imitation and thoughtless conformity. Christianity claims that individual freedom and self-giving love can be combined in a single personality, and it is towards this combination that the Christian college must strive.

"Strong character," says Ernest M. Lijon, "can be built only around a body of strong basic convictions."[4] The Christian college exists for the purpose of assisting young people to develop such convictions. But in many Christian colleges, especially those with firm theological commitments, there is serious misunderstanding of the conditions out of which strong basic convictions arise. Unless education is merely indoctrination or imitation, it will never do for the teacher to seek to provoke strong convictions by offering the student his own as infallible guides. As the student's experience expands, he will discover that there are other opinions, also capable of being represented as infallible; and if he has not learned a methodology of criticism he will, as Lijon rightly predicts, only "become more bewildered than ever in his efforts to choose among drastically different projections of infallibility."[5]

The level of a college's expectancy influences student performance, not only in study but also in conduct. Much of the indiscipline of students can be traced to the absence of standards in the institution. But there are two ways to establish and enforce standards. One is to impose them by authoritarian promulgations and to enforce them by a system of sanctions. The other is to elicit acceptance of the standards by the student and to obtain self-enforcement through inward motivations. Every sensitive educator knows that the latter, though more difficult, is the only acceptable way.

But how does one internalize moral and aesthetic standards? How is character formed? How can a value system be revised? Lijon's answer is a perceptive one:

> As I read the research of others and examine our own, I am increasingly aware of how consistently *decision-making* is believed to play the central role. If, therefore, effective character education is to be achieved at the college level, it must be directed toward the student's crucial decisions.[6]

---

[4]Ernest M. Lijon, "Crucial Decisions of the College Years," *Liberal Education* 51:1 (March 1965): 81.

[5]Ibid., p. 81.

[6]Ibid., p. 77.

Character develops through decision making. And the role of the teacher who would be influential in the formation of character is a maieutic one with respect to the student's decision-making activity. The teacher who wishes to be useful in the formation of character must leave the student free to make decisions of his own. Teaching must not be doctrinaire, yet it must press the student for a decision. Teaching itself must be decisive, not in the sense that it establishes authoritative guidelines for decision, but in the sense that it vindicates the view that opinions *can* be held, that responsible decisions *can* be reached. Teaching must be calculated to clarify the alternatives from which the student may choose; it must supply data on the basis of which the student may make his choice; and it must then require him to make up his mind, as he is able.

In the Christian college the choice of basic convictions is an essential element in learning. Anyone who works in such a college ought to have well-formed opinions concerning the educational conditions which contribute to the formation of Christian character. Despite the urgency of such concerns in Christian higher education, there is surprisingly little systematic study of the principles of character education among Christian educators, and it is rare that a comprehensive plan of action has been established on an institution-wide basis. Yet the distinctiveness of the Christian college—indeed, the foundation of its justification—is precisely its opportunity to go beyond the efforts of other educational institutions in seeking to coordinate learning experiences in the cognitive domain with the formation of Christian personality.

THE CULTIVATION OF MATURITY

The aims of education finally center in the personal development of the student. Education is the process of helping students to acquire the autonomy, the competence, the sensitivity, and the discipline of mature human beings. The analysis of the objectives of the Christian college centers, therefore, on the definition of Christian maturity.

A useful point of departure for such a definition is afforded by Arthur Chickering's *Education and Identity*, one of the most influential books in American education in the last two decades. Chickering views education in terms of seven major vectors of development for the young adult. He recommends that educational programs should be specifically organized, conducted, and evaluated in terms of these vectors of human development: achieving competence, managing emotions, becoming autonomous, establishing identity, freeing interpersonal relationships, clarifying purposes, and developing integrity.

The human worth of education from this point of view is that it gives to the educated person a sense of competence, a pattern of emotional maturity and self-control, a capacity to establish his beliefs and values through the exercise of self-directed (autonomous) judgment, a concept of himself through realistic understanding of his abilities and ideals, skill in relating helpfully to other persons in social contexts, clarity in vocational and life purposes, and a system of values for defining standards of personal integrity. That is a high ideal for education. It takes us a step beyond the concept of education as the process of mastering subjects. And it is a concept which must be placed at the heart of any endeavor to conduct a program of education within the context of the church.

The essential question for a free society—a society in which one is permitted to pass judgment on the forms of institutional life—is: What sort of individual is being created by the institutions which exist? This question must be asked, too, of our educational institutions, and specifically, in the context of the church, of the Christian colleges. What effect does the institutional structure of the college have on the dispositions and the mentality of the individuals who participate in its processes? Does that structure free individuals for the full realization of the possibilities within them? Are the manifestations of such fulfillment comprehensive, systematic, and predictable or are they sporadic, occasional, and fortuitous? Are the individual's sensibilities being sharpened or dulled? Are his mind and his hands becoming more adept? Is his curiosity being aroused? Is his concern being directed toward responsible action? Is he becoming more autonomous, more responsible, more free? Such are the questions which must be pressed as we evaluate the quality of American institutions. Institutions must always be judged in terms of their utility for realizing individuality. "Individuality," as Dewey once said, "is not something originally given, but is created under the influences of associated life."[7]

Chickering's concept of vectors of human development can be adapted for purposes of a statement of mission for the Christian college. There is, for example, a way for the Christian college to view

---

[7]John Dewey, *Reconstruction in Philosophy* (New York: Henry Holt, 1920), pp. 154, 155.

MAJOR DEVELOPMENTAL VECTORS FOR THE YOUNG ADULT*

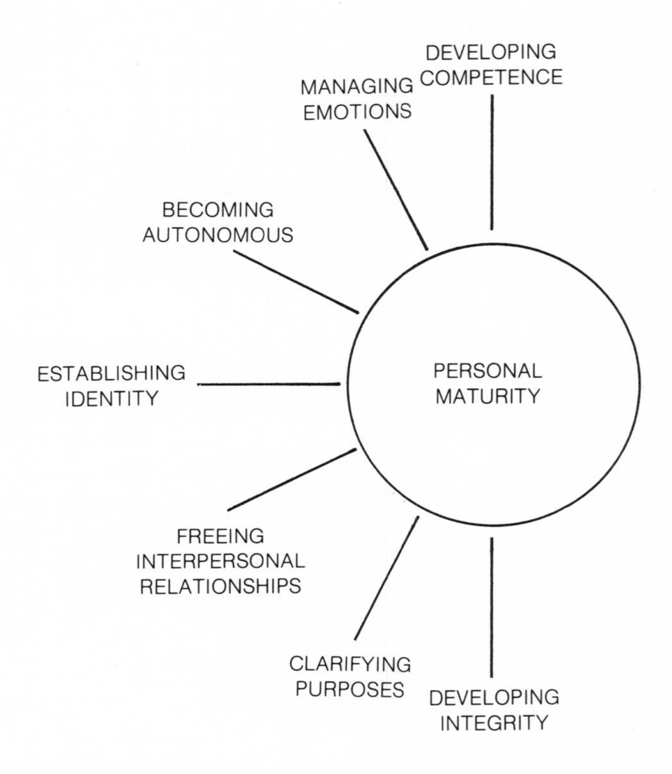

*Based on Arthur W. Chickering, *Education and Identity* (San Francisco: Jossey-Bass Inc., Publishers, 1971).

the competence at which, in Chickering's model, education aims. This is not to say that the learning which is the foundation of competence may have an inherent Christian character, viewed in terms of its subject matter. Rather, it is to observe that an individual may come to view his competence from the point of view of a Christian understanding of vocation. He may learn to see his competence, say, as a mathematician or as a neurosurgeon, as a gift of which he must be the steward. The gift, of course, calls for further cultivation and development, and a new dimension of duty therewith appears. But the discovery and cultivation of the gift become for the individual an occasion for obtaining a sense of worth and ultimately for developing a sense of vocation. The aim of Christian education is, from this point of view, to assist individuals to discover and develop a sense of competence and to dedicate that competence to the service of God and of men in the name of Christ. If a program of Christian education is not leading individuals to such a discovery of competence as a gift which places them in God's debt, then that program is failing to carry out an important aspect of the mission of Christian higher education.

Again, there is a Christian way to construe the emotional maturity and control at which education, viewed in Chickering's way, is aimed.

Processes of Personal Christian Maturation

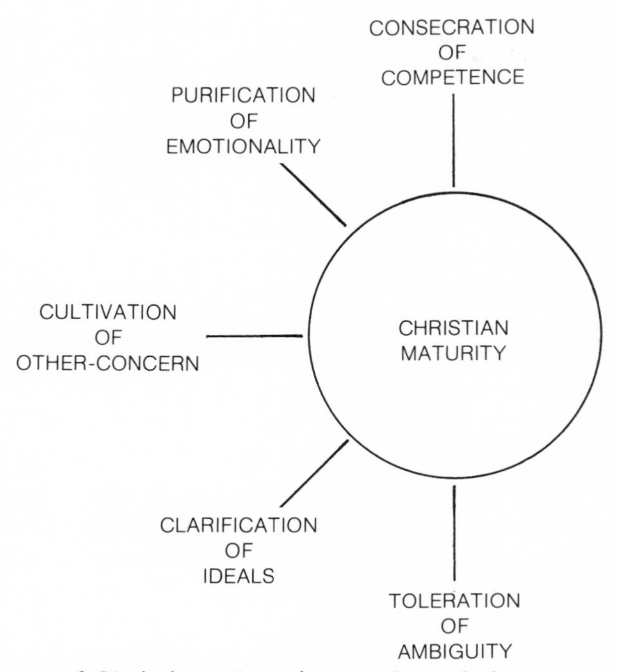

A program of Christian education ought to help persons to develop a pattern of emotional life which is consistent with Christian discipleship. Innocence is the state of the person who has not experienced such impulses as hate and avarice. Spirituality, on the other hand, is the state of the person who, having experienced such impulses, has learned to manage them. It is spirituality, of course, at which Christian education aims. Viewed positively, the aim is to cultivate the Christian graces of love, joy, peace, patience, and humility, which are the fruit of God's spirit when present in a human life.

A Christian pattern of emotionality is an important element in the skill in interpersonal relationships which it is another aim of education to release. The Christian way is to add to affability considerateness, to etiquette respect, to tolerance love. The Christian life is always a life in togetherness, and the task of cultivating Christian maturity must therefore include a specific address to the social dimension of experience.

Furthermore, the cultivation of Christian maturity includes the clarification of a system of Christian values and ideals through which an individual may come to an understanding of himself and may define his own standards of personal integrity. Beliefs about reality and obligation define the inner man from which Christian behaviour springs, and the critical consideration of these beliefs is, therefore, an indispensable element in Christian nurture. The Christian college must be especially concerned to provide opportunities for confrontation of these issues so that, as a result of the development of a coherent belief system, personality may become more fully integrated.

Finally, the Christian college must be especially concerned about the individual student's developing capacity to tolerate the ambiguity and uncertainty which are inherent in human existence. The Christian walks by faith, not by sight, and the capacity to trust God in the absence of warrantable proof is required of the follower of Christ. Many persons of limited experience, of course, are unaware of the complex and problematic aspects of existence. Education first creates ambiguity by so expanding the horizons of experience that the problematic aspects become apparent. Then education seeks to cultivate the capacity to tolerate ambiguity through a synthesis which reconciles acceptance of finiteness with insistence on critical judgment. Christian education is content neither with blind faith nor with iconoclastic criticism, but only with trust which recognizes the finiteness of man.

A conscientious teacher, of course, wishes to see his students come to assurance. And he will, above all, wish to discourage that masquerade of skepticism which is one of the most offensive characteristics of the partially educated. But the process of coming to assurance is not less important than the end result. And assurance where only uncertainty is justified is nothing but prejudice. So a conscientious teacher must come to terms with students who are in the process of working through their doubts.

The teacher cannot expect to dispel their doubts through his authoritative truth-saying. Quite to the contrary, the teacher is likely to discover that his authority with students is inversely proportional to the claims he makes to authority. It is in the admission of error that a teacher may become a model for a learner, and it is in the admission of doubt that a teacher may be permitted to join with a student in a common quest for greater truth. The teacher who cannot admit to uncertainty and ambiguity will find that he is cut off from students in the process of their growth. What students want in their teachers is not thinking machines which crank out infallible proofs, but living (and therefore fallible) human beings who dare to accept the risk of disclosing themselves in their uncertainties and in their questionings. Through such a disclosure the authenticity of a creative interpersonal relationship may develop, with benefits to the growth of both parties to the relationship.

The task of being God's instrument for fostering the development of Christian personality is the highest calling which has been given to man. The college which espouses such a purpose has a greater reason to be than any other educational or social institution. Furthermore, an educational institution which gives itself to such a purpose will discover a vital connection with concerns which are of fundamental importance to adolescents in process of development. Some of the young are self-conscious about this search for personal identity and value-determination; many others are not. But all can readily recognize the importance of the process of maturation in terms of both their immediate and their future lives. Not all of them value development in the direction of Christian maturity—so, of course, not all of them ought to seek the distinctive educational service of the strongly Christian college. But in a Christian college it is possible for those who teach and those who are taught to be united through a shared concern about a progressive development of personality in the direction of Christian ideals for human life. This concern is what the vocation of the Christian college is all about.

Chapter 4

GENERAL EDUCATION IN THE CHRISTIAN COLLEGE

The curricula of most American colleges are lacking in any essential organizational unity. The term "curriculum" suggests a purposively contrived course, leading to the achievement of a goal; but in most colleges it is impossible to discern the structure of education, the organizing principle which gives meaning to curricular planning. Students are shunted from registration period to registration period, having obtained enough assistance to sign up for the number of courses they think they can manage and to keep whittling away at the graduation requirements, but with scarcely any sense of the meaning of it all. And the faculty's understanding of the total curriculum often goes no further than their awareness of the system of requirements, to which they refer all questions about program planning. The requirements themselves usually represent compromises emerging from a conflict of party interests within the faculty and can be given no cogent and consistent justification by reference to a single educational idea.

The disunity and disorganization of the curriculum of a Christian college are, in the last analysis, only another symptom of that failure of nerve which is the underlying weakness of Christian higher education today. It is a sign that the faculty have not been so controlled by their belief in an integrating educational principle that they have been willing to accept the labor and inconvenience involved in actually implementing that principle in the program of instruction.

Admittedly, it is difficult to establish a curriculum of purpose. To do so requires steadfast resistance to some well-established social and educational trends. Most colleges have found it easier to go with the stream.

One of the trends which make it difficult to plan a curriculum purposively is the pressure of professionalism in education. Our society thinks of education more and more in terms of productivity. Educational systems are expected to supply trained personnel for industry and the professions. And the increasing complexity of the professional requirements has resulted in growing pressure on the colleges to diversify their course offerings. College after college has yielded to the demand by installing programs of doubtful relationship to underlying institutional objectives, on the ground that the program was necessitated by something called "the constituency." Expectations laid on the college from without, rather than systematic educational convictions defined from within, have been determinative of curricular development, and unity has correspondingly suffered.

It is by no means to be assumed that every course of study which is useful to society or demanded by "the constituency" is necessarily in conflict with a college's basic purpose. But time after time colleges can be seen abandoning their ideologies and yielding to the pressure of professionalism. This is nothing but a failure of nerve. The colleges defend themselves by protesting that accomodation is necessary for survival. But there is a point when it becomes appropriate to ask, "Why survive, unless there is a distinctive effort which gives meaning to the struggle for survival?"

Actually, the "constituency", whose demands are the foundation of so many institutional policies, is one of the myths of modern education. The "constituency" is often a couple of letters received by the president. G. R. Elliott reflected first-hand knowledge of the way colleges actually operate when he expressed the opinion that the reason material and vocational interests so often control policy in liberal arts colleges is that "these interests are *believed in* by their promoters more religiously than the college as a whole believes in humanity and wisdom; such is the plain, hard fact."[1] The facts belie the idealism of the

[1]George R. Elliott, *Church, College, and Nation* (Louisville: Cloister Press, 1945), p. 52.

Christian college movement. At many points in the curriculum Christian colleges have followed the course of expedience rather than of principle.

A second trend which makes purposive structuring of the curriculum difficult is the pressure towards specialization in scholarship. The trend is a natural corollary of the advancement of learning. In modern scholarship the highest standards are attained only through concentration on a limited field of learning. Within his field of specialization a mature scholar is confident of himself; outside it he becomes uncomfortably doubtful of his competence to judge. Accordingly, in almost every college the planning of parts of the curriculum is turned over to specialists. The result is then added up and made to fit within whatever institutional restrictions are found necessary, and the product is a curriculum. The fragmentation of scholarship leaves most college faculties without that form of interdisciplinary understanding which would permit a college-wide curricular consensus.

The departmentalized preoccupations of college faculties are not due to selfishness, jealousy, or imperial ambition. If the problem were a form of moral deficiency, it would actually be easier to solve. But in fact, the root of the problem is in the integrity of the scholar and in the specialization of learning—both of which are, from another point of view, major strengths in our educational system. Every college discovers, therefore, that the scholarly community resists efforts to bring extra-departmental concerns to bear in the appraisal of departmental activities. And every college finds that the faculty is doubtful of its ability to devise an objective plan for a total-college curriculum. When the inevitable periodic review of graduation requirements comes up for faculty debate, it is almost a foregone conclusion that the decisions will be made by an accommodation of departmentally oriented opinions.

The importance of an integrated curricular organization should not be exaggerated, of course. A curriculum is only a plan, a skeleton, a schedule. The key to the instructional situation is emphatically the teacher. A soundly constructed curriculum is no guarantee that instruction will be effective, and a good teacher can achieve results even with a badly organized curriculum. Nevertheless, organization is necessary for maximum efficiency in any institution. Furthermore, the Christian college needs an integrated curriculum in order to project the image of a distinctive educational service to a public which is not always able to tell the difference between one college and another.

Whitehead's twin proposals for curricular development apply with special force to the small Christian college today: "Do not teach too many subjects" and "What you teach, teach thoroughly."[2] The besetting sin of curriculum planners in the small colleges is the imitation of the large universities. But it is both hopeless and imprudent for a small college to seek to duplicate the diversified curriculum of a multi-purpose university. Instead it must build a curriculum which expresses its particular institutional character and exploits its unique institutional assets. The small college must work out its own salvation.

THE CHRISTIAN COLLEGE AND LIBERAL EDUCATION

It is entirely possible that a Christian college can serve a distinctive function by offering curricula with a professional, technical, or vocational emphasis. But it is more likely that the resources, traditions, and purposes of the Christian colleges can be exploited best through curricular concentration in the humanities and the natural and social sciences. For the foreseeable future, the main thrust of Christian higher education undoubtedly will continue to be in the context of liberal education.

The concept of liberal education is an elusive one. For one thing, the concept is historically conditioned; its content has changed very significantly in a hundred years. For another thing, even at any given point in history the exact limits of the concept are difficult to determine. There is, therefore, a perennial debate concerning what courses of study should be included in a program of liberal education. If liberal education is understood as education aimed at freeing the human spirit, it is possible to justify including a very wide variety of subjects under the label. The fruitlessness of the debate about subject matter has left some people doubtful that the concept of liberal education is definite enough to be of any use in curricular planning. But such a conclusion is unwarranted. The idea can be given a definition which is both delimiting and adaptable, if emphasis is placed not on the content, but on the methodology of liberal education. A college may then build a curriculum designed to give free rein to this methodology.

Liberal education involves an instructional approach which is humanistic, historical, and philosophical. In the Christian liberal arts

---

[2]Whitehead, *The Aims of Education*, p. 14.

college liberal education must also implement a theological approach. These, then, become the over-all instructional emphases which should be preserved in the curriculum of a Christian college.

Humanistic

First, the curriculum of a Christian college should be oriented towards the human situation. Christian higher education is constituted for the sake of persons and the society of persons. It should be conducted, therefore, in the spirit of Socrates, who said, after devoting himself to the pursuit of the principles of natural philosophy, that it would be more fitting for him to devote himself to the study of man—indeed, of himself. The proper study of mankind is man. The Christian scholar, too, has a special vocation to engage in scholarly pursuits which are of human significance.

Curricular programs in the humanities are clearly germane to this sort of concern. The language, literature, art, philosophy, and religion of man are the core of humanistic learning. The descriptive study of human behavior in the human sciences yields understanding of both individual and society. Natural science, too, is a humanistic concern to the extent that it represents an attempt by man to understand the world and man's relationship to it. The critical issue, however, is not what *subject matter* is humanistic—since on the details of this there is an almost endless possibility of debate—but what *concerns* are humanistic. Scientific study may become technical and data centered and cease to be a humanistic enterprise. Similarly, the humanities may be taught in a routinized manner and may degenerate into a fact-gathering chronology or into formal analysis for its own sake. A humanistic concern, however, should be conspicuous throughout the curriculum of a Christian college.

Historical

A second emphasis in the curriculum for the Christian college should be the historical. Man cannot be understood except against the background of history. Furthermore, historical research is the foundation of scholarship in any field. A historical orientation is the point of departure for virtually every learning experience at the collegiate level. Historical studies must therefore be a major emphasis in the organization of the curriculum. A historical perspective should be established for the treatment of virtually every issue.

This does not mean that professional historians and courses conducted by the history department must be accorded a position of special favor in the college. Nor is it implied that the treatment of every issue must be chronological. There are different ways to organize an effort to convey a historical understanding. Nevertheless, all learning is social and implies dependence on the past. History, in the broad sense, may be accepted as another basic organizing principle for curricular construction in the Christian college.

Philosophical

In the third place, liberal education must be philosophical, not in the sense that it must develop a technical philosophical apparatus and focus on the traditional subject matter of the technical discipline of philosophy, but in the sense of Whitehead's dictum that general education must convey a philosophic outlook.

A philosophic outlook focuses more on general principles and less on details. It seeks meanings, not merely sequences; it offers interpretations and evaluations, not merely descriptions. Professional students of philosophy do not always have a philosophic outlook. Formal training in philosophy is not necessarily a philosophical education. By the same token, almost any subject matter can be approached with a philosophical outlook.

What makes education liberal is precisely this approach. The vast majority of scholars, however, have only a limited capacity and interest for the kind of integration which philosophical interpretation (in the nontechnical sense) involves. Most scholars are either timid about their competence for philosophical analysis or preoccupied with the details of specialized learning. It is a distinctive college that actually succeeds in making philosophical perspectives controlling for the program of instruction.

Theological

Finally, for the Christian college the course of study must be emphatically theological. Indeed, theology must be the queen, not in the scholastic sense that it is the point of reference for a synthesized Christian philosophy, but in the analytical sense that the ultimate objective of the Christian in scholarship is the clarification of theological meanings. Again, it is not formal study in theology that is in view here. Rather it is a theological understanding, with or without the technical apparatus of professional theologians, that is to be sought.

Such an understanding should be the central concern of the program of learning in Christian higher education. A clear understanding of the content of the Christian faith should be the most urgent concern of all who study and work at the college. All kinds of learning experiences should be employed as tools for clarifying that faith and should be regarded, indeed, as indispensable for a full understanding of its implications. Theological reflection should provide the setting and occasion for the integration of the whole range of collegiate learnings.

OUTCOMES OF GENERAL EDUCATION

A well organized curriculum includes a core which expresses the college's understanding of the educational outcomes deemed essential for every student. In many colleges this core is only loosely structured; in others it is tightly organized. A more structured core curriculum of general education, however, is likely to result from the development of a more precise definition of educational objectives. Structure is also a likely outgrowth of the pressure for greater efficiency in college operations. For both theoretical and practical reasons, curricular study in the small college must give close attention to the creation of a coherent structure for the general education curriculum.

The distinctiveness of a program of general education in a Christian college does not consist merely in the addition of some credit requirements in fields not represented in other collegiate programs—for example, in religion. The distinctiveness of the Christian college needs to be stamped on the entire program of general education. Particular emphases in the general education core need to be defined by reference to a theological concept. The aims of particular courses of study need to be cast in a theological dimension. It is the totality of a curriculum, not merely isolated parts of it, that expresses the Christian identity of the college. Yet in the curricula of most Christian colleges the distinctives of a Christian higher education are all too imperfectly articulated.

Whenever one attempts to delineate the desired outcomes of an educational program, there is risk of being carried away by one's own idealism. Summaries of the aims of education typically describe a paragon who probably does not and cannot exist. Realism requires one to remember that any ideal is always difficult to actualize. A definition of educational purpose does serve, however, to establish a goal towards which activity may be directed. Even though its realization may be doubtful, a clear statement of purpose will guide the faculty in devising a curriculum which will enable a student to proceed as far in the approximation of the ideal as his circumstances and abilities will permit. It has been observed, furthermore, that the goal of liberal education is not an "educated" person, but a "potentially educated" person—that is, a person who is equipped for carrying on the rest of his education on his own. In this chastened sense, even very ambitious goals for general education may be realizable.

General education should be understood not as an educational program designed for everyone, nor as a sampling of a little of this and a little of that in order to broaden experience. General education is an integrated effort towards the communication of the unity of thought and experience. The outcome of general education should be a systematic grasp of this unity. The task of general education in the Christian college, so conceived, is a profound one.

Critical Thinking

The program of study should be designed to convey to every student an understanding of and respect for the process by which knowledge is acquired; intellectual curiosity and a thirst for truth; and the ability to think critically, to reason logically, and to evaluate opinions and arguments accurately.

The Christian college must find a way to view this objective in harmony with its own theological assumptions. Theological conservatism does not require theological dogmatism. "Faith which is unwilling to face indisputable fact is but little faith," said Albert Schweitzer. "Truth is always gain, no matter how difficult it is to accommodate ourselves to it." Reverence for truth is a virture not only for the scholar, but even more for the Christian. Coleridge's perceptive remark is confirmed by all of church history: "He who begins by loving Christianity more than truth will proceed by loving his own sect more than Christianity and end by loving himself most of all." Fearlessness in the pursuit of truth must be the dominant trait of a Christian intellectual community.

A superficial theological perspective sometimes occasions uneasiness about the applicability of a rational method in religion. There are those who would discredit rationality on the ground that man's finite reason cannot be admitted as the final arbiter of belief. But one need not make reason absolute in order to insist on its indispensability within the range of its competence. Indeed, religious belief and practice are often purified by an encounter with rational criticism. There is much in man's religion that needs to be purged out, not simply because it is inconsistent with a standard of revelation but also because it is meaningless, absurd, or self-contradictory. Christianity has nothing to fear from an encounter with intellect. There is nothing anti-intellectual about Christianity, even though Christianity itself is not a product of intellect. Rather Christianity regards intelligence and criticality as an inherent part of human nature. Hence it is part of the task of Christian education, as the endeavor to release man for the fulfillment of his rational powers, to cultivate intellect.

The foundation of critical thinking is an unquenchable thirst for the truth. The insistence on truth is an essential Christian virtue. Falsehood in all its forms is incompatible with the outlook of one who serves the Christian God. A truly critical spirit is always optimistic; it evaluates opinions in the hope that truth can be uncovered. The pessimistic skepticism of those who doubt the objectivity of truth is a symptom of a pseudocritical spirit. The aim of Christian higher education is to foster criticism in the proper sense—to cultivate the ambition to possess truth and to disclose a methodology for realizing that ambition—and to view criticism as a God-given responsibility. Any educational effort should seek to enhance the processes of critical thinking. Christian higher education should explicitly justify this concern and establish an added motivation for critical activity as part of its service to the God of truth.

Communications

The program of study should be designed to allow every student to acquire a command of language sufficient to express his ideas clearly and to communicate them effectively; the ability to participate in the communicative process as speaker, writer, hearer, or reader by virtue of discipline and skill in the use and interpretation of words.

The Christian religion is emphatically a religion of the word. The object of Christian belief is the *kerygma*, the message preached. Mastery of language is a basic tool not only for purposes of communication generally, but also for the specific form of communication on which the life of the church is based.

Carelessness in the use of language is the basis of many failures in communication. It is also responsible for many conceptual confusions and impossible opinions. The rigorous analysis of words is a fundamental requirement of all intellectual activity. But it is also demanded by the need for clarity in the understanding and communication of the Christian message.

The ability to express one's ideas clearly and effectively, however, may give one a sense of power which poses its own temptations. The art of persuasion must be subjected to an ethical scrutiny, lest it be employed in ways which are inappropriate and for purposes which are improper. Gorgias protested that he was only a teacher of the art of rhetoric and that he could not be held responsible for the purposes which the art was made to serve by his students. But no Christian teacher can absolve himself from the responsibilities of moral education. Truthfulness will be to him no less important than forensic effectiveness. Furthermore, the Christian teacher of the arts of persuasion will be careful to warn the prospective Christian witness not to presume upon the divine function in religious communication. The Apostle took special precautions in his use of persuasive utterance, lest the faith of his hearers should rest in the wisdom of words rather than in the power of God (1 Corinthians 1:17; 2:5). This principle should define the setting in which the art of effective communication is taught in the Christian college.

The mastery of language is the foundation of all advanced learning experiences. Jacques Barzun rightly regards articulate precision as the essential and distinctive mark of intellect. An inadequate mastery of American English is a serious liability for the college student. His powers of both expression and comprehension are curtailed by his linguistic incompetence.

Similar limitations are imposed by unfamiliarity with a foreign language. Babel prevents many a learning experience and restricts one's cultural heritage. A major concern of education should be to break down the tower of pride and the attendant cultural narcissism and to enlarge the scope of possible experience through the mastery of language. Study of a foreign language should not be regarded by a Christian student simply as a requirement to which he has to yield. It should be motivated by respect for another language and culture and humility about one's own. Accordingly, foreign language study must not be the "lick and a promise" which it has become in so many

American colleges. Study of the language should be consummated in meaningful use of the language so as to unlock the secrets of the culture and psychology of the foreign tongue.

The Christian view of the significance of language and respect for the art of communication ought to result in a high estimate of the value of language study. Yet in most Christian colleges linguistic pursuits have fallen into the same kind of disrepute which they have acquired elsewhere in American society. Especially those Christian colleges which look towards the more advanced forms of learning experiences should devote much time and energy to the restoration of the highest regard for the study of language.

History

The program of study should be designed to convey to every student an understanding of the historical roots of contemporary culture, especially of western civilization, and of the major developments of world history; the capacity to explain and interpret historical events.

The foundation of understanding the present is understanding the past. Knowledge of the historical antecedents of current events is essential for an accurate interpretation of their significance. Such knowledge also suggests responsible approaches to the solution of contemporary problems. History affords illustrations of the application of alternative principles in society and state and affords an empirical basis for appraising the utility of similar hypotheses in the present. But history should be studied not only for the sake of its relevance for contemporary problems. It is worth studying as the record of human culture and civilization. Nothing human can be foreign to the Christian scholar, and reverence for the human cannot help but inspire the keenest historical curiosity. History comes alive when it ceases to be a catalog of dates and facts and becomes the story of mankind.

Ortega y Gasset has warned, with his customary brilliance, that man cannot be understood merely as a datum to be described under the scientific rubric of a thing-having-a-nature. What explains a person's conduct, his performance of his task, is, in part, the ideas, the beliefs, the convictions on which his life is grounded. "The diagnosing of any human existence," declares Ortega, "whether of an individual, a people, or an age, must begin by an ordered inventory of its system of convictions."[3] Historical investigation, of course, is the basis of such an inventory, for life-determining convictions are historically derived. Hence if the proper study of mankind is man, history is the inner core of that study. Science, says Ortega, has come to a full stop before the strange reality of human life. Science cannot comprehend humanity in its essence.

> Man is not a thing. . . . It is false to talk of human nature. . . . Man, in a word, has no nature; what he has is . . . history. Man finds that he has no nature other than what he has himself done. . . . [Hence man is] forced to concern himself with his past, not from curiosity nor in the search for examples which may serve as norms, but because it is all he *has*.[4]

The Christian's concern about history ought to be of a higher quality than that of most people. Christianity is a historical religion, not only in the sense that the Christian faith is centered in a crucial historical event, but also in the sense that all of history is regarded as a stage for God's redemptive activity. Yet the controlling motivation of the Christian historian is not to trace the workings of divine providence in history and to justify the ways of God to men. Rather his keen interest in history is an expression of his interest in man. "Among the richest benefits to be secured from a careful study of history within the Christian framework," writes Richard W. Solbert, "is a deeper understanding and appreciation of the doctrine of man. History provides rich resources for observation both on the nature of man and on his behavior in the redeemed and unredeemed state."[5]

The Christian scholar brings to the study of history a set of sensitivities which lend a special reverence to the study. Among these are the humble assessment of the worth of one's own time and culture and the eagerness to learn from the experience of other men; the sense of fairness and honesty and the concern for careful workmanship, which Weber said was characteristic of the Protestant ethic; and the optimistic confidence in the meaningfulness of history and the disposition to interpret particular events and circumstances in the perspective of life's meaning and purpose. The cultivation of such sensitivities should be

---

[3]José Ortega y Gasset, *Towards a Philosophy of History*, p. 168.

[4]Ibid., p. 185.

[5]Richard W. Solbert, "History" in Ditmanson, et al., eds. *Christian Faith and the Liberal Arts*, p. 181.

one of the distinctive objectives of general education programs in history in the Christian college.

Human Sciences

The program of study should be designed to convey to every student an understanding of the main factors which influence human behavior; the elemental principles of social and political organization; the significance of cultural and social variations among different peoples of the world; the main causes of emotional disturbance and instability and of social disintegration; and the relevance of the Christian faith for personal and social problems.

A superficial and un-Biblical construction of the Christian doctrine of salvation has led many Christians to draw back from the personal and social implications of the gospel. The fundamentalist mind has at times associated the social applications of the Christian message with an erosion of orthodoxy, and the evangelical churches have thought of redemption not only in eternal but also in temporal terms. Yet the eternal life held out as a possibility in the Christian gospel is clearly conceived in the Bible to be a here-now possession of the believer. The temporal relevance of the Christian faith, for both personal and social concerns, is a cardinal tenet of evangelical doctrine.

The world in which we live is, however, far too complex to permit an account of this relevance apart from an extensive orientation in the human sciences. The social and psychological sciences may be regarded as a study of the means which are appropriate for the achievement of certain purposes. Social scientists study the factors which influence human behavior and thus indicate means by which behavior might be redirected in more suitable patterns. They analyze the consequences of public policies and thus suggest ways in which social and political institutions might be made to serve human ends. Knowledge of these relationships, which are often immensely complex, is essential if one is to show the applicability of Christian principles in the life of man.

Disciplined reflection is needed in order to construe the methodological assumptions of social science in a manner which is compatible with Christian faith. For example, the social sciences tend to operate with the deterministic assumption that human behavior can always be explained causally. This assumption will need to be construed by the Christian scholar in such a way as to make proper allowance for the notions of freedom and moral responsibility, which are essential to the Christian idea of man. Social scientists inevitably find analogies to human behavior among sub-human animal species, and the Christian scholar will need to show how the implications of these resemblances can be harmonized with the Biblical view of human nature.

Christians who work in the social sciences often settle for a compartmentalization of thinking on these matters, for the problems are immensely difficult. But both at the advanced level of social research and in general education programs in the social sciences, a thoroughly integrated concept of the unity of Christianity and the social sciences is necessary if the human sciences are to be given their due with respect to the church's work in the world.

A major aim of general education programs in the human sciences at the Christian college should therefore be to allow the Christian student to have an unhesitating respect for the method and findings of science in the matter of human behavior, by enabling him to see how the scientific methodology can be coordinated with the theological dogma. From the standpoint of the Christian college, general education has not succeeded until the student believes that experimental psychology and statistical research are no less essential than theological analysis in enabling the church to address itself to the modern situation. The Christian scholar should have an avid appetite for knowledge about mankind and should be eager to master whatever techniques are appropriate for the acquisition of such knowledge. There is no such thing as "Christian sociology" or "Christian economics," but there is such a thing as viewing the social sciences Christianly, that is viewing them as a tool for purposes of Christian ministry.

Natural Sciences

The program of studies should be designed to convey to every student a general descriptive knowledge of the physical environment, its processes and its order; a habit of rigor and exactness in observation and description; an appreciation of the role of science in human society; an understanding of the history and fundamental concepts of science.

The revolution in science education from the elementary level up poses a new situation for curriculum planners. Natural science and mathematics now play a larger role in American society than has been the case in any preceding generation. The explosion of knowledge is nowhere more apparent than in science and technology. Literacy in science is now a requirement for everyone.

The demands of technology pose a painful dilemma for many liberal arts colleges. The amount of time that is necessary to achieve minimal goals in science education encroaches on the time that is required for the broadening of experience. We seem to be forced to choose between technical and liberal objectives; but when faced with such a choice, we find either option distasteful. Thus the current demand for scientific education requires unusual efficiency and ingenuity in curricular planning. Most college faculties are understandably frustrated by the circumstances.

The Christian college must find a way to provide rich opportunities in science education which will equip every student for effective participation in the life of the space age. A far higher level of technical competence is required than was necessary for general education a generation ago. At the same time, the Christian college cannot afford to forfeit its distinctiveness for the sake of technological concerns. Science education at the Christian college must place special emphasis on the humanistic and cultural implications of scientific discovery. To achieve the combination of technical competence, sensitivity to human and social values, and Christian understanding is no simple assignment. But the performance of this task, difficult as it is, will give a distinctive—and indeed a superior—quality to the general education program in science in the Christian college.

The basis of an adequate integration of Christian faith with modern science is a clear distinction between scientific explanation and philosophical interpretation. Christianity, of course, posits the reality of the supernatural and is incompatible with philosophical naturalism, the view that nature comprises the whole of reality. But it is naturalism, not natural science, that is the adversary of orthodox faith. The confusion of the two is responsible for the so-called warfare between religion and science. Some scientists, of course, have also been philosophical naturalists, but it is with their philosophy, not their science, that the Christian faith is at odds.

Both sides in this debate are guilty of the confusion. The critics of Christian faith have at times supposed that the content of the faith has been scientifically more determinate than it is. On the other hand, defenders of the faith have often misinterpreted the significance of scientific explanations of natural phenomena and have presumptuously labeled them as heterodox or misapplied them for an apologetic purpose. A primary objective of general education should be to remove such misunderstandings. On the one hand, Biblical passages which allude to the physical environment need to be carefully exegeted. On the other hand, the metaphysical neutrality of natural science needs to be systematically expounded.

Careful analysis in both contexts will disclose that any essential tenet of Christian faith is in harmony with any fairly established principle of science. Apparent inconsistencies between science and Christian faith can be traced either to misinterpretation of the theological data or to some inadequacy or misapplication of the scientific investigation. For example, the Christian scientist will approach his study in the light of the conviction that God created and controls the world. But honesty requires him to recognize that the specific method and duration of creation are not disclosed, either in the Scriptural account or in the findings of science.

The Christian's commitment to supernaturalism does not require him to pre-judge the conclusions of scientific studies regarding the age of the world, the relationships between various forms of life, or the processes of biological adaptation. Scientifically derived explanations of natural phenomena must be evaluated simply on the available evidence in pursuit of an objective scientific method. The baselessness of philosophical interpretations constructed out of scientific findings can be disclosed through the same kind of criticism. Thus the most rigorous scientific study can be conducted within the framework of theistic presuppositions. Scientific education in Christian colleges sometimes displays a timidity which indicates that insufficient attention has been given to these elementary distinctions.

A Christian should be expected to approach scientific study with enthusiasm and abandon. For one thing, he believes that this is God's world. A desire to know God provokes a desire to know God's works. To one who sees with the eyes of faith, the study of nature inspires reverence, awe, and gratitude. But furthermore, the Christian should be expected to approach scientific study enthusiastically because of the human importance of the study. Human life is unbelievably richer in our generation because of modern science. Indeed, the recognition of the social and human importance of science and technology in our society has been institutionalized in a colossal and unprecedented program for the support of scientific research.

The welfare of both individual and society is based on the progress of science. The Christian, who is keenly concerned with welfare, accordingly will value scientific study as a tool of progress. Problems of disease, overpopulation, production, transportation, communication—the list is far too long even to be enumerated—all can be attacked with the resources of scientific knowledge. To promote the advance of scientific research, therefore, can be a Christian vocation, since through it man and society may be served.

Properly conducted, scientific education is particularly suited to the aims of liberal and humanistic education. Sometimes humanists have questioned the value of natural science, which they tend to conceive as mechanical and routine. But science is not simply the clerical compilation of facts. Science is the search for order in nature. The development of a scientific outlook, then, involves advance in the direction of general principles and unified explanations.

In the sciences one finds an unlimited opportunity for exercising critical acumen and a boundless reach for curiosity and imagination. The combination of freedom and discipline is nowhere more appropriate than in scientific study. And nowhere is there greater occasion for aesthetic rapture at the contemplation of grandeur and order. That vision of the order of the world, of course, can be informed by a religious outlook. Scientific study, properly conducted, can release the human spirit for the highest artistic and intellectual attainments and at the same time can provide an occasion for a religious interpretation.

Literature and Philosophy

The program of studies should be designed to allow every student to develop the ability to understand and interpret literary and philosophical masterworks; to analyze theoretical questions and to evaluate alternative answers to such questions; to evaluate literary productions aesthetically and critically.

Great literary and philosophical works are to be appreciated not only as carriers of ideological and theoretical interpretations but also as works of art. The artistic quality of the production should not fail to provoke a response in the reader. But the student of literature and philosophy is in an especially favorable position to clarify, compare, and evaluate the alternative world- and value-hypotheses which are presented to reflection. The systematic outlines of these alternatives, as well as nuances within each outlook, can be readily disclosed through a careful selection of readings.

General education should aim at developing sensitivity to such alternative interpretations of life-meanings. It should seek to cultivate tolerance in the sense of openness to unfamiliar and initially implausible understandings and a preparedness to engage in critical reappraisal of an accepted outlook. An outlook which is self-evident simply because it has not been examined or because it has not been compared with alternative interpretations is unworthy of an educated person. Honest inquiry is necessary for the development of intellectual, emotional, and moral competence. Convictions which have stood the test of a comparative analysis will always be stronger for the encounter. Maturity in belief comes only after the horizons of one's experience have been extended to include the other point of view.

Our culture is in a relativistic reaction at present. There is much misunderstanding of what reappraisal of one's beliefs signifies. For many adolescents it signifies recognizing that one person's interpretations of life's meaning is no better (or worse) than another's. But in evaluating the great ideas, education requires a balance of freedom and discipline. Thought, while free to inquire, must be rigorously disciplined to truth. The current contempt for every ism is no proof of urbanity; it is itself an ism—and it is not a special achievement of the twentieth century. The rejection of systematic thought must itself be scrutinized through a systematic investigation. Education must seek to establish a better basis for a life-outlook than caprice or emotion or arbitrary choice.

Literary and philosophical studies are especially useful for showing the relatedness of the diverse areas of human concern and experience. In one sense literature and philosophy have no subject-matter of their own; the data treated are drawn from other disciplines and from life concerns generally. The subject-matter of literature and philosophy may be of a historical, sociological, political, religious, aesthetic, emotional, or scientific nature. What is distinctive are the method and purpose of literary and philosophical analysis. Accordingly the study is inherently integrative and is especially important for imparting to the student a sense of the coherence of experience.

Literature, of course, has a special character and calls for appreciations which go beyond the theoretical and philosophical. If philosophy is concerned with reflection, literature is concerned with experience, in an indeterminate sense. Artistic and emotional appreciations are implemented in the analysis of literature. But the aim of literary study is to achieve a unified basis for the interpretation of experience. Not only thought, but also emotion can be made to cohere in a self-consistent structure of experience.

Literary criticism, indeed, could profit from closer contact with systematic thought. Whether from the artistic or the philosophical side, criticism is consistent only if it is made by reference to principle. Criticism is often arbitrary and self-contradictory, however, because the criteria of worth are not clearly and distinctly conceived. The sense for the unity of experience is therefore an essential aim of literary as well as philosophical study.

It hardly needs to be pointed out that such integrative studies are especially suited to the purposes of the Christian college. A characteristically Christian approach in literary and philosophical criticism will go a long way towards the achievement of the aims of Christian higher education. Unity in thought, value, and emotion can be achieved on the basis of Christian faith, and literary and philosophical study affords a particularly suitable occasion for the consideration of this unity. Literature and philosophy should therefore receive strong emphasis in the general education program of a Christian college.

Fine Arts

The program of studies should be designed to enable every student to acquire an understanding of the forms of art in the great traditions; the capacity to appreciate and enjoy beauty; the ability to employ aesthetic forms in self-expression.

Financial pressures sometimes force colleges to reveal the priorities in their scale of values. When budgetary restrictions impose the necessity of determining which of a number of goods are of lesser or greater value, the arts are often squeezed out first. The artistic dimension of campus life and of the curriculum is often thought to be nice, but not necessary.

Whitehead has eloquently belabored the short-sightedness of such an attitude. An efflorescence of art is the first activity of nations on the road to civilization, he said. Yet we are prepared on the basis of financial expediency to pauperize the masses of the population artistically. "The stupidity of the whole procedure is," comments Whitehead, "that art in simple popular forms is just what we can give to the nation without undue strain on our resources. . . . It would require no very great effort to use our schools to produce a population with some love of music, some enjoyment of drama, and some joy in beauty of form and color."[6] In the light of the place of art in civilization and in view of a comparison of natural and educational expenditures for various purposes, one can only say that the present state of education in the arts in most colleges is just another illustration of the failure of nerve.

Part of the problem is some extremely superficial thinking among some college faculties concerning the nature of the fine arts and their place in liberal education. It is quickly assumed that the objective of education in art, music, and dramatics is the development of proficiency in performance and that such training is of dubious relevance for the liberal arts. The error is made by faculty members both inside and outside the fine arts departments. But it is by no means necessary to conceive of education in the fine arts in such narrow terms.

As is true in any field, technique always follows principle. Whether the performance is in evaluating the validity of an argument, or conducting a program of research, or playing a musical instrument, a proficient performer is master of the principles in novel circumstances. In every field a teacher can either settle for rote imitation or insist on creative mastery of general principles. So there is no need for education in the fine arts to limit its concerns to "mere performance."

Furthermore, each of the arts has an extensive body of theoretical materials, as intellectually exacting as is involved in any field. Music involves not only musical theory but also the psychology and sociology of music. An artist must be something of a physicist, as well as master of the principles of form. An actor cannot perform well without a kind of understanding which comes only from wide reading and study. In addition, each of the fine arts has its own historical materials, which require to be viewed in the light of a wider historical understanding. There can be no question, therefore, about the substantive character of study in the arts, and it would be a profanation of the entire discipline to think of it only in terms of training in performance technique. The proper study of the arts involves a content and method which are thoroughly commensurate with the most rigorous scholarship in the sciences.

For purposes of general education the study of the arts should concentrate on the history and literature of the arts, with a view to

---

[6]Whitehead, *The Aims of Education*, p. 50.

enhancing the student's capacity for appreciation and criticism. Technical mastery of musical theory and of the principles of art is not as essential for this purpose as some musicians and artists claim. More advanced knowledge of principles undeniably allows more refined discriminations, but the eye and ear can be trained for general appreciation and evaluation with only a limited technical apparatus and vocabulary. General education courses in the fine arts should be organized not as a foundation for specialized study at a later stage, but as a presumably terminal experience designed to make artistic experience vital and significant for a life-time.

In the Christian college a special effort should be made to exhibit the role of art in religion. Art should, of course, be valued also for its own sake, as one of the works of man. It is not enough to say that the Christian should value art because it is useful in religion. Yet the distinctive approach to artistic education in the Christian college will inevitably emphasize the religious significance of art.

There are some conceptual confusions in these matters which the general education program in art should be at special pains to eliminate. The genius of the Reformation was, from one point of view, the recovery of the distinction between aesthetic experience and religious experience. The sense of beauty is not the same as the awareness and worship of God. The finest aesthetic quality in Christian worship is much to be desired, but not because with this quality worship is rendered authentic. The sign of true worship is that the will of God, as revealed in his Word, is honored. Said Luther, "Gladly would I see all the arts, especially music, in the service of Him who gives them, as He created them." But it was of Scripture that Luther said, "It is the cradle in which Christ lies."

Art can be adapted to the purposes of worship to the extent that it enhances the effectiveness of the communication of God's Word. But a religious communication is not simply an aesthetic communication. Christianity is a religion of words, not of feeling. "If the heart of the matter can be set forth without words," E. Shillito accurately observes, "then it must be added that the Word is not what it was at the first nor what it has been wherever it has come with power into human life."[7]

Luther was at first indifferent to the cultus of the church, and

[7]E. Shillito, "The Preaching of the Word" in Nathaniel Nicklem, ed., *Christian Worship* (London: Oxford University Press, 1936), p. 210.

Calvin was polemical in attacking it. A similar reaction against traditional aesthetic forms has been characteristic of many groups of Protestant Christians. Worship in many Protestant churches is painfully inartistic and even anti-artistic. The cruder forms of musical and artistic expression are apparently deemed less likely to divert attention from the essential religious subject-matter. Eccentricity and spontaneity in the service of worship are thought to allow for greater freedom in the movement of the Spirit. Order is suspect; disorder is condoned. The worship of many churches is predominantly characterized by didacticism; the hymns, prayers, anthems, and responses are regarded as "preliminaries" to the sermon. Such patterns of worship reflect an inadequate understanding of the place of art in religion. Luther's mature outlook is the right one: all the arts should be placed in the service of God, but simply as a means of heightening attentiveness to the Word of God.

Aesthetic experience can never be substituted for religious experience, but it can contribute to it. Aesthetic experiences serve to heighten our powers of awareness, concentration, and sensitivity. Attentiveness and discriminating awareness are essential for edifying encounter with God's Word, and an aesthetic experience is often the means for focusing attention and heightening interest. Furthermore, aesthetic experiences may enhance feelings which are appropriately attached to the understanding of God's Word. Art can be a suitable expression of religious passion, of religious awareness infused with an appropriate feeling. The use of aesthetic forms in worship requires the ability to identify the feeling or mood which is appropriate and it also requires knowledge of the artistic means for expressing or stimulating that feeling.

The utility of art in religion is a limited one. But this is not to say that artistic concern in the churches should be allowed to stand at a low level. The churches have always been a major custodian and patron of the arts; part of their cultural responsibility is to create a center for artistic expression and enjoyment. And the religious activities of the churches, though of a different nature from aesthetic activities, can be made more effective by the cultivation of a proper artistic quality.

If art is to serve a religious purpose, it must first meet the indispensable condition of religious service, namely self-forgetfulness. Luther is famous for the saying, "God created the world out of nothing; so he whom God will use must first become—nothing." This principle also applies to the use of art for purposes of religious communication. The use of art in religion should follow the principles of style. Style in speaking and writing should be suited to the purposes of communication. Style should never call attention to itself. The virtues of style are clarity, energy, and simplicity-with-order. These same qualities should characterize the use of music, drama, and art in religion. When artistic production calls attention to itself, it ceases to be of any utility in religion. The communication of this kind of understanding of the religious value of art should be the distinctive objective of general education programs in the fine arts at the Christian college.

Physical Education

The program of studies should be designed to enable every student to acquire an understanding of the elements of physical health; a habit of discipline in physical exercise; enjoyment of recreation and play; increasing skill in a lifetime participation in physical activities.

The training of the body and the protection of health are a part not merely of prudence, but also of Christian duty. A Christian's body is the temple in which the Holy Spirit dwells. Maintenance of bodily strength and the development of maximum physical prowess are an essential element in the discharge of Christian obligation and the realization of a full Christian personality.

Physical education has an indispensable role in Christian education not only as a means of disciplining the body but also as a means of developing the capacity to play. Christian life is more than Spartan self-denial or Puritanical self-discipline. A Christian understanding of life will also express itself, in the appropriate setting, in playfulness. There is a kind of play, of course, which is a symptom of purposelessness or frustration about life, neither of which belong to the Christian ideal. Nevertheless, the very assurance of the Christian and his dedication to the pursuit of eternal values enable him to achieve that perspective of detachment from which a healthy sense of humor springs. The enjoyment of life is one expression of Christian joy. Play belongs to Christian life.

Physical training is secondary, of course, to the development of understanding in the implications of Christian faith. "Train yourself in godliness," the young pastor was advised, "for while bodily training is of some value, godliness is of value in every way, as it holds promise for the present life and also for the life to come" (1 Timothy 4:7, 8). Yet despite a certain tendency towards asceticism which is detectable in his own manner of life, Paul did not discount the significance of physical training and healthiness even with respect to the preparation for eternity. Every student in a Christian college must be helped to train and develop his body, as a secondary, but nevertheless, essential part of his duty to himself and to Christ.

Estimates of the educational value of physical education tend to run low among many academicians. In many colleges there is considerable conflict over the assignment of academic credit for physical education courses, especially for the courses usually required for freshmen. The debate is complicated by the fact that often the basis on which college credit is assigned is not clearly stated. Some educators tend to think of a credit as recognition for time spent in activity systematically planned by academic people. Others assume that the awarding of credit and the assignment of grades are indispensable if student participation is to be sufficiently motivated. What is needed, however, is clarity about the educational utility of physical activity programs at a deeper level of theory. Physical education courses can be so organized that they are genuinely educative at the collegiate level. When conducted in such a manner—as contrasted with the practice of throwing out a ball so that the youth can play—physical activity courses can be welcomed without reluctance or embarrassment into the collegiate curriculum.

Physical education courses conducted in the proper manner (in terms of educational suitability) will emphasize the understanding of general principles governing physical development and health and the development of skill and enjoyment in the "carry-over" sports. The perspective in which a general education program in physical activity should be conducted is not the demand of freshman enthusiasm and energy, but the requirement of a lifetime of physical well-being. Preparation for a lifetime of enjoyable participation in physical activity is the ground on which physical education requirements in college study can be justified and should be the aim by reference to which the general education program in physical education is constructed.

Religion

Finally, the program of studies should be designed to convey to every student an understanding of the fundamental principles of the

Christian faith as revealed in the Scriptures; a systematic grasp of the basic philosophical and ethical implications of that faith; the ability to discriminate between the Christian faith and competing ideologies; a practical and historical understanding of the nature and mission of the Christian church.

Throughout the curriculum the integration of faith and learning is the distinctive concern of the Christian college. Responsibility for achieving this integration cannot be turned over to one department but must be accepted by the entire faculty. Nevertheless, there is need for systematic and concentrated study in the materials of the Christian religion.

The religious neutrality of most of American education has left large gaps in the general education of even the most lettered. The churches' occasional and unsystematic efforts at religious education are clearly inadequate, even for the average church member. The intensity of study that is required can be achieved only in a school. But educational institutions are usually hesitant to approach a subject matter which might be construed as sectarian. Even church-related colleges are sometimes affected by the academic stance of noncommitment in matters of religion. The unique opportunity of Christian higher education, however, is to give to the study of religion its rightful place in general and liberal education.

From the Protestant point of view the foundation and touchstone of the Christian faith is the biblical revelation. Hence for the Protestant college biblical scholarship must be the foundation of the general education curriculum in religion. This does not mean, of course, that the only acceptable organization of the program of study is an expository one. It means rather that, whatever organizational pattern is followed, an inductive study of the biblical materials is basic. The fundamental objective of the general education program in religion, in other words, should be to enable the student to understand the Bible.

The subject matter of general education courses in Bible and religion has a tendency to exhibit the professionalism of graduate education in the field. This tendency must be steadfastly resisted. General education courses in religion should emphasize the relevance of the biblical teaching for the life-situation of man, they should stress ethical application, and they should lend themselves to the development of a comprehensive philosophic outlook. The subject matter for primary emphasis should be the elements of Christian doctrine, the main principles of Christian personal and social ethics, the outlines of church history and the principles of ecclesiology, and comparative analysis of the Christian faith by reference to non-Christian philosophies and religions. In each case religious studies in the general education program should be rigorous but not technical, biblical but not doctrinaire. Enough time should be allowed for such studies to permit the development of a productive and critical understanding. Of special concern should be the aim of giving the student a methodology and motivation for inductive study of the Bible on his own.

Large segments of American education are dominated by the opinion that theological understanding is inimical to creative and rigorous scholarship. The Christian college is uniquely placed to demonstrate the essential importance of religious study within liberal education and to insist that without a theological understanding learning is incomplete.

Chapter 5

STRUCTURE IN THE CURRICULUM

Although general education is an essential part of the curriculum, a college education is not merely a general education. A broad learning experience is essential, but it must be supplemented by a program of specialized study aimed at the development of competence.

SPECIALIZED EDUCATION

A college education should permit a student to achieve the competence of one who knows. But given the diversity and complexity of modern scholarship, universal competence is unattainable. Specialization is unavoidable if competence is to be attained. An essential aim of higher education must be to assist the student to acquire sufficient mastery of some field of learning to enable him to keep pace with and make his own contribution to our rapidly changing and expanding knowledge.

The purposes of specialized education include the following:

- to enable the student to develop the ability to do independent research and to make his own contribution to knowledge
- to cultivate in the student a sense of the unity of thought through the integrated and systematic investigation of a field in depth, and to give the student a concrete understanding of the nature of scholarship

• to allow for a proper division of labor in scholarship and to give the student a sense of mastery over at least one aspect of human learning

• to enhance the utilitarian value of a college education by giving the student a special competence which he can put to practical use.

Competence, of course, is a relative term. There is one level of competence which is appropriate to undergraduate education, another which is appropriate to graduate study, another which is appropriate to advanced research. Correspondingly there are varying degrees of specialization and intensification at these different levels. At the undergraduate level specialization allows a student to concentrate *on* a given field. At the graduate and research levels specialization means concentration *within* a field. Then as science matures and its content is enriched, fields themselves become sub-divided, and further specialization is required. Competence is not a static concept, and it is therefore impossible to define the scope of specialized study, even on the undergraduate level, once and for all.

The four-year course of study should be about equally divided between general and specialized education. There may be differences of opinion, however, concerning the manner of the division. Most colleges allow general education to be concentrated in the first two years, specialized education in the last two. There is no necessary reason for this distribution, however. Similarly, many colleges employ the categories of "major" and "minor" in organizing the program of specialized education, the major being constituted of the equivalent of about one full year of study and the minor of the equivalent of about a half year of study. Again, there is no necessary reason for the provision of "majors" and "minors" in the curriculum. There is room for a variety of approaches in the implementation of specialized curricular programs.

The indispensable principle which must be followed in curricular organization, however, is that intensive study in a specialized field of scholarship needs to be supported by supplementary studies at an advanced level in a related field. The purpose of the program of supplementary studies (often labelled the "minor") is not to guard against over-specialization or to supply a secondary half-way competence in addition to the major concentration. Rather the aim of the program of supplementary studies is to enhance the student's mastery within his specialization. Consequently the program of supplementary studies needs to be selected with a view to its supportive relatedness to the specialization. The supplementary program must be regarded as part of the student's total field of concentration.

The choice of a field of specialized study is properly connected with the choice of a vocation. The purposes of specialized education must therefore include vocational preparation. The so-called antithesis between vocational and liberal education is a spurious one. Specialized education in a liberal arts college is unavoidably associated with vocational purposes.

Educational *vocationalism* is something very different. When a narrow vocational preoccupation causes instruction to lose its freedom and creativity and to settle for imitativeness and routine application of procedural rules, the essence of liberal education is lost. Training which is controlled by vocationalism may enable the student to deal with a single type of problem effectively, but not with the variety and novelty of problems with which the liberally educated person is equipped to deal. A liberal education must have a vocational orientation, in the sense that it gives the student a competence which he can put to use, but it cannot be reconciled with vocationalism, in the sense of training which concentrates on procedures rather than principles.

There is room, therefore, for vocational curricula in the liberal arts college, but these curricula need to exhibit the distinctive stamp of liberal education. Vocational preparation in the liberal arts college must go beyond creating the ability to perform a fixed function under direct orders from a superior and in obedience to established rules. If, as Whitehead says, education must be concerned with the imaginative consideration of learning, vocational preparation must always be calculated to sharpen and enhance the imagination.

The distinctively liberal approach in vocational preparation is to emphasize general principles in their adaptability. The complexity of modern society, indeed, requires the capacity for analysis and imaginative reorganization which comes only from a mastery of over-all principles. Vocational curricula are entirely appropriate for the liberal arts college, if the methodology of study focuses on the imaginative consideration of the general principles underlying the career.

The Christian doctrine of vocation serves to reinforce such an interpretation of the nature of specialized education. Preparation for a career of usefulness is inherent in the idea of Christian higher education. A diversity of callings can be construed under the ministry of the church in the world. Much more is involved than the staffing of ecclesiastical institutions and agencies. The whole range of possible service in the name of Christ needs to be included. To the extent that resources can be marshalled, programs of specialized education in the Christian college should be aimed towards an integration of competence in the exercise of such callings with a creative understanding of the content and implications of the Christian faith. In this way the Christian college can help to produce the leadership needed for the work and witness of the church.

Specialized education at the undergraduate level should aim at comprehension of the distinctive issues and characteristic principles of a given field. Coverage of the entire field is not required. The survey approach is of doubtful value, both in the conduct of general education courses and in the organization of a major. Progress is more likely to be made through a careful selection of materials for intensive analysis. Thorough investigation of a specific issue inevitably brings to bear understanding of broad principles. A careful selection of such issues, with a view to their utility for evoking comprehension of characteristic issues, can be made the organizational basis of the major. Specialization at the undergraduate level should emphasize the principles which govern the field as a whole. Mastery of these principles can then be made the basis of more specialized, intensified, and practical approaches in professional activity and advanced study.

The integration of career preparation into the traditions of liberal education remains an unfinished task at most Christian colleges. Frequently, specialized and career preparation programs merely co-exist alongside general or liberal education programs, without being effectively unified with them. The mutual enrichment of these two systems of learning, as contemplated in an integrative idea of education, remains largely an unrealized hope.

Two conditions must be satisfied before integration can occur. First, the same collegiate rigor and quality must be maintained in both specialized and non-specialized courses of instruction. In both, the focus of concern must be on the permanent and significant rather than the transient and trivial. Superficiality in either sector of the curriculum will obstruct integration. Second, career preparation and liberal education must be viewed as but different aspects of a single process of human development through education. The program of instruction must avoid the sterility of either preoccupation with abstractions without regard for practical utilization or assimilation of techniques of immediate or short term applicability without regard to general principles. The cultivation of intelligence and the stimulation of curiosity must be viewed as essential purposes of specialized and professional education no less than of liberal education. And the demonstration of the usefulness of knowledge must be viewed as no less essential for liberal education than for specialized and professional education.

The college's curricula in specialized education and career preparation should be designed so as to foster achievement of the following educational outcomes: (1) mastery of basic tools and skills which are the foundation of competence; (2)understanding of the fundamental principles in a variety of circumstances; and (3) understanding of the interrelationships of principles and recognition of the methodology and context out of which principles emerge and are revised. The programs should not be addressed to the development of a narrow or mechanical competence which is applicable only in a restricted environment and is soon obsolete. Emphasis should be placed, rather, on the need for adaptability of specialized skills and on the development of technical competence as a flowering of general or philosophical understanding. The aim should be to enable the graduate to fulfill the widest possible range of career roles.

The aims of programs of specialized education and career preparation are not discontinuous with those of general education. These aims include the following: (1) to provide an orientation to the vocabulary and basic principles in a professional or scholarly field; (2) to provide a foundation for further study and growth; (3) to equip the specialist for adaptation to the changing requirements and varied demands of the world of work; (4) to exhibit the key ideas, underlying assumptions, and broad generalizations which give meaning to particular facts and flexibility to techniques; and (5) to cultivate the attitudes and motivations of responsible professional practice. Such aims for specialized and career preparation programs are closely related to the aims of liberal education. Indeed, it is entirely possible to conceive of specialized or career preparation programs of a liberal arts college as one of the contexts in which the aims of liberal education might be effectively pursued.

Obviously, if specialized education and career preparation are to be effectively integrated with liberal education, sufficient time will have to be allowed within the total undergraduate experience to allow the student to cultivate the discipline and awareness of the liberally educated mind. Every specialized curriculum needs to provide adequate opportunity, within the general education core program or within the specialized courses themselves, for students to assimilate the concepts, principles, and understanding which will facilitate the imaginative consideration and creative application of specialized competence.

Career preparation and liberal education are sometimes polarized because of static or rigid conceptions of either of the two components. Conflict also grows from the heightening of demands for specialized or non-specialized competence in the face of the limits of available time in the undergraduate experience of students. Curricular design must come to terms with such polarization through integrative planning which recognizes the distinctive role of each component in a total program of personal development through education.

An additive approach to curriculum development is not adequate for the purpose of adapting the ideals and traditions of liberal education to the requirements of contemporary society. The undergraduate curriculum must exhibit the integration of professional and liberal education, of specialized and general education, so that the graduate will be equipped not only for entry into a career and for short term performance in a career, but also for adaptation to career roles which cannot now be foreseen and for a life-time of practical effectiveness.

THE PRINCIPLE OF PARSIMONY

The operation of many American colleges reminds one of the analogy of the leaky vessel in Plato's *Gorgias*. The vessel is so full of holes that the water level can be maintained only by continuously replenishing the supply. An incalculable number of dollars annually passes through the system of American higher education in a manner suggested by the analogy. The supporting public keeps pumping in money, which keeps running out through the leaks in the system. The process is repeated year after year; the public is continually asked to make up for the college's operating deficit, through either taxation or voluntary contributions. The system is irrational and wasteful. It ought not to be allowed to continue.

The focal point of wastage in the colleges is the curriculum. By far the largest proportion of a college's expenditures is in salaries, and it is in the maintenance of unnecessary salaries that the colleges are committing their most grievous fiscal sins. Many colleges have larger staffs than they need. In the instructional budget the overload of staff arises from the fact that the curriculum includes more courses than are needed. The proliferation of courses in the typical undergraduate curriculum has thus eroded the efficiency of the colleges and has seriously hampered the effectiveness of many institutions.

Parsimony in the organization of a curriculum is mandatory from the financial standpoint, especially for the smaller colleges. For the Christian college it is dictated, furthermore, by the Christian ideal of stewardship. But it is also justifiable on educational grounds. The factors which have made for proliferation are not central to the idea of the Christian college. They have emerged from circumstances external to the college and its philosophy of education. A Christian college can remain true to its educational ideals and convictions while refusing to yield to these pressures.

The dominance of the universities in the American academic scene in recent years is one root of the problem. If the nineteenth century was the age of the college, the twentieth century is the age of the university. Of course, universities are also greatly troubled at present over the alarming rate of course proliferation in their own curricula. But university curricula, especially at the graduate level, exhibit a degree of specialization which reveals the influence of educational diversification and advanced research. The dominance of the university system in American higher education creates the impression that the mark of excellence, both in curricular organization and in scholarship generally, is a comparable degree of specialization.

The faculty of a small college is inclined to seek a curricular pattern which is oriented towards the ideals of the graduate programs with which they are familiar. Recruitment for faculty positions seeks to make allowance for the specialized competences of prospective faculty, and specialization within a department is assumed to be necessary to attract scholars of the highest quality. New recruits in college teaching are especially conscious of the specialization of their training and experience and are attracted to positions which allow them to exploit their competence. Thus the university tradition has created patterns which tend to associate quality with quantity, and many small colleges have been affected by these patterns. Excellence tends to mean specialization, and specialization means the proliferation of courses.

A second root of the proliferation of courses is the elective system in the curriculum of higher education. There is much to be said for this system. It was part of the reform that enabled Harvard College to become Harvard University. It allows freedom and flexibility in program planning so that the course of study can be adapted to the particular needs, purposes, and interests of the individual student. Actually, however, the elective system is often the reflection of the autonomy of departments and the symptom of the breakdown of wholeness in the total organization of a college. Conflicts of departmental interests are most often compromised by an adaptation of the elective system. In many cases, when the student is given an elective, the faculty has not been able to resolve the differences of opinion as to what should be required. Nevertheless, the elective system has its merits, and something would be lost if it had to be abandoned.

The small college, however, is not served best by the elective system. The small college does better to establish strict limitations on the electives which are allowed to the student. The distinctive feature of the Christian liberal arts college is the attempt to contribute to the integration of experience, and the elective system does not expedite this attempt. There is nothing sacred about the elective system, especially from the standpoint of the Christian college; and despite its advantages in some respects, it has positive disadvantages which justify its being curtailed. It will be found that if the elective system is controlled, one of the strongest pressures making for curricular proliferation will have been removed.

A third root of the proliferation of courses in American colleges is an unimaginative application of the survey approach in undergraduate instruction. Both in introductory courses and in the major, there is a great disposition among college teachers to want to "cover the field." Again, it is undeniable that there are positive advantages in comprehensive coverage. But Ortega y Gasset was certainly reflecting a mature educational judgment when he wrote, "Selection is the essence of teaching." The teacher can cover topics only selectively. This principle has not yet been given its due in the organization of the American college curriculum. It should be the point of departure for curricular study, rather than the conclusion to which debate regretfully comes. Whitehead once said, "God has so made the world that there are more topics desirable for knowledge than any one person can possibly acquire. It is hopeless to approach the problem by the way of the enumeration of subjects which everyone ought to have mastered. There are too many of them, all with excellent title-deeds."[1]

This is not to say, of course, that the educator should abandon the effort to distinguish between the fundamental and the superfluous, the important and the nonessential, the central and the peripheral. The selectivity of education means precisely that the teacher ought to be able to identify that "which everyone ought to have mastered." The point is rather that the basis of the organization of the curriculum should be a principle which expresses the unity of thought, rather than a distributive principle which expresses the importance of various kinds of learning. If importance is the criterion for determining what should be included in a curriculum, it is difficult to justify the exclusion of anything. But if there is a central, unifying curricular motif, it can be shown that some materials are, relatively speaking, more germane. It is not possible to cover everything in a small-college curriculum, either in a program of general education or in a program of specialized study; hence it is important to discover a unifying concept which will lend purpose to the selection of topics.

The principle of parsimony brings us back to the recurring theme of the need for a distinctive educational concept in the Christian college. "The problem," says Jerald Brauer, "is that the Christian college is trying to be all things to all men, not in order to witness to the vitality of the faith but in order to keep the doors open. This cannot go on."[2] The basic problem in curricular development is the determination of the range of knowledge which it is the college's objective to treat. If it is made too narrow, there is risk of pedantry and proliferation. If it is made too wide, there is risk of a loss of rigor and scholarly excellence. The balance of thoroughness and selectivity is difficult to strike. And it is easy to oversimplify the problem in books on educational philosophy. But the solution to this problem may be the key to the future of the Christian college in America.

Mark Van Doren has said that the absence of intellectual design is the one intolerable thing in education. Design is indispensable for both

[1]Whitehead, *The Aims of Education*, p. 39.

[2]Jerald C. Brauer, "The Christian College and American Higher Education," *The Christian Scholar* 41: Special Issue (Autumn 1958): 240.

instructional effectiveness and institutional efficiency. Design in the program of general education means the attainment of efficiency in the strategy for achieving the integrative goals of education. An analysis of characteristic emphases and functions in various types of study and of their relationships to other disciplines will contribute to unity in curricular implementation. A curriculum which is efficiently integrative will be comprised of parts which are interdependent and mutually reinforcing.

All disciplines, notes a St. Olaf College Self-Study Committee, have relationships to other disciplines.[3] The study of the ways in which these relationships are sustained needs to be reduced to more of a science, along the lines, for example, of the very helpful suggestions developed by the St. Olaf Committee. Some courses of study, the Committee observes, are primarily *receptive-focal.* They draw materials and principles from other fields and focus them on work in a particular field. Here the coordination of various learnings is the means of making the student more effective in the performance of a given task. Other studies are primarily *contributive.* These disciplines have only a formal subject-matter of their own, but their application is basic to other studies which are *receptive-contributive.* In some ways they draw upon other fields. Integration in learning experience here is a matter of a reciprocal application of materials and principles drawn from different disciplines. Finally, there are *synoptic* studies, in which a concerted effort is made to see things in a connected whole. Some studies may be accidentally synoptic, or perhaps synoptic in a limited scale, but philosophy and theology are disciplines which are inherently and intentionally synoptic, both in method and in content. They aim at an interpretation of knowledge and experience as a whole. Such fields seek integration through disciplined reflection of the widest possible scope.

The classification of components of the curriculum under categories such as these, and the correlation of their respective roles in the general education curriculum in the light of their functionality for specific educational objectives, comprise a project which it has scarcely occurred to college faculties to undertake. Yet a purposive effort in general education waits for such an analysis to be conducted.

---

[3]St. Olaf College Self-Study Committee, *Integration in the Christian Liberal Arts College,* (Northfield, MN: St. Olaf College Press, 1956), pp. 163-70.

The primary curricular concern of a faculty should be to achieve maximum efficiency and systematic purpose in the organization of the program of general education. The faculty should first create a core curriculum, comprised largely of specifically required courses, whose main objective is the integration of learning on a philosophico-theological basis. Thereupon study should be devoted to the reorganization of the various specialized programs, which should be designed by reference both to an internal principle of organization and to the content of the general education core. In both programs the curricular options presented to the student in the small college need to be stringently limited.

The principle of parsimony means the abandonment of the elective system in favor of a coherently organized curriculum. Undoubtedly it will be said in some quarters that such a principle in curricular organization is retrogressive. Indeed, it is a step backward if the norm for measuring instructional excellence is the multi-purpose university. But it is not a step backward if it is based on the creation of a distinctive educational unity within the college. A closely structured curriculum was characteristic, indeed, of the American colleges of the nineteenth century. But the principle of parsimony does not ask that we simply roll back the clock and return to an anachronistic form. A creative reorganization of the curriculum in the mid-twentieth century can take advantage of the progress made by the general education movement and can recognize the extension of the aims of education to include individuals and professional purposes not envisaged by the nineteenth century college.

The curricular reorganization demanded by the principle of parsimony is not retrogressive but reconstructive. It can be made the new departure for a fresh approach in American higher education. It can be the means by which small colleges can attain new heights in educational excellence, through an efficiency which will enable them to compete with more wasteful institutions. If careful study is devoted to the problems, structure in the curriculum can be achieved with both greater efficiency and greater effectiveness. The mandate to explore this possibility should be given the highest priority by Christian college faculties in planning for their future.

EDUCATION IN VALUES

The curricular distinctiveness of the Christian college centers on the nature of its provision for value formation through education. The foundation of an educational program designed and conducted to foster the clarification or formation of values in students is an understanding of the method by which questions of value may be addressed through critical scholarship and of the psychological processes of values clarification.

Education is characterized by the primacy of its preoccupation with intellect. Education is basically concerned with improving the student's power to think and thereby to enhance his capacity for living. The educator's approach to the question of values is, therefore, necessarily by way of *thinking* about values. The foundation of a program of education in values is an understanding of the relation between thinking and valuation.

The relation between thinking and valuation is of primary importance from the point of view not only of educational theory but also of value theory. The indispensable requirement of valuation is intentionality, the free choice of the valuer as mediated by his understanding of the nature of the choice and his critical assessment of the considerations bearing on the warrantability of the choice. A program of education in values, therefore, must apply the methodologies and results of scholarship to the critical study of value judgements.

There are several levels at which scholarship may be applied in the study of values. At one level scholarship, as the investigation of the relationships between means and ends, may be applied in the determination of value in an instrumental sense. At a second level scholarship, particularly psychological and sociological inquiry, may be applied in the observation, reporting, explanation, prediction, and guidance of valuational behavior of individuals. Scholarly study *about* values and valuation is a major aspect of the science of human behavior. But there is also a third level for the application of scholarship to the study of values, viz. the analysis of the critical basis of value judgements. Here the object of investigation is the value judgements themselves, not merely the beliefs, feelings, or attitudes of a valuing subject; and the questions have to do ultimately with intrinsic value, not merely with the instrumental value of means. Here the applicability of scholarship is much more debatable in scholarly circles and much more difficult to state precisely.

Education in values is not merely a matter of communicating right or true answers to questions about value and about God or of enabling an individual to become aware of his personal system of values. The teacher of values must also communicate the *foundations* of value judgments—the process of thought which will enable a reflective person to become settled in his ethical, aesthetic, and religious convictions. The focus of a program of education in values is on moral reasoning, on the basis of aesthetic criticism, on the methods of theological analysis and on the place of valuation in the life of the mind.

Thus, the enterprise of moral education is not merely the identification or communication of a system of rules of conduct. It is also the determination of the rules of procedure or the canons of evidence which we may use to assess the merits of a moral view. The morally educated individual should be able to explain what sorts of demands are placed on a person when, having put forward a moral view, he is asked to justify it. Similarly, the task of theological education is not merely to impart a set of orthodox beliefs concerning God and his relationship to the world. The task is also to clarify the methodology for distinguishing between meaningful and nonsensical theological propositions, between "radical revelation" and the culturally conditioned theological enterprise, between the Word of God and the cultural accretions of human interpretation of the Word of God.

An analogous situation holds in scientific education. The teaching of science is not merely a matter of getting people to repeat scientific truths. It is also a matter of helping them to understand science, to be clear about the methods of scientific inquiry, and to be able to reason scientifically, so that they can comprehend the meaning of the scientific truths which they possess. Similarly, educating people in history, literary criticism, or philosophy is more than pumping true propositions into their heads; it is teaching them to know what counts as sufficient grounds for a belief in these fields.

A program of education in values, therefore, must concentrate on assisting students to master a method of *thinking* about values. As John Wilson says of moral education:

> Any basis for moral education should consist of imparting those skills which are necessary to make good and reasonable moral decisions and to act on them. We are not primarily out to impart any specific *content*, but to give other people a facility in *method*. This is what eventually happened with science, and this is why science and

> education in science eventually prospered; and this is what must happen to morality.[4]

The foundation of a unified program of Christian higher education is a theological understanding which permits the integration of Christian faith with advanced scholarship, the permeation of the educational process by a Christian interpretation, and the penetration of the life of the campus by the central ethical and theological convictions of the Christian church. The separation of an effort in theological education from the rest of the educational program is contrary to the idea of a Christian college. Such separation is disfunctional from the point of view of personal development through education and is based, furthermore, on a mistaken understanding of the nature of theological method. The idea of a Christian college presupposes that there is a theological method which can be validated as coordinate with other forms of scholarly inquiry. Without such a method theology is reduced to pontificating its dogmas and theological education is merely doctrinaire. But possessing such a method, the student can comprehend the basis of his religious belief. The integration of faith and learning in the Christian college of liberal arts requires the achievement of a theological construct which is fully in harmony with contemporary scholarship.

A program of education in values must provide for an integration of cognitive and affective learning. Both components are essential in the total development of the student. On the one hand, the cognitive study of values should be organized in recognition of the ways in which the affective development of students may influence their capacity to give attention to general principles. Furthermore, the aim of the program of values education should be understood not only in terms of the development of cognitive understanding of the basis of moral, aesthetic, and religious belief, but also in terms of the appropriation by the individual of a coherent system of values and beliefs by which he may guide his decisions and his actions.

From the point of view of planning for affective development it should be remembered, on the other hand, that the cognitive study of values must be a conspicuous element in any effort to provoke reap-

---

[4]John Wilson, et al., *Introduction to Moral Education* (Gretna, LA: Pelican, 1967), p. 27.

praisal and clarification of personal values and beliefs through education. Particularly in the college setting, conflict over values should be generated by critical consideration of the foundations and implications of value judgments. Particularly at the more complex stages of affective development, the integration of affective and cognitive processes is of the utmost importance. Educational strategies for guiding students in the formation of values should recognize the close interdependence of these two domains.

The program of education in values must also be based on knowledge of the psychological processes through which moral and religious values are developed. Educational strategies will be more likely to be effective in fostering maturity in moral and religious belief if they:

- *Sustain a rhythm of differentiation and integration, questioning and resolution, challenge and response, which stimulates adaptive growth.* Development occurs as individual adaption to unfamiliar and stressful situations. As long as habitual responses are satisfactory no new adaptation will occur. But where an individual is confronted with a challenge which exposes the inadequacy of habitual responses, creative adaption is demanded. Such challenges are painful, of course, but it is only through stress that progress is possible. Of course, the stress may not be so great as to cause collapse. And sometimes guidance towards a more adequate response must be supplied by someone of greater experience. But without some frustration and doubt, no individual can grow in grace.
- *Provide for an enlarging exercise of independent judgment and individual decision with respect to both program planning and critical evaluation of beliefs.* Spiritual development proceeds from faith to faith. In the early stages of development it may be best for the exercise of free choice to be hedged about with disciplinary restrictions, but there must be a progressive relaxation of such constraints to allow a broader and broader rein to the individual's own choice. It is only through having the opportunity to make mistakes that individuals may gain autonomy.
- *Recognize the uniqueness of individuals, with respect to both educational needs and rates of learning.* Most education in the United States is too stereotyped to be worthy of the name. Education, as distinguished from mere training, is an attempt to lead an individual into the realization of his potentiality. Training, on the other hand,

attempts to produce individuals of a desired type. The effectiveness of training is measured in terms of approximation to an ideal type which represents the aim of the training program: the standard is an ideal civil engineer or an ideal historian. But the ideal types by reference to which the aims of education, viewed as training, are defined are nothing but abstractions. So are the statistically derived descriptions of the student whom such programs ostensibly serve. The student, too, is an abstraction which, for all its philosophical splendor, does not exist in the real world. What education deals with are real, live students, who do not fit into stereotypes of statistical profiles and who do not respond to educational stimuli merely as members of a class.

Flexibility and recognition of individual differences will be conspicuous features of a system of education designed to foster personal development. What is in evidence in most colleges, by contrast, is a curriculum characterized by repetitiveness and a set of policy requirements characterized by impersonal rigidity. When contemporary students resort to games to beat such a system, they are only experiencing the sterility of an academic regimen which never had any value for human life.

- *Organize the form and sequence of instructional activities not only by reference to the logical (or chronological) division of the subject-matter, but also by reference to the kinds of instructional method best suited to attaining educational goals.* No one instructional method is, by itself, adequate as a means to achieving the variety of educational aims which must be recognized in a developmental program of education. A discussion technique is optimal for the achievement of some, but not all, educational objectives. Some educational aims are best achieved through a lecture method. A wide range of learning experiences is required in a comprehensive program of education. A well-structured curriculum, therefore, will provide not only for a comprehensive and organized treatment of subjects, but also for the systematic and strategic use of the full range of instructional methods. When students are thrown without explanation into a large lecture section, they should be expected to resent it and to collapse. But if the choice of a lecture method can be defended on educational grounds, and is not merely an economic expedient, then once the explanation is provided to the student he will be able to see how the lecture course can contribute uniquely to his development. One cause of the ineffectiveness of so much instructional activity in American colleges and universities is the inadequacy of our provision for strategic use of particular instructional purposes in a manner which exploits their distinctive advantages.

• *Employ a method of evaluation of student achievement which minimizes a system of rewards based on standing relative to other students and maximizes evaluative feedback which the student finds personally corrective and edifying.* We do not need to abolish grades. But we need a radical new departure in grading in order to break the fixation on grade averages which has emasculated education as a means of personal human development. Teachers owe their students a conscientious evaluation of their work which reveals to the student his substantive strengths and weaknesses. But the competitiveness of the grading system which has been the bequest of teachers to their students is one of the most pernicious features of the American educational system. The reform of the course-credit-grade system is the most overdue item of unfinished business on the agenda of American education.

• *Emphasize a content of study which identifies fundamental questions, throws light on complex issues, and demands critical evaluation of basic interpretations of human existence.* It is to deal with such matters that the Christian college is peculiarly called. No other institution in American higher education can be expected to do so. The churches do not have the resources. Only in the colleges of clear Christian profession can a young person find the opportunity for fundamental engagement with the great issues of Christian thought. Many adolescents have developed a keen interest in such issues. The Christian college that prepares itself for a comprehensive and orderly treatment of these matters will find another way to establish a strong and vital connection to the real-life concerns of adolescents.

Chapter 6

THE CHRISTIAN TEACHER

The heart of the educational process is the teacher. A well-structured curriculum, an efficient and enlightened administration, convenient and attractive physical facilities and equipment, and fiscal soundness are all essential to a good college, but in the last analysis these are of educational significance only to the extent that they release a teacher for more effective performance of his instructional function. The key to the success of any educational enterprise is the competence and personality of the classroom teacher. Hence concern about the quality of classroom instruction is properly the first order of business for an educational institution. Once they have achieved clarity concerning the nature and purposes of Christian higher education, the Christian colleges will need to find or train the teachers who will be able to implement the idea. Without Christian teachers there is no Christian education.

EDUCATION WITHOUT INSTRUCTION

Public debate over educational programs in recent years has quickened concern about the quality of instruction. The debate has had a number of very wholesome effects and has helped to create a welcome mood of openness to suggestions for reform. Yet despite many workshops and pronouncements, the performance of classroom teachers still lags at a great many colleges.

Furthermore, there is a great deal of confusion, both in the colleges and in large segments of the public, about the conditions which make for effectiveness in teaching. It is often assumed that what makes for good teaching is the provision of small classes and an attendant closeness of student-faculty contacts, or a student-faculty relationship which is tenderized by humaneness and openness, or a requirement that teachers take courses in educational psychology and teaching methods to augment their scholarly competence in the subject field. Yet in college after college these conditions are satisfied and teaching remains ineffective.

What students and teachers are saying about each other indicates that all is not well in the classroom. Students accuse teachers of providing the very thing which teachers accuse students of demanding—a substitute for education. Students complain that they are being cheated through the disorganization, abstractness, incompetence, absenteeism, or indifference of their instructors; that they are not being sufficiently pressed or disciplined; that their classes are dull, uninteresting, and irrelevant. Teachers, on the other hand, protest that students are not prepared to consume the sort of instruction which they aspire to give them; that their instructional endeavors are repeatedly frustrated by student disinterest and indiscipline; that students think of college as a headquarters for part-time employment opportunities, recreational activities, and sociability rather than as a center of learning.

Such accusations betray the fundamental self-contradiction in the instructional situation. There may be debate as to who is to blame, but the fact is undeniable that students and teachers alike are aware that the rigor has gone out of many classrooms. Teaching has been counterfeited. It has become, as Denis Baly notes, nothing but the merchandising of academic "packages." A college degree has come to be conceived quantitatively—in terms of recognition for the accumulation of a certain number of units of study. To use Barzun's phrase, a major segment of American education today is offering education without instruction.

Exposure Without Experience

For one thing, education too often offers the student exposure without experience. The present level of understanding about the nature of education is betrayed by the prevalence of physical metaphors in the description of the function of the teacher. Teachers speak of themselves as "influencing" students—influencing their beliefs, their plans, their choice of goals, their values—as if the categories of cause and effect were appropriate for describing learning. Teachers speak—especially at the time of registration—of "channeling" students in certain directions—as if the human personality were subject to steering at the will of another. Teachers speak of "exposing" students to certain ideas and experiences—as if the student's mind were like a photographic plate, waiting to receive an impression from without.

Such metaphors are seriously misleading. It is impossible to imagine Socrates speaking thus about his own role as a teacher. Yet in classroom after classroom, teachers think of themselves as "exposing" students to something. Remembering what things were like in graduate school, the teacher still talks fondly of studying something "in depth," but he resigns himself to the fate of the undergraduate instructor. He yearns for the opportunity to really get into the subject, but he is prepared to settle for a survey.

Contact Without Discipline

But in the second place, there is education without instruction because the college classroom is often the scene in which teacher and student experience contact without discipline. Education is, indeed, an encounter between a teacher and a learner. In recent years, however, American education has become preoccupied with the social aspects of the encounter. The purpose of the encounter—mastery of the subject matter, disciplined understanding of which is the mark of the educated—is forgotten and in its place is left a new justification of contact—the socialization of the immature.

In *The House of Intellect* Jacques Barzun quotes at length from an article in an educational bulletin, "Contact: a Focus for Guidance." What the child needs, according to the author of this piece, is "contact" with an adult. By "contact" is apparently meant, Barzun notes, "the conveying of feeling through some exchange of words or gestures." The approach best calculated to establish contact is, in the words of the educationist, "a forgiving and forbearing atmosphere in which each child feels his uniqueness appreciated."[1] Of course, no one can be

[1]Barzun, *The House of Intellect* (New York: Harper Torchbooks, 1961), pp. 101, 102.

against kindness, acceptance, and tenderness. No one can prefer a rude and inconsiderate teacher. But what is missing in all this talk about "contact," Barzun notes, is any reference to the subject matter which brings teacher and student together. The teacher wants the student to feel accepted; the student wants to know the teacher as a human being; but where is the concern for learning about, say, geography?

Barzun has perceptively identified one of the sources of this changed conception of the role of the teacher. What has happened, Barzun claims, is that philanthropy—one of the enemies of intellect—has taken control of the schools. "The notion of helping a child has in the United States displaced that of teaching him."[2]

Contact without discipline is sometimes all that passes between teacher and student. Both are more concerned to be understood as persons than to recognize the austere discriminations which intellect requires. Philanthropy becomes an excellent rationalization for avoiding judgment and discipline, both of which can be made to appear discriminatory. Education too often has become content with subjective standards of evaluation, drawn from the opinions of the student or from the pooled ignorance of the class. The meaning of excellence, the quality of genius, against which a person's most creative accomplishments may be measured, is then not encountered in its starkness.

Contemplation Without Commitment

There is education without instruction also when classroom teaching encourages contemplation without commitment. A major weakness of classroom work in American colleges is the noncommittal and indecisive tone of much instruction. Certainly, the sign of scholarship is judicial impartiality and critical objectivity. The beliefs of the scholar have to be derived from evidence; unexamined or unsubstantiated beliefs can be accepted only by the thoughtless. But education cannot remain undecided, always collecting data, never drawing conclusions. Yet many students find it possible to pass through their courses without ever being required to make up their minds about central issues. It is not surprising that such courses should be thought dull.

Sceptical indecision threatens to cut the heart out of instruction in American schools. It is being forgotten that education must aim at a responsible and judicious choice between alternatives. A mature scho-

---

[2]Ibid., p. 102.

lar knows what to believe, and he also knows when doubt is justified; but he cannot act as though all opinions were equally credible or equally dubitable. Education ought to lead not to a sophomoric relativism, but to the firming up of convictions and the settling of opinions.

Indoctrination Without Dialectic

At the other extreme from the uncommitted classroom, however, is the doctrinaire classroom, the classroom in which education without instruction takes the form of indoctrination without dialectic. While some teachers pronounce a plague on all doctrines and discharge an opinionless graduate, others advance doctrine from sheer dogmatism and discharge an opinionated graduate. Many instructors who are decisive are merely doctrinaire. The faithful teacher must steer a middle course and strike a happy balance between decisiveness and criticism.

The Socratic teaching is an example of the balanced view. Socrates's whole life was dedicated to a refutation of Sophism, which made truth relative and rhetoric the highest learning. In reply Socrates sought to demonstrate that truth is so, that convictions can have a universal warrantability. Certainly there are conflicting opinions, Socrates admitted, but this does not mean that truth is in conflict with itself. For there is a difference between knowledge and belief. Knowledge *is* attainable if one takes the necessary pains. Education is dedicated to the vindication of the distinction between knowledge and opinion. The learning of the rhetorician may be useful in persuading another to adopt one's opinion, but the only learning which belongs to education, said Socrates, is the learning of the philosopher or the scientist, which issues from the pursuit of truth.

From the Socratic standpoint, the method for both the discovery and the communication of truth is dialectical. The process by which truth comes to be possessed is the process of deciding between conflicting alternatives. The movement of teaching, then, is the clarification of alternatives, combined with a stimulus (often achieved through the use of irony) which provokes the learner to decide. The process is dialectical and critical and it places the onus of discovery on the learner. The teacher is the mid-wife, helping the learner bring to birth the idea which his intelligence conceives.

The tenor of the Socratic dialectic was most conspicuously elenctic, for learning becomes possible only after misunderstandings, prejudices, and confused assumptions are cleared away. Opinions held by the many have to be challenged in order that truth may be possessed. Socrates's zeal for refuting false beliefs and exposing mistaken conceptions earned him a reputation for scepticism, and the misunderstanding eventually led to his martyrdom. But it is clear that Socrates's scepticism was only heuristic and provisional. He was convinced that *elenchus* was simply the preparation for knowledge, and he was careful to warn that the refutation was not an end in itself. It was only part of the critical, dialectical process by which truth was discovered.

Teachers of the Socratic type are frequently misunderstood. And the Socratic methodology is frequently misapplied by professional teachers. It tends to be assumed that there are only two possibilities, either authoritarianism or relativism, and the teacher who rejects the former alternative is presumed to endorse the latter. Both the pupils and the enemies of Socrates jumped to the conclusion that because he challenged authorities he rejected all objective standards for beliefs and moral decisions. Idolized by the iconoclasts and maligned by the reactionaries, the Socratic teacher longs to encounter the individual who can understand—the one who can accept a universal truth on another basis than dogmatism.

There are always those classrooms where the Socratic balance is struck. Yet the decline of Socrates's maieutic art in the educational world is one of the most lamentable facts of our times. The most common forms of decisiveness in the classroom are advocacy, exhortation, and pontification. Unable to preserve the dialectical motif, education is often nothing but indoctrination.

Education becomes indoctrination when the teacher forgets that the method by which a conclusion is derived is no less important than the correctness of the conclusion. The aim of education is not merely orthodoxy in belief—not even orthodoxy by reference to the most unchallengeable canon of truth. The aim of education is also critical independence—the ability to cite the grounds on which specific beliefs can be vindicated and to employ a methodology of critical appraisal.

Such are the deficiencies of instruction in American college classrooms. One might hope for a better performance in the Christian colleges, where social intimacy and Christian concern augment the ordinary service motivations of the teacher. Considering Max Weber's thesis about the Protestant ethic, one might expect Christian teachers to be more highly motivated than non-Christian teachers in regard to the achievement of professional excellence. The person who can view teaching as a Christian vocation might be expected to add a dimension of quality and of religiosity which would make his work distinguished. One might expect to see a greater ambition, a higher idealism, a more rigorous self-discipline, a deeper concern for the welfare of students as individuals. One might expect to see the marks of the Christian man shining in the personality of the Christian teacher. One might expect to see churchmanship and theological astuteness influencing the directions in which scholarship is applied.

But there is no evidence that teaching is actually more effective at the Christian colleges. On the contrary, teaching is frequently less effective on such campuses. Although not always by their design, scholars at smaller Christian colleges are usually free from the preoccupations and dispositions which may lead their colleagues at multipurpose, research-oriented institutions to neglect their teaching responsibilities. But there is no evidence that outstanding competence in teaching is particularly related to religious profession. Nor is there any evidence that small classes such as are often characteristic of Christian colleges are any guarantee of superior instruction. On the contrary, some of the worst teaching in American higher education takes place in classes of fewer than ten enrollees; and in a very small college where the faculty has not mastered the special art required in this type of teaching, the high proportion of small classes may only make teaching worse.

In fairness it should be acknowledged (as the Danforth report is careful to do) that teaching is excellent in many Christian college classrooms and that there are Christian colleges which are, on the whole, "doing a good job" in preserving a concern for teaching. But Christian colleges cannot be content with commendations for "doing a good job." Colleges which concentrate on undergraduate teaching have momentous stakes in achieving unmistakable superiority in teaching. "Undergraduate college faculties," warns the Danforth Commission, "should not rest until the quality of their teaching is unmistakably superior to that found in multipurpose institutions."[3] It is not unmistakably superior now.

Many religious colleges are being forced by the current competition for qualified scholars to settle for a lower level of competence than

[3]Pattillo and Mackenzie, *Church-Sponsored Higher Education in the United States*, p. 209.

their recruiters seek. Salary limitations and the shortage of teachers sometimes lead church-related colleges to compromise either their theological and religious standards or their academic standards when making faculty appointments. Usually it is the religious requirements which are made to bend first. As the Danforth report says, "People who think that rigid sectarianism is the principal defect of church-related higher education are fifty years behind the times."

FUNCTIONS OF THE COLLEGE TEACHER

The promise of Christian higher education centers on an ideal concept of the teacher. Yet this ideal is singularly difficult to state. The instructional situation is full of paradox. On the one hand, educational theory affirms the decisive importance of the teacher in the learning process. On the other hand, the conscientious teacher, as exemplified, for example, in the Socratic ideal, protests that he cannot himself impart wisdom and that all genuine learning comes from within the learner himself. Specifying the functions of the teacher in an ideal sense has always given pause to philosophers.

Thinking about a model teacher is fraught with immense difficulty. Recent research has shown, as Joseph Adelson has noted, that there are many styles of effective interaction between student and teacher and that no one of these styles exhausts the ideal. There are teachers who are extremely successful in illuminating a subject matter, with tremendous benefits to student learning, but who fail to inspire. There are other teachers who stir and enchant, but fail to produce intellectual discipline or scholarly rigor. Who is to say which teacher is more effective?

Indeed, there is reason to doubt that it is useful for a teacher to think of himself in ideal terms, as though he were a model whose learning or personality should be emulated by the student. Anecdotes about model teachers or model teaching behavior are memorable in academia, but the question is whether they should be made paradigmatic. The role of models in the psychology of learning needs to be carefully assessed. It is true, as Axelrod notes, that there are times when a student's development centers on discipleship or, alternatively, on a rejection of discipleship. At such times the dialectics of dependency/rejection center on the teacher as ideal type, and the student's development is decisively influenced by his contact with the teacher. On the other hand, there are times when modelling creates a blight on growth, when "the master, now within, retains his influence beyond the point where he is needed."[4] Ideal concepts of the teacher become counterproductive when they result in the prolonged dependency of the learner.

Axelrod suggests three ideal types for teachers: (1) The teacher as *shaman* keeps the attention of students upon himself, inviting the student's identification and emulation. (2) The teacher as *priest* is the agent of scholarly or disciplinary authority, challenging the student to consecrate himself to a collective ideal. (3) The teacher as *mystic healer* cures intellectual disease in the student and acts to release every student's inner potential. Such models are edifying, each in its own way. But the suggestion that any of them is paradigmatic simply ignores the complexity and paradoxicality of the instructional situation.

A more edifying approach to articulation of the ideal of the teacher would be to consider what instructional services are required by learners in order to enable them to achieve intended educational goals. The concept of the functions of the teacher stems from the theory of learning. A theory of learning is a *descriptive* account of how human learning and development take place. A theory of instruction is a *prescriptive* account of the means which are recommended for securing the learning of individuals. Such an account may not be simplistic. A plurality of teaching strategies and styles is required by the complexity of the learning process.

Some general principles of learning are part of the conventional wisdom of American education. Alvin Eurich has stated those principles as follows: (1) Whatever a student learns, he must learn for himself—no one can learn for him. (2) Each student learns at his own rate, and for any age group the variations in rates of learning are considerable. (3) A student learns more when each step is immediately strengthened or reinforced. (4) When given responsibility for his own learning, the student is more highly motivated; he learns and retains more. Or, as John Dewey once expressed it, "Since learning is something that the pupil has to do himself and for himself, the initiative lies with the learner. The teacher is a guide and director, who steers the

[4]Joseph Axelrod, "The Teacher as a Model," in Nevitt Sanford, *The American College* (New York: John Wiley & Sons, 1962), p. 401.

boat, but the energy that propels it must come from those who are learning."[5]

There is widespread assent to such an understanding of the learning process, but much of the instruction offered in American classrooms fails to implement these principles. Instructional activity in American colleges tends to be teacher-centered rather than student-centered, with emphasis on assigned tasks and manipulation of the classroom environment to effect learning. A student-oriented approach to teaching, on the other hand, would de-emphasize the role of the teacher as communicator, as expert resource, or as motivator and would emphasize the role of the teacher as manager of the learning process. The teacher needs to be not only a competent scholar in his discipline, but also a careful student of the learning process so that he will know how to make the decisions that are required of a manager of that process.

The tendency to believe that a study of methods will correct operational deficiencies is one sign of that "faith in machinery" which Matthew Arnold said was characteristic of the modern world. Oblivious to the question of ends, modern man has placed his faith in means and has exerted himself to the utmost in seeking to improve his methods. Remarkable technological advances have resulted from this bias, but technology tyrannizes if the ends which it is intended to serve are not clearly in view.

It is not a study of methods, in fact, that is needed most by college teachers today, but a study of ends. Once teachers become clear about the aims of education and about the functions of the teacher, suitable methods for achieving these aims and performing these functions will readily suggest themselves. The study of teaching needs to focus not on techniques but on principles, not on the tactics of the teacher but on the essential nature of the teacher's task.

The functions of the teacher are to *organize* the materials of learning, to *mobilize* an appropriate set of instructional activities, to *motivate* the learner, and to *evaluate* the achievement of the learner. Effectiveness in teaching is significantly improved if a teacher is clear in his own mind about what is involved in each of these functions and makes explicit provision in his educational planning for carrying them out in due course.

---

[5]Dewey, *Democracy and Education*, p. 160.

Organization

The first task of the teacher is to organize the materials of learning. The first principle of instruction, as Jerome S. Bruner has recently emphasized, is that effective teaching requires a scheme of organization which exhibits the structure of the subject matter. A deliberately designed instructional effort is the most effective as well as the most efficient. "Aimlessness," as Paul Klapper has said, "is the most important single cause of ineffectiveness in teaching and of frustration of educational effort."[6] A sense of the order and coordination of parts is indispensable to learning, a sense of the purposiveness of the activity is an important motivation for study, and a sense of accomplishment is one of its chief rewards. Too many students sit in classes in which aimless instruction is depriving them of all three experiences.

The aimlessness of college teaching is symptomatized by a number of conditions. There is the notorious neglect of long-range planning, which leaves an instructor discovering two weeks before the end of the term that he has more than half of his material yet ahead of him. There is the discrepancy between the instructor's ambition and the student's ability, which results in an inadequate adjustment of the materials of study to the actual needs, purposes, and aptitudes of the students to be served. There is the pedantic preoccupation with isolated details, at the expense of coherence and generality. There is the immutability of methodology, resulting in the repetitiveness and routine which are the bane of academic life. All these maladjustments in the process of undergraduate instruction arise ultimately out of the absence of purpose in the organization of a program of study.

The basis of order in teaching is an operational definition of course objectives. This definition will be controlled by a number of general points of reference: the purposes of the college as a whole, the objectives, interests, and abilities of the students, the requirements of the subject, the competence and orientation of the instructor, and the relation of the course to other courses in the curriculum. Decisions will have to be made about the relative priority of various kinds of objectives: cognitive, affective, manipulative, vocational, preprofessional, general-educational, pregraduate, interpretive, methodological, imita-

---

[6]Paul Klapper, "The Professional Preparation of the College Teacher," *Journal of General Education* (1959): 229.

tive, creative, assimilative. The statement of purpose will have to be made operational and concrete so that it will be clear what experiences and patterns of behavior are to be secured. And it should not be forgotten that educational aims are not clearly defined until the instructor knows how to measure the successfulness of his effort.

Following the articulation of the purposes of the course in operational and measurable terms, the instructor must select the materials which he deems suitable for the achievement of those aims. The instructor will need to assess materials in the light of questions like the following: Is the material appropriate for the purposes outlined? Is the material of maximum utility for the efficient achievement of these purposes? Is the material manageable—is the instructor capable of treating it, are the students able to comprehend it, and are the resources needed for understanding available to the student? Finally, is the material capable of arousing a lively interest in the student?

A number of different patterns may be followed in the organization of course materials. One might follow a *historical* organization of the materials, emphasizing chronological development. One might organize the materials around a number of key *issues* and follow the "problems" approach. One might take a *systematic* approach, organizing the materials of the course with a view to expounding a particular outlook or interpretation in its systematic outlines. Or one might follow a *textual-interpretive* approach and organize the course around a collection of textual materials which are to be interpreted and criticized. Each approach has distinct advantages of its own. What is indispensable, however, is that there should be an identifiable pattern of organization, deliberately and consistently chosen.

Clarification of the structure of the subject matter is one of the most important contributions which a teacher can make to the learning of a student. Awareness of structure is an aid to the learner's comprehension of the meaning of details. It is also an aid to retention and recall. Assisting the student to organize data and to identify the orderly relationships of details is a major responsibility of every teacher. As Whitehead has said,

> One secret of a successful teacher is that he has formulated quite clearly in his mind what the pupil has got to know in precise fashion. He will then cease from half-hearted attempts to worry his pupils with memorizing a lot of irrelevant stuff of inferior importance. The secret

of success is pace, and the secret of pace is concentration.[7]

Mobilization

Having organized the materials of learning, the teacher may then proceed to the second task, namely, that of determining a set of appropriate learning activities and conducting such activities in an effective manner. Careful design of teaching-learning activities and skill in conducting these activities are important requisities of the successful teacher.

Axelrod distinguishes two main modes of teaching activity which emerge from an analysis of the images which university teachers hold of themselves. On the one hand, there are teachers who approach their task primarily in a *didactic mode*, which emphasizes the presentation by the teacher of knowledge which the student is expected to assimilate and master, or direction by the teacher of the student's motor-kinetic activity so that skill will be developed through supervised repetition and practice. On the other hand, there are teachers who approach their task primarily in an *evocative mode*, which emphasizes the strategy of teaching the student in a process of inquiry and discovery. Those teachers who are competent in the didactic mode are called *craftsmen* by Axelrod; those who have achieved excellence in the evocative mode he calls *artists*.[8]

Axelrod distinguishes further among several prototypes of evocative teachers, depending on the ways in which the various elements of the teaching-learning process are emphasized. The first of these prototypes emphasizes the *subject matter*, to which both the teacher and the learner are expected to accomodate themselves. In terms of this prototype, the personal identity and characteristics of the teacher should have little bearing on the students' learning. What is important is knowledge of the field, its principles and its facts.

A second prototype of evocative teaching focuses in the *teacher*, who by his personality and behavior demonstrates to the students what intellectual and scholarly competence is like. The teaching/learning

---

[7]Alfred North Whitehead, "The Rhythmic Claims of Freedom and Discipline," in *The Aims of Education and Other Essays* (New York: Mentor, 1949), p. 46.

[8]Joseph Axelrod, *The University Teacher as Artist* (San Francisco: Jossey Bass Publishers, 1973).

process in this prototype is instructor dominated. The instructor is always at the center of activity, always dominating, always controlling.

The other two prototypes distinguished by Axelrod are *student* centered. In the first of these the central concern is with the development of the student's mind. What characterizes the activity of teachers who follow this prototype is concern for the intellectual development of students. Such concern is expressed in teaching which focuses on the analysis of language, the evaluation of evidence, and problem solving. Knowledge is viewed here not so much in terms of product, but more in terms of process.

Finally, Axelrod suggests, there are teachers who organize their activities from the point of view of concern about the total development of their students as persons. The separation of intellectual development from emotional and social development seems to such teachers to be artificial and futile. Furthermore, such teachers allow themselves to be drawn much more intimately into the individual as well as the group experiences of their students and tend, accordingly, to minimize the distinction between teacher and learner.

The organization of teaching/learning activities by a teacher will follow some such prototype of teaching. Not all teachers will proceed in the same way; not all will place equal stress on the various educational objectives which might be of concern. What is common to all effective teaching, however, is deliberate planning of teaching/learning activities as an expression of the teacher's considered conviction that the selected approach is the most appropriate one from the point of view of the student's growth. Merely following personal inclination, style, or habit is not enough to satisfy the requirements of effective teaching. In whatever mode is appropriate the effective teacher must find ways to deal responsibly with his students as individuals in a process of development.

The teacher is an artist, who knows how to apply a variety of instructional tactics and can adapt his style to the special demands of the instructional situation. No one method in instruction is adequate for all educational purposes and for all learners. Effectiveness in teaching requires mastery of a variety of instructional skills. The method of lecturing is suited for certain purposes and certain audiences, the method of discussion for others. A teacher who is prejudiced in favor of one method to the exclusion of others is foolishly restricting his effectiveness. Every teacher should take special pains to develop his skill in a variety of teaching techniques.

Classroom lecturing, though presently in a period of some decline, will always be a major tool of undergraduate instruction. Mastery of the art of lecturing—and wisdom in choosing the circumstances for its exercise—will be the mark of a good teacher. But skill in individual tutoring and in the guidance of group discussion is no less indispensable. So is skill in directing students in bibliographic study, in the analysis of written materials, and in writing papers. A good teacher needs to be a master of all these techniques. The reason for a diversified instructional skill is not simply that variety increases interest. More important are the facts that different methods are adapted to different purposes and the needs of different learners and that every course of study involves purposes which call for a variety of approaches.

Motivation

Effective teachers know how to implement motivational appeals which inspire the learning of the student. Of course, the student must accept responsibility for his own education. The conditions for learning—the aptitude, the concentration, and the discipline—must all be supplied by the student, and in the absence of these conditions even the best teacher will be ineffective. Students, too, are responsible for the quality of their educational motivations. Nevertheless, one sign of an effective teacher is his awareness of the motivational factors affecting learning and his ability to control these factors so as to increase the likelihood that the student will become involved.

The most important single obstacle to learning in college is the lack of concentration. Indeed, there is something to be said for the view that educational aptitude is simply the power to focus the mind's attention. The inattention of students is sometimes so habitual as to be beyond remedy, but generally the causes of distraction can be removed through carefully planned effort. A student's ability to concentrate may be revolutionized through the flowering of a latent interest or through the recognition of the life-importance of a certain kind of study. Poor concentration can be caused by personal anxiety or conflict in non-academic situations, by weariness resulting from overwork, by unsatisfactory living and working conditions. A sensitive teacher should be able to identify such factors and suggest adjustments which might assist the student to alter them. Sometimes there is conflict between teacher and student which distracts the student from learning. An adjustment of the teacher's manner or method may be all that is required to remove the conflict. Adolescents are typically distracted by their resentment of authority and their desire for independence, and a gifted teacher will know how to help in the management and guidance of such a disposition.

Many factors affect students' interest in classroom work, but the decisive factor is the reality-relatedness of the activity. Effective teaching enables a student to establish a context of relevance and applicability which will give meaning and point to a given study. What sustains an intellectual interest is the sense of the utility of learning. The teacher is, as Gilbert Highet puts it, a bridge between the school and the world. Not infrequently the discipline of classroom work creates in the adolescent the impression that the academic world is far removed from the world of actual experience, and a mood of purposelessness may set in, which enervates academic motivation. Hence, the teacher must, from time to time, draw aside the curtain and allow the student to see the relevance—the life-importance—of his study. It is only by so doing that a teacher can help to create a life-interest in a study. There is a kind of interest which can be evoked in students by the attractiveness of a teacher's personality, by liveliness in classroom activities, by friendly encouragement and personal attention. But a life interest has to have another base. A program of study will attract and hold a student's interest permanently only if it is relevant, and its relevance is a matter of its relatedness to the reality in which the student lives and breathes.

One of the most effective means of motivating scholarship is at the same time one of the most difficult to control. This is the association of the student's activity with a high tradition of culture and learning. A teacher at a school possessed of a fine scholarly tradition is able to exploit pride in the institutional heritage and turn it into an effective motivation for learning. In a college whose traditions are ill-defined or even anti-intellectual, this means will be less available, but even there an alert scholar will be able to locate some aspect of the institutional heritage which can be made the point of appeal. The advantage of doing so is that the student can be helped to think of himself as a member of a community of high attainments. He may be able to identify living illustrations of high ideals of scholarship and may be led to accept responsibility for continuation of a high level of performance. One of the ways, therefore, in which a teacher may inspire his students is by revealing and reinforcing a high academic tradition with which students may identify. The excellence and vitality of the teacher's own scholarship are certainly one of the most important elements in such a tradition.

A successful teacher is one who understands and appreciates students and helps them to want to learn. One of the most elementary principles for establishing a motivation for learning is that the teacher must help the student to obtain a sense of satisfaction through achievement—not by giving him artificial praise and trumped-up encouragement, but by permitting him to use what he has learned in experiences which are inherently rewarding. Such experiences are the vindication of competence. Sequential practice, which enables a student to exploit something which he has learned and to put it to use at a level of greater complexity, provides a sense of accomplishment and an awareness of progress. A perennial sense of defeat, inadequacy, and disappointment, on the other hand, will eventually destroy ambition.

Evaluation

The task of evaluating student work is one of the most arduous of the responsibilities of a teacher. The vast majority of teachers regard the grading of papers as the drudgery which is unavoidably associated with the job and they are anxious to obtain whatever relief they can from these duties. The ideal situation is thought to be having an assistant to perform these onerous tasks, while the teacher is left free to do "nothing but teach." Increasingly, resentment against the necessity of evaluating student achievement has become the primary factor affecting the relationship between teachers and students in American colleges and universities.

The indifference of college teachers to grading is often a sign of the vagueness of their conception of the objectives of a course of instruction. In the absence of a concrete formulation of the educational outcomes being aimed at, evaluation of student work has only a subjective basis and can be justified only under the necessity of reporting a grade to the registrar. If, however, an instructor has a clear, definite, and positive understanding of the purposes of a course and if that understanding can be articulated in pragmatic terms, it will require only planning and effort to devise instruments of measurement which will indicate the degree to which these purposes are being achieved.

One root of the breakdown of the system of grading is a misunderstanding of its purpose. The primary function of educational measurement is widely thought to be that of certifying the completion of a certain unit of work at a certain level of perfection. This understanding is especially prevalent among students and in society at large. It is this concept of the function of grading, not grading itself, that needs to be attacked by educators.

The primary function of educational measurement is not certification but correction. A well-formed instrument of educational measurement provides a summary of what is of essential importance in any course of instruction. Preparing for an examination is one of the most effective disciplinary techniques for focusing student attention on what is of the highest priority. Examinations correct student waywardness. And if an instructor is organizing his own affairs properly, the development of instruments of measurement will be part of his own self-discipline in selecting materials for relative emphasis. The process of grading is one of the most practicable means for keeping perspective on the most important materials of a course of instruction. But the examination also serves an educative function by identifying areas where additional work is needed before competence is attained. Educational measurement, in short, is part of the strategy for achieving the aims of education.

The main value of the *Taxonomy of Educational Objectives*, produced by a number of psychologists and educators under the editorship of Benjamin Bloom,[9] is that it suggests concrete ways in which classroom teachers might create instruments of educational measurement which are systematically adjusted to the aims of education. From a psychological or philosophical standpoint, the idea of a taxonomy is highly problematic. A theoretical classification of psychological processes by type is almost certain to break down. But if the *Taxonomy* is accepted as a practical proposal for considering possible areas of concern and as a tool for developing instruments of educational measurement, it is capable of revolutionizing classroom teaching.

The Bloom taxonomy classifies cognitive, affective, and motor-skill activities by genus and species and illustrates procedures for measuring ability to perform these activities. Comprehensive and sys-

---

[9]Benjamin Bloom, ed., *Taxonomy of Educational Objectives: I. Cognitive Domain* (New York: David McKay Co., 1956); *II. Affective Domain* (1962).

tematic measurement of the achievement of educational goals can be attained only if care is taken to note the various forms of human activity, to assess their relative importance by reference to the goals of a specific program of instruction, and to create instruments for measuring ability to perform the respective activities. Careful study will suggest evaluative items suited to each level of activity within any subject-matter field.

A conscientious teacher who realizes the importance of educational measurement will consider that it is no more important for him to do research in preparing his lectures than it is for him to do research in preparing comprehensive and reliable instruments of educational measurement. Rather than abolishing grades, an educational institution ought to consider enlarging and diversifying its grading practices. An instructor might even be asked to assign a grade indicating the level of achievement in each of the major types of learning objectives, in order that the student may gain a clearer understanding of his strengths and weaknesses. Grades might then be reported not in the form of a number or a letter, but in the form of a paragraph or essay of critical evaluation. In any case, an irresponsible retreat from the whole activity of educational evaluation is nothing but the abdicaton of teaching. More, not less, attention needs to be given to the criteria and methods of educational measurement.

External discipline by a teacher, under the threat of institutional sanctions, is a poor substitute, of course, for the voluntary self-discipline of the student. It is the latter rather than the former which should be made the basis of school learning. But it is self-contradictory for a teacher to expect a student to apply rigorous standards in self-criticism, while the teacher himself is lax in his own appraisal of the student's work. Rigorous evaluation by both teacher and student is what is needed for the elevation of scholastic standards.

What should be demanded by a classroom teacher? In a rigorously disciplined educational system a teacher would be expected to demand *accuracy*. The practice of many college teachers suggests, however, that the present generation is dubious about the principle. Precision and exactness are admitted to be necessary for certain purposes, but, relative to the entire body of scholarship, the range within which accuracy is regarded as unforgivable is being progressively narrowed. Whether under the influence of philanthropy or of art, the present crop of teachers is developing a marked disposition to regard it as petty to insist on accuracy in every detail. An enlightened teacher, it tends to be assumed, will be generous and forbearing in dealing with his student's errors.

There is a corresponding erosion of the demand for *thoroughness* in undergraduate study. College teachers seem to have resigned themselves to doing no more than scratching the surface, and they have adopted a habit of thought which leads them to expect students to do the same. Superficial and incomplete treatments are accepted because it is deemed unreasonable to demand more. Slovenliness in scholarship is being countenanced, with respect not only to accuracy but also to thoroughness.

But the greatest defeat of educational evaluation in the college classroom is the absence of the demand for *articulateness*. Without articulateness there is no learning, as Barzun contends, yet the educational situation today reflects that "flight from articulateness" which has become characteristic of our entire society.

Teachers too seldom demand articulateness from their students, and, in fact, they perpetuate inarticulateness by their teaching and evaluating methods. Teachers everywhere are distressed over the inability of their students to write; yet these same teachers are notorious for their inclination to ignore the ineptness of student papers on the pretense that a "subject-matter professor" ought to grade only on "content," not on "form." Errors of mechanics, expression, organization, and so forth are supposed to be corrected by the English department; apparently it is beneath the dignity of instructors in other departments to concern themselves with such matters. In college after college, responsibility for the teaching of writing has been abdicated by the faculty, while they continue to beat their breasts over the incompetence of their students. What efforts are expended through freshman writing courses are generally inadequate due to the formalism and artificiality of the exercises. Ideas which cannot be precisely articulated are not yet fully formed. So a teacher who settles for an obscure communication is countenancing indiscipline in thought as well.

But finally, the teacher must demand *decisiveness* and commitment. Making up one's mind always carries with it the risk of error, and the young are especially doubtful of their preparedness for decisiveness in scholarly study. Yet truth becomes knowledge only by being possessed, and the act of possessing it involves the commitment of the will.

A bird will never fly until it abandons the nest and takes the risk of depending on its own wings.

There are, of course, right and wrong times for decisiveness. The wise teacher will know when it is time to stir up the nest. Unfortunately many committed students are prematurely decisive, while the large majority of students maintain tentativeness far too long. The situation reflects the general inattention of teachers to the intricacies of educational timing.

The intellectual and cultural deficiencies of the schools and of society in general can be attributed to the disregard of the ideal of perfection. The causes of this disregard are varied and complex, but, no doubt, the growth of mass production techniques throughout our system of production and the dominance of a narrowly conceived instrumentalist philosophy are significant factors in the obfuscation of standards. These factors certainly make themselves felt in our system of education.

We have reached the stage where it sounds reactionary for an educator to insist on a rigorous application of standards. Such a proposal will be scornfully received by many as idealistic, inflexible, and doctrinaire. Education has become too philanthropic and too democratic to tolerate the exclusions and discriminations which are entailed by a rigid application of standards. It is by stimulating individual creativity, curiosity, and interest that teachers hope to develop intellect, and the means of such stimulation is thought to be an accepting and encouraging approach to the student. It is assumed that austere insistence on some standard of perfection will frustrate the student's initiative, destroy his self-confidence, and leave him bogged down in discouragement. The failure of the philanthropic approach will probably not be realized until we reap the harvest of a whole generation of undisciplined minds. It is not that no one warned us, however. It was Matthew Arnold who said that culture, and especially intellectual culture, has its origin not in curiosity, but in the love of perfection.[10]

THE VOCATION OF THE CHRISTIAN TEACHER

Such are the concerns and the methodology of college teaching. An effective college teacher will be clear about his function relative to the

---

[10]Matthew Arnold, "Culture and Anarchy," reprinted in *The Portable Matthew Arnold*, ed. Lionel Trilling (New York: Viking Press, 1949), pp. 473ff.

student's learning and will be able to comprehend and implement appropriate methods for carrying out those functions. Clearly if colleges and universities are to achieve distinction as centers of effective teaching, they will need to devote themselves to the refinement and application of these principles, and they must make it a central aim of college planning to recruit and discipline a corps of outstanding teachers, possessed of superior competence not only in scholarship but also in instruction.

A good teacher, says Gilbert Highet, must know his subject thoroughly. He must also know students, and he must know how to teach. He must, furthermore, like students and like to teach. He must have wide interests and a wide sensitivity, a strong sense of humor, a streak of kindness, a dependable memory—and willpower.[11]

An effective teacher is characterized by rigorous scholarship, albeit a scholarship of the type which lends itself to the organization of teaching/learning activity, and not necessarily of the type which fosters the development of a field of learning. But an effective teacher is also characterized by a certain ethical quality—by a sense of responsibility towards truth, towards society, and towards students as individuals. In this combination of scholarship and duty lies the integrity of the teacher.

To such qualities the Christian teacher adds the consecration of his whole life to the work of ministry in the name of Christ. The vocation of the Christian teacher is to be God's instrument in the cultivation of Christian maturity.

How Christ is formed in a human heart is a mystery which remains impenetrable. Hence the strategies of the Christian teacher can never be fully systematic. The teacher may become the most consummate artist, still the spirit blows where it lists. The Christian teacher places his hope in the power of God's word to redeem, not in the persuasiveness of what the Apostle Paul calls the "wisdom of words." And he knows that it is best for faith to depend not on human agency but on the power of God. It is for this very reason that no mere teacher can guarantee the result.

Were a human teacher adequate to redeem a soul, the method of Christian teaching might be direct. But Kierkegaard is profoundly

---

[11]Gilbert Highet, *The Art of Teaching* (New York: Vintage Books, 1950).

correct in analyzing all authentic religious communication as an indirect communication. The principles of indirect communication are themselves subject to analysis up to a point, and the Christian teacher needs to develop skill in applying them. But inherent in the idea of religious communication as indirect is the readiness of the agent of all such communication to let God be God. One may plant, another may water, but God gives the increase.

The vocation of teaching within the context of the Christian church is identified in the New Testament as a gift of the Spirit. Both the obligations and the endowments of the Christian teacher are of God. The academician who has heard Christ's call judges that his whole life is his as a gift. He then confesses that since Christ has been given to him by God's grace, he can no longer live for himself, but must devote himself to seeking out that one to whom he, in turn, may become Christ's gift.

An aesthetic consciousness, to use the Kierkegaardian term, is not an adequate basis for the vocation of the Christian teacher. Neither is an ethical one. The righteousness of God moves from faith to faith. The Christian teacher must bring to his task more than an interest in his subject and more than the faithfulness of a master of the art of teaching. He must also bring faith in the gospel as the power of God unto salvation.

The study of how God works through the teachers of the church to effect the work of redemption should be the central concern of Christian college faculties. The dialectics of religious communication are the pulse of a vital Christian college. The development of skill in the employment of these dialectics is what is distinctive about the vocation of the Christian teacher. To Highet's list of the essential qualities of the teacher the Christian college must add those which relate to religious communication. The identification and cultivation of these qualities are the greatest needs of the Christian college movement today.

Chapter 7

THE STUDENT CULTURE

The life of Christian discipleship is nurtured through the community of spiritual commitment. What saves a man is the Word of God, but the bearer of the Word of God is, as Luther loved to stress, the church as a community of faith. It is through the writing and speaking of faithful personalities that the Word of God is communicated to mankind. As Bonhoeffer has put it, "God has willed that we should seek and find His living Word in the witness of a brother, in the mouth of man."[1]

What makes the educational objectives of the Christian college distinctive by comparison to those of other educational institutions is the college's participation in the redemptive mission of the church. The college, too, assays to be an instrument of redemption, a community through which the Word of God may address itself to man, a center for the nurture of an authentic Christian discipleship.

The Christian colleges are uniquely placed to establish an open Christian society for the purpose of Christian nurture. Few of them, however, are taking full advantage of their opportunity. Many of the church-related colleges have by now abandoned their former attempt to form a Christian community, and the sectarian institutions which

[1]Dietrich Bonhoeffer, *Life Together* (New York: Harper and Row, 1954), p. 23.

are still engaged in the endeavor often seek no more than a regimented behavioral conformity and a socialized campus tranquility. The fact that a free community of Christian faith does not exist at the typical church-related college is another example of the failure of nerve which, we have been saying, is the fundamental weakness of Christian higher education today.

INSTITUTIONAL AIMS AND THE STUDENT SUBCULTURE

Even a small college is a relatively complex social institution. The diversity of the college's relationship to society and the heteronomy of subgroupings within the college community greatly complicate the task of description. Sociological and economic analysis has only recently begun to identify these complexities, and the theory of Christian higher education has not fully learned to recognize the insights which have been obtained.

One of these insights is the recognition that the culture or "climate" of a school is at best a synthesis of less inclusive cultures which arise through the grouping of individuals within the school. Sociological analysis discloses, for example, the existence of a faculty culture, perhaps a rather different administrative culture (which may be especially responsive to the culture of the supporting constituency or to economic pressures), and a student culture. In a heterogeneous student body, there may be several student subcultures, and there are likely to be subgroupings within the faculty as well. On every campus there is a certain amount of tension between such cultures, none of which is finally representative of the college as a whole.

"Whenever two or more people interact on the basis of consensus," a sociologist would say, "particularly when they are confronted with the same contingencies and exigencies of everyday life, a society exists."[2] This society, in turn, becomes a factor which influences the way in which individuals respond to their circumstances. In a college there are several collections of individuals working on common problems. The "college family" as a whole has only rare occasions for being together—perhaps it has no existence except in the sentimentalized imagination of the president. Most day-to-day concerns involve break-

[2]Albert H. Whiting, "The Student Culture and the Educational Enterprise," *Liberal Education* 50:4 (December 1964): 514.

ing up the total group into smaller components. The college is a composite of the subsocieties which are the product of these day-to-day contacts.

Out of their routine contacts with their fellow, students develop a culture of their own, the educational significance of which is often forgotten. The student culture effects a redefinition (and probably a dilution) of the educational demands imposed by the college officialdom. Indeed, one root of the difficulty of creating a homogeneous campus community is the fact that the redefinition of the norms and ideals of the college by students is itself a group process which may operate independently of faculty planning and administrative decisions.

At every college one can observe this process by which students redefine official requirements in their own terms. In their contacts with one another students establish common understandings and agreements about matters touching their roles as students. These agreements determine the minimal accommodation to the demands of the faculty which students as a group are prepared to accept. The student culture, that is, defines the limits within which it is acceptable behavior to ignore faculty or administrative demands and provides what Dean Whiting has called "a social sanction for the reduced view of an educational program."[3] A student who fails to measure up to faculty expectations may avoid any feelings of disapprobation or guilt as long as his own performance falls within the norm accepted by his own peers.

The peer-group consensus is probably not formalized or codified, and the constraint on individual thinking and behavior is probably not effected by a formal judicial system or a set of enforceable sanctions. Still, even without his being aware of it, the individual student derives his concept of what he should do and be from the patterns of the student culture with which he senses a strong identity. It is the consensus of his fellow students as to what is useful or important, rather than the judgment of an academic representative of an older generation, which the student is probably going to accept as the standard for evaluating his activity.[4] Newman once observed that the students at

---

[3]Ibid., p. 515.

[4]Cf. Howard Becker and Blanche Geer, "Student Culture in Medical School," *Harvard Educational Review* 28:1 (Winter 1958): 70.

Oxford were more influenced by one another than by all the dons, lectures, and examinations.

The principle holds not only of the academic aspects of campus life, but also of the religious aspects. The religious tone of a school is not established merely by the official adoption of a theological or ethical norm, or by administrative pronouncements or regulations, or by the domination of a devout faculty, or by the establishment of curricular requirements in religion, or by provision for the collective demonstration of piety. Such arrangements under the egess of the faculty and administration are certainly important to the religiosity of a campus, but what is also needed is a student culture which reinforces this official religious character. Bernard Loomer once wrote,

> The university is not the church. To take one obvious point, membership in a university faculty involves the meeting of certain intellectual standards which do not apply to membership in a church. And yet the kind of community that is needed in a university if members of its faculty are to realize their intellectual goals may perhaps more closely approximate to the community which is the church than we have realized or admitted.[5]

Presley McCoy has said that the purpose of a college is to bring about in the student a "heightened awareness of the fully functioning self."[6] All activities which contribute to the accomplishment of this purpose are educative. Ideally, a college should be so organized that the whole system of daily campus activities, both inside and outside the classroom, contributes to the full functioning of a self and is therefore educative. Intellectual activity need not be limited to the classroom, and the round of artistic, journalistic, athletic, and social activities in which the student engages can be a powerful force in his education. The task for individual planners is to establish a pattern of total-campus life which will express the unity of thought and action, of intellectual awareness and aesthetic appreciation, of mind and body, of faith and learning.

But how can the unity of the Christian college campus be established and maintained? Is it, after all, within the power of the faculty and administration to manage not only the official college culture but

---

[5]Bernard Loomer, "Religion and the Mind of the University," in Amos N. Wilder, *Liberal Learning and Religion* (New York: Harper, 1951), p. 168.

[6]Presley C. McCoy, "College Curriculum and Campus Climate," *Liberal Education* 50:1 (March 1964): 28.

the student culture as well? In one sense of the term "manage," it is impossible to manage students, either individually or collectively, and the effort to do so is both misplaced and unjustified. Some schools do, indeed, succeed in managing students, in the sense that they secure behavioral conformity through the use of sanctions, but such arrangements do not effect cultural unity of the depth which we seek. The human spirit cannot be intimidated or coerced, and a subliminal protest will remain in the soul of the student who consents to abide by the institutional regulation. Under stress that protest will be brought out into the open and the superficiality of the campus unity will then be made apparent.

In another sense, however, the management of the total campus culture is possible, at least within limits. One means for bringing about a rapprochment of the two cultures is the creation of an open campus society in which dialectical processes freely operate. The establishment of openness may then pave the way to the achievement of a wider consensus on values and institutional policies. The foundation of such a consensus, of course, is free communication in a climate of trust and respect for personality. When common understanding through open communication is energetically pursued by the faculty and administration, students are likely to be found eager to contribute to the wholeness of campus life.

Another means by which the officialdom can bring the student culture into closer alignment with the official culture is to organize the broad backdrop of campus experience, which subtly and imperceptibly, yet definitely, shapes student opinion. College publications, the instruments of intracampus communication, campus architecture and decor can all be created in the image of the college's ideals and aims. A campus milieu, stamped by the school's ideals, and a corps of charismatic leaders in all parts of the college who genuinely understand and share those ideals can become an important means of achieving campus unity without intimidation or coercion.

A program of collective worship which displays the highest ideals of Christian life and scholarship and an approach which secures the free and willing participation of all members of the academic community as a matter of conscientious choice can also become a major rallying point of campus unity in the Christian college. Few institutions, however, are having much success currently in maintaining the relevance and acceptance which the chapel service ought to have. In a few colleges considerable time is allotted for this purpose on a systematic basis, but the opportunity for the enhancement of the spiritual unity of the campus through an effective program of common worship remains for the most part unexploited. In most church-related colleges the observance has long since become perfunctory. Most of the Chapel services at Christian colleges are too often dull and uninspiring, planned without sufficient imagination and forethought, and overly preoccupied with institutional relationships and agency-oriented promotion. To sustain a series of daily worship programs on a high plane of spiritual relevance, interest, and variety requires much more planning—and much greater liturgical skill—than most Christian colleges have been able to dedicate for the purpose.

Controversy over chapel at the Christian colleges frequently centers over the merits of voluntary versus compulsory attendance policies. The debate generates emotions which far exceed its importance. Furthermore, the controversy often arises out of a failure to understand the nature and function of the service. If the service is viewed as an occasion for common worship and as a call to spiritual commitment, a system of compulsory participation is no less inappropriate than it would be in the churches on Sunday morning. Participation in worship and commitment in Christian discipleship cannot be coerced; they can only be won, in a manner which allows for the free exercise of a person's will. In point of fact, many colleges which follow a policy of voluntary chapel attendance have a more earnest religious purpose in conducting their chapel services than those which follow a policy of compulsory attendance—although many conservative constituents would be convinced that exactly the reverse was true.

The real issue, however, concerns not so much student attendance as faculty and administrative planning. It is the ambiguity of the concept of the role of the chapel service and the thoughtless way in which the chapel program is administered which pose the real crisis for worship at the Christian college. The creation of a program of worship which deserves the voluntary participation of the communicants is the task of a college chaplain as much as of the pastor of a church. Indeed, it is a basic responsibility of the Christian college faculty taken as a group. This task is largely unfulfilled in most Christian colleges today. Yet a program of common worship, properly conducted and reflecting the highest ideals of the college, is one of the most important elements of cultural unity in the Christian college.

Finally, rigor and consistency in the enforcement of institutional standards of performance are not the least of the means by which the character of the student culture can be brought into closer alignment with the ideals of the official college culture. The student consensus on what must be learned, for example, generally results, as Dean Whiting has noted, from a testing of the limits to which the faculty and administration can be pressed in accommodating their standards to student resistance.

> The degree to which the student culture redirects and dilutes educational aims and efforts is directly related to the degree to which the faculty is indifferent, routinized in teaching practices, and permissive in reviewing, checking, and evaluating student work. It is our belief that, where faculty expectations are uniformly high and are reflected in their requirements, and where the objectives of the educational program are pursued with vigor and confidence, the response of the student to the educational program will be strikingly positive.[7]

What Dean Whiting says about academic matters can also be applied in social and religious matters. The student consensus on what is required in social and religious practice will also be a result, generally speaking, of a testing of the limits to which official positions can be compromised. Where institutional expectations are confidently declared and rigorously enforced, the student response is usually to get in step.

Colleges, like parents, sometimes are unable to see anything beyond the dichotomy between permissiveness and authoritarianism in matters of student discipline. But the very genius of Christian experience is the synthesis of the two antitheticals in an outlook which unifies law and grace. It was a man of highest principle who said, "The sabbath was made for man, not man for the sabbath." So, too, a Christian college may base its life on principle without adhering tenaciously to rules for their own sakes. What is needed in the college is an unapologetic and consistent adherence to standards, modified by a sympathetic and gracious regard for the welfare of students as persons. In that combination lies the key to a college community which is distinctively Christian and yet free.

ADMISSION POLICIES AND THE STUDENT CULTURE

One obvious way in which a college may influence the character of

---

[7]Whiting, "The Student Culture," p. 516.

the campus climate is the selection of the personnel who constitute the college society. The literature of higher education has generally assumed that the idea of a Christian college implies the application of some kind of religious test in the selection of faculty members. But too little has been said about the stake which the Christian college has in the character of its student body. The preceding discussion poses the question, whether or not it is also implicit in the idea of the Christian college that a personal test—an ethical, if not a religious test—should be applied in the admission of students, as well as in the hiring of faculty.

College policies and procedures on admission ought to be set primarily out of regard for the welfare of the individual applicant. Considerations of institutional expedience cannot be ignored, of course, but the college's aim should be to admit all applicants who show promise of being able to complete the program of studies offered. Few colleges are able to guarantee educational opportunity to all who meet this qualification. It is perhaps inevitable that socio-economic factors should also influence the character of the student clientele, especially in those colleges which operate in the private sector. Yet the crucial questions in admissions are not, "How can we keep full?" or "How can we get the best students?" but "Will our college be able to serve this student well?"

Is it appropriate for a college to seek through its admission policies to maintain a distinctive character in the college community? Clearly the answer depends on the characteristics by which the distinctiveness of the institution is defined. A college would not be justified, for example, in seeking a racially homogeneous student body, since race is not a characteristic which is essential to the performance of a recognized educational function. When hedged about by proper regard for civil and human rights, however, a school is certainly within its rights in asking concerning an applicant, "Is this personality likely to strengthen the college community as we conceive it?"

All colleges apply some kind of personal test in the admission, or at least in the retention, of students. The catalogs of many colleges explicitly announce that attendance at the college is "a privilege and not a right," and most colleges, even those operated out of tax money, apply that precept at least when taking disciplinary action against problem students. There are behaviors which simply cannot be tolerated in an academic community. The question is not whether the principle is educationally tenable, but how far it should be applied.

The Christian college has much at stake in being permitted to recruit students as well as faculty who can contribute to the vitality of the community of faith. Some schools concerned about the spiritual character of the campus community will carefully restrict admission to students who, as far as can be humanly ascertained, are Christian in faith and practice. There may be merit in such a policy, but it should not be made normative for every Christian college. Each institution will have its own method of defining the limits of the church and its own arrangements for welcoming "seekers" and for nurturing the faith of the immature. Perhaps it will be enough for the school to require evidence of a kind of moral earnestness of those who seek admission. But some way must be found for articulating and implementing a fair and yet discriminating (not discriminatory) personal test for the admission and retention of students. The integrity of the Christian campus community is involved.

A vigorous disclaimer might well be registered at this point. An admission policy which is selective on religious or ethical grounds might be strongly denounced as discriminatory, overprotective, and unrealistic. A school has no right, it might be said, to demand that students must be its "kind of people" before it will have anything to do with them. Such a demand smacks of bigotry and is incompatible not only with the democratic concept of equality but also with the Christian concept of community.

This is a serious objection to the policy of selective admission and it cannot be dismissed lightly. And it must be admitted that there have been interpretations and applications of the principle of selectivity which render the objection understandable and, in the context of those applications, entirely justified. A word of rebuttal, however, may help to clarify our intention in recommending selective admission for the Christian college.

(1) The policy is not recommended as a means of shielding students from conflict and isolating them from the world. The strategy underlying the policy is precisely the reverse, namely that of seeking to intensify the student's encounter with ideologies which conflict with his own, through narrowing the scope in which that encounter occurs.

The attempt to create a homogeneous campus community should not be viewed as a timorous retreat from reality, but as an attempt to escape the educational anomaly which Everett Lee Hunt has deplored in his *Revolt of the College Intellectual.* Hunt reports the impression made on him, during the early years of his experience in student personnel work, by Clarence Cook Little's book *The Awakening College.* Little took the view, according to Hunt, that "our hope for an awakened college lies in a vastly increased interest in the character and personality of the individual student." The largest and most tragic cause of the frustration of educational effort, according to Little, was the emotional stress experienced by the collegian. He recommended an endeavor to control the stress-producing influences in the campus environment as a means of releasing the student for fearless participation in the dialectics of education.

In dealing with some of the phenomena of adolescence,

> The elders. . .had left youth too much to themselves in a manner quite contrary to the methods of Nature. Nature always protects developing new structures with a fixed and simple environment—an outer shell or chrysalis. But in college we wait until the students have reached the age of the most disrupting physiological and psychological changes and then we change their geographic environment; their social environment, which presents new and sometimes false and unreal campus values; their emotional environment, which often allows and encourages unrestricted experimentation with subtle and powerful forces; and their mental environment. We then require them to clarify and correlate new facts and theories whose significance is not understood.[8]

The strategies of education need to recognize the limitations of adolescent capacity. The aim of a selective admission policy in the Christian college is not to avoid conflict. Conflict is inevitably associated with the educational process. Even in the cloister the world is encountered in all its starkness. But if a student lives in a campus community which does not require him to make all his adjustments at once, he may be better able to manage the reassessment which education requires of him. And reducing the range of conflict may actually mean that the student will experience its cutting edge.

To some extent, of course, the whole idea of a school involves a retreat form reality. There is disagreement only over the question, "What are the respects in which an artificial and contrived social arrangement is desirable for the school years?" Our contention is that

---

[8]Everett Lee Hunt, *The Revolt of the College Intellectual* (New York: Human Relations Aids, 1963), pp. 2, 3.

the creation of a religiously and morally homogeneous campus community may be educationally appropriate because it establishes a social context for an unbiased intellectual and personal reappraisal.

(2) Nor is it the aim of a selective admission policy to guard the reputation of the college with its public or to satisfy the demands of over-protective parents. Certainly there are Christian schools whose selectivity in admissions and austerity in student discipline are dictated by concern for the institutional image, but our recommendation has nothing to do with public relations.

As a matter of fact, the net effect of the procedures we recommend will probably be to increase the complaints of a conservative constituency. We have recommended a selective admission policy not as a means for establishing external controls over individuals, but as a means for creating a free and open Christian society. Regulation of student conduct takes place at every school, but the ideal of freedom requires the form and scope of such regulation to be kept to the minimum necessary for the proper organization of group living. Far from increasing the regimentation of individuals for the sake of institutional ends, an admission policy which certifies the reliability of the individuals who comprise the student body will enable the faculty and administration to minimize the arrangements for external control of student conduct. It is true that most of the schools which follow a selective admission policy also maintain a high degree of regulation over students, but that combination is anomalous. It is not the arrangement advocated here.

Whitehead once said that "the only discipline, important for its own sake, is self-discipline."[9] All education must operate on this assumption. The educational intention of a selective admission policy, therefore, cannot be mere behavioral conformity for the sake of an institutional reputation. The intention is rather to enhance the freedom of the society of learning, to protect responsible young people in their right to make their own choices, even wrong ones. And the school which follows a selective admission policy in the manner we intend will continue to discover that, as Whitehead also said, the torch of learning has started many a conflagration.

---

[9]Alfred North Whitehead, "The Rhythmic Claims of Freedom and Discipline" in *The Aims of Education*, p. 44.

(3) It is more difficult to meet the charge that a religiously or ethically selective admission policy is discriminatory. The charge often grows, however, out of a concept of education which a Christian college simply cannot accept. No college would be charged with discrimination for following an admission policy which was selective on academic or intellectual grounds, but it would be charged with discrimination (and quite properly) for following an admission policy which was selective on racial grounds. Our critic of selective admission on a religious or ethical basis views a religious or ethical test as analogous to a racial test. He assumes that neither religion nor race is relevant in determining an applicant's qualifications for membership in an academic community. We have argued, however, that a religious or ethical test for admission to a Christian college may be appropriate from an educational standpoint. (A racial test is emphatically not appropriate, since it is not educationally relevant as a criterion of selection.) The charge that a religiously or ethically selective admission policy is inherently discriminatory, therefore, really takes issue with the whole concept of a Christian college as we have been expounding it.

The right of a college to choose its own constituency has always to be guaranteed, as long as its selectivity is limited by considerations of civil and human rights. The requirement of nondiscrimination on the basis of *race*, *color*, or *national origin* has been imposed upon all educational institutions, whether public or private, since the Civil Rights Act of 1965. But the recent legal definitions of civil rights have been careful to preserve the right of religiously oriented institutions to preserve their religious distinctives without being charged with discrimination. The Christian college which acts to preserve its integrity as a Christian community, therefore, cannot be charged with discrimination under current definitions of public policy.[10]

(4) Our proposal for an admission policy aimed at establishing a Christian campus community presupposes a concept of the church which has been forthrightly repudiated of late by such writers as Harvey Cox. Cox wishes to stress that the church is an event rather than an institution; it is the "people of God in motion." The church is a kind of *diaspora*, distributed throughout the secular city, rather than a

[10]Whether it is entitled to public support out of tax funds is another matter. See the discussion of this issue in chapter 9, below.

discernible community, maintaining a separate identity over against the secular city. Cox's concept of the church calls for the creation of new structures through which the church may carry on its ministries; the traditional structures, he thinks, have been shown to be "crippling."

What the "future shape of the church in the university" should be, Cox is unwilling to prescribe in detail. But it is clear, he thinks, that "the future witness of the church will be in the secular university," not in some restored form of the Christian college. The Christian college or university, he is convinced, is an anomaly, and the hope of creating a Christian campus community is misguided. "The idea of developing 'Christian universities' in America was bankrupt even before it began."[11]

Cox's analysis has won a surprising endorsement among church leaders, as Christian communities have become more and more aware of their isolation from the main currents of secular life. New forms of Christian ministry are clearly called for and new structures will have to be invented. Cox's work is valuable in many ways, not the least of them being the forcefulness with which it calls attention to the church's propensity towards conservatism and divisiveness. It must be agreed that one of the major tasks confronting the church at present is the creation of agencies through which it can effectively serve in the secular university, whose dominance in modern culture is guaranteed by well-established social trends.

But Cox has also argued that the traditional idea of a Christian community is no longer viable from a theological and ideological standpoint. In this view he is at fundamental issue with all that has been argued in this book. Imperfections in the forms of Christian communal life are always recognizable; but one might recognize these blemishes and still labor for a closer approximation to the ideal. The ideal itself is what appears to Cox to be bankrupt.

Our purpose here is not to deny the viability and necessity of new forms of Christian ministry in the academic world. It is, however, to defend the viability of an approach which is currently discredited by critics who fail to understand its meaning. In seeking to create a dynamic and open Christian community, a Christian college may find itself going "against the stream" of modern culture. The idea of a

---

[11] Harvey Cox, *The Secular City*, revised edition (New York: Macmillan, 1965), pp. 193, 194.

Christian college is not a popular one in the present age. But the critics who say that the idea is bankrupt or self-contradictory are tragically wrong. One form of Christian ministry in education—though by no means the only form, of course—will continue to be the Christian school, conceived as a community working together, as Ferré puts it, to help the world to find and to do God's will.

STUDENT PERSONNEL ADMINISTRATION

The control of the campus climate under a characteristic institutional ideology is a total-college concern. The endeavor to enhance the unity of the college community must be shared by the entire professional staff and must be a major occupation of the leadership of the college in all its parts. Student personnel officers, however, are strategically placed to exert special influence over the development of the student culture, and a word may be in order concerning the approach which should characterize student personnel work at the Christian college.

In his book on *The Smaller Liberal Arts College*, Lewis B. Mayhew has forcefully criticized the current tendency of smaller colleges to organize their student personnel services along the pattern established in the larger universities. To some extent this tendency is to be explained by the role of the larger universities in defining the criteria of institutional evaluation with which the smaller institutions have to contend, especially in connection with the accreditation process. But it is also to be explained by the tendency to imitation which characterizes large segments of American higher education.

There is no need for the smaller Christian college to imitate the large multipurpose universities in the organization of student personnel services. The circumstances surrounding student life are fundamentally different in the two types of institution, and institutional purposes may dictate a very different order of priority in the use of available resources. The Christian college is probably well advised to start from scratch in devising its own idiosyncratic organization for student personnel administration. It should seek the simplest organization commensurate with the functions required.

Some basic assumptions about student personnel work find particular application in the program of a Christian college. In the first place, it may be assumed that student personnel services should be conducted in concert with the total operation of academic life. On many campuses one can observe a demoralizing dualism between the student personnel and the academic sectors. Whatever is the cause of this schism, if it exists, the unity of the campus community requires that it must be eliminated. It may be assumed, therefore, that the fundamental aim of student personnel work is to enable students to achieve a maximum unity in their collegiate experience. It is therefore obvious that the educational and theological concepts which are appropriate for the Christian college ought to be conspicuously in evidence in the conduct of its student personnel services.

A second assumption is that student personnel work must be conducted in respect for the individuality of students and their rights as persons. It is for the sake of students as persons that the college community is composed. Yet it is easy for student personnel services to become impersonal and formalized, more concerned with the enforcement of institutional regulations and with bureaucratic convenience than with individual good.

One demonstration of a college's respect for the individuality and the rights of students is the allowance of maximum play for the exercise of student freedom. If it is true that the clarification and vindication of personal ideals are achieved through the exercise of choice in decision-making situations, the college which is primarily concerned about the maturation of personalities must provide the largest possible opportunity for students to make their own decisions. Student personnel work should assign to the student responsibility for making his own choices and, of course, the responsibility, also, for living with the consequences of his choices. Permissiveness-and-punishment is God's method of teaching, Ferré observes,[12] and the same method is also valid for student personnel work at the Christian college.

Another way in which a student personnel officer can display respect for the individuality and rights of students is in the responsible use of confidential information and the protection of the student from an invasion of his privacy. A dean who manages to convince a student that he is respected and valued as an individual may elicit a high degree of candor and openness in his communications with the student. That kind of honesty can be the basis for a most helpful exploration of the

[12]Ferré, *Christian Faith and Higher Education*, p. 102.

student's real anxieties and goals. But the relationship can be quickly destroyed through a slip in the maintenance of a confidential trust. If that trust is breached, the ministry of the dean is finished.

Of course, there will be points where individual freedom will come into conflict with the freedom of other individuals and with the social good. At those points, clearly, there will be call for institutional regulations which restrict individual freedom. There is no such thing as absolute freedom in any human society, and it cannot exist in a Christian college any more than in urban traffic. We are thus led to a third assumption about student personnel work, namely, that whatever regulations are found necessary for the proper organization of group living on the campus should be clearly and unambiguously formulated (together with a clear indication of the penalties imposed for violation), thoroughly published and disseminated, and fairly and consistently enforced. Arbitrariness, or the appearance of arbitrariness, does more than anything else to alienate an adult from the young. Most of the conflicts between students and their colleges grow out of a breakdown of communication concerning what is required. Mayhew writes that it is, in his opinion, very likely that

> An institution may adopt virtually any policy regarding regulation of student conduct it desires and still have a contented, effective student body, so long as the policy is clear and the students understand it even before they attend the institution. The colleges where considerable unrest is found are those that are ambivalent about student conduct.[13]

Finally, it may be assumed that student personnel work should be sensitive to the emerging patterns of change, both in society as a whole and in the particular constituency of the college. Educational and social structures which were established generations ago have been permitted to persist in many colleges long after they have ceased to be relevant to the real needs of students. If it may be doubted that the fraternity system is still viable for American education, the same is true of a whole series of anachronistic regulations which have been perpetuated in the more sectarian Christian colleges. The inflexible adherence to out-dated regulations on the part of these institutions has often had the opposite effect from the one intended; it has led the young to lose their respect for law, since their experience testifies that laws are always

---

[13]Lewis B. Mayhew, *The Smaller Liberal Arts College*, p. 66.

unreasonable. Sensitivity to the winds of change will enable a student personnel officer to live by principles which are actually relevant to current circumstances and to the needs of present day students.

RIGHTS AND RESPONSIBILITIES OF STUDENTS

Colleges exist primarily for the sake of students, although college operations do not always implement this principle. Sometimes secondary concerns become over-riding and students are used as means rather than served as ends. Especially for the Christian college, however, the primary emphasis ought to be on service to individuals. Hence an account of the ministry of the Christian college must include a clear recognition of the rights of students.

The student demonstrations of the late 1960's drew public attention to the issue of the rights and responsibilities of the college student. The students, of course, tended to be primarily interested in the assertion and protection of their rights. Harassed college administrators, on the other hand, tended to think primarily about the responsibilities of students. Often the faculty, who seek a closer relationship with students and may well be suspicious of the administration, took the side of the demonstrators, while legislators and boards of control responded with demands for severe repression of anarchistic exhibitions. Now that we have moved away from the emotionality of those days we may reflect about what they taught us concerning the responsibilities of the campus.

What are the rights of a student? Clearly there are a number of rights, both natural and legal, which must be guaranteed to students simply as persons. Currently American society is engaged in a fresh attempt to state more precisely what these rights are and how they are to be protected. The struggle now going on in many colleges is, in one respect, part of the larger attempt at redefinition of the fundamental human and civil rights. A thoroughgoing review of these issues, involving all parts of the college community, is very much in order at present and would contribute much to the unification of the campus. The public at large also has a profound interest in the clarification of the rights of students as persons, especially in view of the expanding encumbrance of public funds in the educational enterprise.

For example, it is a matter of fundamental concern to the public whether every individual has a right to an education up to the limit of his ability and endurance. There has been a growing tendency in

American educational circles, or at least in American legislative circles, to assume that individuals do have that right. A less publicized protest lurks within the faculties of most colleges, however. No doubt, public institutions are more directly and immediately involved in the adjudication of the "universal education" issue, but the operations of private colleges are also clearly implicated. Even with respect to its own limited constituency, a Christian college must come to some conclusion concerning the rights of its college-aged constituents to an education suited to their gifts and callings.

But what of the rights of students as students? As in other social relationships, these rights are based on the contract, either explicit or implicit, into which the student entered with his college when he was admitted. Of course, most adolescents do not have a very clear conception of the obligations incurred by contractual agreements, and in most cases the terms of the agreement between a student and his college are not explicitly stated. The colleges tend to presume that the freshman applicant has a comprehensive understanding of what is involved in becoming a student at the college. But, of course, few of them have such an understanding, and it is often some time before the student discovers all the unexpressed implications of his admission. He then begins to realize that in becoming a student at this particular college he has implicitly submitted to a series of regulations which he neither understood nor anticipated when he applied. He then engages in a series of experiments to find out what the college will, after all, permit him to do or not to do. Sometimes the student becomes greatly irritated over the existence of unexpected requirements and rebels against the whole system of regulation. Considering the character of our times, it is not surprising that the reaction should be, on occasion, one of extremism and violence.

The situation calls for a return to the basic questions: What is it to be a student? or more specifically, What is it to be a student at this particular college? What is the nature of the agreement between a college and its students which in turn defines the rights and responsibilities of students? One obvious answer is that a student is, first of all, a learner. He has not yet reached maturity, although he is rapidly coming to sense his emerging adulthood. He presents himself at the college for the purpose of being taught, in relation to both classroom concerns and his larger experience. The college admits him with this understanding and thereby accepts the responsibility of providing the resources which he needs in order to learn. The student has the right to be treated as a learner and to be given the opportunity to learn.

But the student is more than a learner. He is also a personality in development. In admitting an individual as a student, and especially in inviting him to live in the college's facilities, the college accepts responsibility for his general welfare as well as responsibility for his instruction. It is pointless to debate the question whether acceptance of this responsibility places the college *in loco parentis*. There are obvious ways in which an institution cannot stand in place of an individual's parents. The question to be debated concerns the ways in which and the degree to which the college bears responsibility for the welfare of the student as a developing individual. Clearly some degree of responsibility is entailed by the college's acceptance of the individual as a student. Each institution must make its own determination of the extent of that responsibility.

In general, then, the student has the right to be treated as an immature individual emerging into adulthood. The college must be prepared to accept him in this "twilight zone." The educator should be prepared, for example, to encounter individuals who are painfully experiencing the pressure of measuring up to higher standards of performance than those to which they have been accustomed and who are likely at times to break under the strain. College students are encountering a stiffer and less familiar form of competition from that which they knew in high school. Whereas once they could rely on face-to-face contact and the generosity and goodwill of their examiners, now they are obliged to achieve a new level of accuracy and precision in their efforts at verbalization and to deal with a more impersonal grading system. The classes in which they sit usually include fewer low achievers and more high achievers than they encountered in high school, with the result that classroom competition is more intense than they have previously known. And they are under considerable parental pressure to achieve a record which will justify the expenditure required to keep them in school and to qualify them for a position of productivity and influence. The student's awareness of the heightened competitiveness of college study expressed, for example, in an inordinate anxiety about grades, is one of the phenomena which educators should expect to confront as they deal with developing student personalities.

The educator should also expect that the students with whom he deals will be lacking in a clear point of loyalty and commitment, ambiguous about their basic values and life-purposes, and generally inept in laying comprehensive long-range plans. There will be exceptions to the generalization, of course, but students tend to have a limited comprehension of the aims of education, an uncertain aim themselves, and a superficial understanding of the way in which education will assist them to achieve their goals. Lacking any consuming commitment to a purpose outside himself, the student becomes preoccupied with himself—his own feelings, thoughts, and conflicts. The immaturity of college students is readily detectable in the self-orientation and self-consciousness which so often characterize their speech and their writing.

The educator should expect to deal with a young adult just emerging from adolescence into an as yet undefined independence. Often the symptom of that emergence is a disengagement with the past and its restrictions. Sometimes the break is marked by rebellion and hostility, but in other cases the separation is more peaceful and amicable. The student, bent on the vindication of his independence, comes to regard any representatives of the System, as well as its rules and ideological assumptions, as his enemy, or at least as alien to his own individuality. The educator should expect students to be deeply sceptical of moral generalizations and precepts. In part this scepticism is the product of the moral relativism which characterizes American society and which has become dominant in the schools. But it is also an expression of the emergent independence of one who is conscious of belonging to another generation and who thinks of moral precepts as the dogma of a passing age. Only too often college teachers and administrators who are forgetful of these facts make the serious and often tragic mistake of taking far more seriously than they ought the scepticism and iconoclasm of the young.

Finally, the educator at the Christian college should expect students—even those with a devout background and an extensive religious education in the church—to display a religious outlook which is largely uncritical and uninformed. Religion is not being taught to the young from a scientific and critical standpoint, either in the schools, in the churches, or in the homes. Students will tend either to think of their religious beliefs as already formed, while they persist in them dogmatically, or to sense their illiteracy in matters of religion, while they see little reason for correcting the deficiency. It is interesting to discover that the same generalizations about the religious beliefs of college students hold, regardless of whether the students are in a Christian college or a public university. What differences in religious understanding can be detected between these groups are generally attributable to the influence of courses taken by students at the Christian colleges. The basic task of the religious educator is much the same in either context, namely, that of helping the students to achieve a more comprehensive and critically adequate religious interpretation.

The educator may be pleasantly surprised to discover that the students with whom he deals are less immature than this portrait suggests. But he should *expect* things to be as we have described them. He should be prepared to treat students with the respect due an adult human being, but he should also expect them to act as something less than adults in a variety of ways. In enrolling such a personality, maturing though not yet mature, the college also accepts certain obligations for the protection of the developing individual. Correspondingly, the student has a right to the care and guidance of those who are more experienced than he.

The rights of the student as a student, then, include the right to responsible instruction, the right to sympathetic and reliable guidance, the right to protection from dangers and risks beyond his comprehension or control, and the right to a modicum of comfort and entertainment as defined by the current standard of living. Does he also have the right to participate in the determination of educational policy, the definition of the objectives of the institution, the establishment of institutional standards, the evaluation of institutional programs, and the projection of plans for institutional development? Certainly, responsible student opinion on such matters will be considered in any well organized college. There is a growing tendency to include student representatives on crucial committees and to allow authentic student participation in institutional planning. The question is, again, not one of kind but of degree. One can observe a wide range in the competence of students for dealing responsibly with such questions. Thus some students and student bodies can be brought more intimately into collegiate councils than others.

But it should not be forgotten that students are still learners and that learning rather than doing should be their primary occupation during the college years. Whitehead warned that during the period of youth, when imagination is learning to be disciplined, a person should be free from responsibility for immediate action, free to ignore the compromises of principle which are implicit in administering the college as an organization.[14] The student should be allowed to devote himself to untrammeled inquiry. He should not accept too early the perils and the distractions of the life of the activist. He will have his chance to act in due time.

Rights always imply responsibilities. The two concepts are correlative. If one person has a right, some other person has a responsibility with respect to the protection or realization of that right. The rights of students reflect the responsibilities of college officials and faculty members towards students. But life is such that everyone who is accorded a right in one respect is also obliged to accept a responsibility in another respect. The rights of students are therefore hedged about by the responsibilities of students. No student has the right to think and do as he chooses—nor does anyone else in society. When students seek to assert an absolute right, even the most tolerant of educational institutions will find it necessary to censure them. Expulsion is always a possibility for any college student who insists on a limitless freedom. It is entirely within the rights of a college, therefore, to expect those who wish to be admitted to the college community to familiarize themselves with the ideals and standards of the community and to exact from them the promise that, if accepted as students, they will respect and foster those ideals through a disciplined life and their most conscientious work as students. A student, too, is part of an institution, and if he refuses to accept the responsibility which membership in the college community entails, he may be required to withdraw. Some such understanding is implicit in the contract under which a student gains admittance to any college, and it ought to be given a characteristic construction in any college which is serious about its Christian objectives.

The nurture of the youth should be the primary objective of a Christian college. Sensitivity to their needs, appreciation of their worth, and understanding of the stages of their growth will cause college officials and faculty members to treat students with the utmost patience and solicitude. Growth will be sought, not by the brutality of

[14]Whitehead, *The Aims of Education*, p. 94.

the shock treatment, but by the tenderness of a long-term nurture. It was always thus that Jesus taught—except when he encountered hypocrisy. Of him it was said, "A bruised reed he will not break, and a dimly burning wick he will not put out."

Chapter 8

THE ORGANIZATION OF LEARNING

Enlightened and energetic administrative initiative is often the key to excellence in a college. Boards of trustees, who often think of their organizations in terms of line responsibilities, may tend to exaggerate the importance of the president and his staff. Yet there is much evidence that the administrative function may be controlling for the climate of a college. The abilities, personalities, and values of the chief administrative officers of a college exercise a determining influence upon the operations of the college and the character of the college community.

Administrative competence and efficiency, however, are not noteworthy in the Christian colleges. Instead there are widespread complaints about the arbitrariness of boards, the anti-intellectualism and absenteeism of presidents, and the weakness of deans. Often enough such accusations are undeserved; yet what Mayhew says about the small liberal arts college in general applies with special force to the Christian colleges in particular:

> Possibly the most serious lack in the privately supported liberal arts college today is educational leadership. The president, who is legally responsible, is so preoccupied with management matters as to be unable to keep abreast of educational thinking, much less translate it

> into educational action. The academic dean, frequently one of the weakest links in the administrative chain, has too generally been an older respected teacher, given the post of dean in his declining years. The abdication of the leadership role has meant that the faculty itself carried on the educational program too generally along lines demanded by tradition. Unless this problem of leadership can be solved, in view of the contemporary condition of rapid social change, the privately supported liberal arts college may very well find itself outclassed by the state supported institutions and unable to maintain itself as an educational force.[1]

The Danforth Commission on the Church Colleges reported the results of a questionnaire submitted to the Danforth and Kent Fellows who are now teaching at church-affiliated colleges and universities. The Commission reported that "the area of administration is one in which the evaluations tend to be highly critical. At least one-half of the respondents are dissatisfied with the administrative leadership of their institutions."[2] The instructors criticized the college officialdom for its lack of single-minded dedication to academic excellence, its subservience to the demands of the college's constituency and of a business-minded culture, its preoccupation with "trivial rules of conduct . . . and a hundred other inane but distracting things," and its incapacity for self-criticism. A few appraisals were strongly affirmative; furthermore, faculty criticism of administration may need to be devaluated in view of the irrational origins of a certain amount of faculty-administration hostility. Yet the candid among the presidents and deans of the Christian colleges would be prepared to admit that there is a considerable amount of truth in the verdict of the majority of the Danforth and Kent Fellows.

SIGNS OF ADMINISTRATIVE MALFUNCTION

In the small college the coordination of planning centers in the office of the president. And the specific focal point of coordinated planning is the institutional budget. Much depends, therefore, on the manner in which the presidential functions are performed and on the system by which the budget is determined. Even in a small institution, however, the organization is much too complex to allow one person to

---

[1]Mayhew, *The Smaller Liberal Arts College*, pp. 79, 80.

[2]Pattillo and Mackenzie, *Church-Sponsored Higher Education in the United States*, pp. 158, 159.

involve himself operationally at all levels. And the fund-raising and public relations responsibilities of the president result in an absenteeism which makes his personal involvement in college planning often unsystematic. The president cannot avoid depending on his staff to assist him in performing the coordinating function.

The problem in many of the Christian colleges is that the staff which is most directly associated with the office of the president and with budgetary planning often has only a limited comprehension of educational philosophy and methodology. The common mistake of small college presidents is to appoint financial officers with a view not to their educational understanding but to their business competence. If the president's office is to produce a budget which represents a genuine institutional consensus on the educational plan for the year, it must be developed on the basis of educational as well as fiscal considerations. Too often, however, the president's chief fiscal adviser, though qualified from the fiscal standpoint, is lacking in the educational understanding which this position requires. As a result educational considerations do not exercise the control over budgetary decisions which they should. The formulation of the budget is seldom a total-college activity and instead is a function of another department of the institution. The prevalence of this condition in the smaller colleges is a decisive proof of the breakdown of the total organization and the fragmentation of administrative work into departmental activities.

A second symptom of administrative malfunctioning is the arbitrary exercise of authority in establishing and applying college policy. The concept of authority is of limited application in educational theory. Nevertheless superficial thinking about the nature of authority in the governance of educational institutions has caused a great deal of alienation and misunderstanding, has created a great deal of confusion, and has frustrated a great many creative and innovative impulses in American colleges and universities.

Respect is accorded to competence. If a person knows something, his opinion gains authority. Nobody will deny this. But the limitations of human knowledge impose a limitation on any individual's exercise of authority in education. It is not possible for an individual, or for a small group of individuals, to command the competence which is required for the satisfactory solution of the very complex issues which bear on educational policy. Nor is knowledge in these matters the exclusive province of a few. Competence is distributed broadly in a college staff.

An administrator who exercises his authority without consultation cuts himself off from knowledge which might be a corrective for his own sometimes wayward opinions. Consultation with colleagues increases the likelihood of reliability in judgment. The authority of an individual of higher rank in the organizational hierarchy may be the decisive element in the relationship between employer and employee or in a military chain of command, but it has much less meaning in the case of relationships among educational colleagues. As Harold W. Dodds says, "Consultation aimed at integration of diverse viewpoints usually gives better results than the participants could have contributed as individuals."[3] In a community of learning governance cannot be by fiat; it can only be by conference.

A list of the strengths of the Christian colleges would not include a reputation for adeptness in the consultative process. On the contrary, one of the loudest complaints about the operation of these institutions is addressed to the inadequacy of their arrangements for obtaining a staff consensus. The Danforth Commission has urged the church colleges to adopt a "new, more flexible concept of college administration," emphasizing a "group-leadership pattern" in place of the traditional "pyramid pattern." "In our judgment," the Commission concluded after surveying the church-related colleges and universities, "the time-honored principles of college administration are much too rigid and doctrinaire to cope successfully with modern conditions of administration."[4] Most of the presidents of the Christian colleges, however, will have a difficult time understanding the pattern proposed. The more strong-minded ones will fear the "group-leadership pattern" as a threat to their positions. The more weak-willed ones will fear it as an unknown which they do not know how to manage. It is unfortunate that most Christian college presidents fall into one or the other of these polarities.

No administrator can ever forget that he is first of all an educator and that even in his dealings with his colleagues he is a participant in a teaching-and-learning process. Even though he is an authority in his

---

[3]Harold W. Dodds, *The Academic President—Educator or Caretaker?* (New York: McGraw Hill, 1962), pp. 16, 17.

[4]Pattillo and MacKenzie, *Church-Sponsored Higher Education in the United States*, p. 202.

field, no scholar can teach effectively (except in a limited scope and sense) unless he carefully restrains the exercise of the authority to which his competence entitles him. Similarly, an educational administrator may have knowledge of what is required in college policy, but if he attempts to exercise his authority to force conformity to his informed opinion, he will eventually encounter resistance and disappointment. Only an educational consensus which goes deeper than mere conformity to an authoritatively promulgated opinion can finally satisfy an educator. This is why the dialectics of the conference table are indispensable in policy-formulation.

If authority is ever exercised in education, it is inevitable that it will be exercised only over a limited scope. People will bend to another's will if they must, but they will still insist on their right to be persons. Wherever authority is exercised, whether by a classroom teacher, a department chairman, or an administrative officer, the people affected will act to restrict the range of its effects. Authority can be exercised only over parts of an educational institution; and the effect of trying to apply the concept of authority in educational administration will, therefore, be to carve up the institution into bailiwicks, presided over by assorted individuals. Even if it is governed by enlightened minds, an institution operated in this manner will have no essential unity.

What unity requires is that each individual participant in the life of the institution—regardless of his rank—must be disposed to correct his opinion or his action by consideration for the collective consensus. The consensus is reached, of course, only by conference. And the conference requires leadership if it is to be productive and efficient. But the leadership which is needed is initiative in stimulating the growth of the group consensus, not an authoritative declaration to which the group must accede. The distinction is a fundamental one for the theory of educational administration. Without a center of initiative committees waste time. But it is in the form of initiative, as distinguished from mere authority, that leadership should express itself in college work.

A college which succeeds in exploiting the possibilities of the consultative approach will possess a number of meaningful brainstorming centers, which will help to identify institutional problems and to suggest fresh approaches to their solution. Reports will cease to be designed to protect the reputation and prestige of the reporter; instead they will be designed in a manner which will suggest questions for collective discussion. The personnel who are responsible for the actual operation of the college's plan will have a forum for calling attention to problems as they arise operationally and for participating in the formation of policies which will be realistic and practical. Consultation will sharpen the growing edge of educational innovation. The breakdown of the consultative process, on the other hand, will in time suppress the creative impulse.

Closely related to a mistaken concept of the nature and grounds of administrative authority is an inadequate concept of the delegation of responsibility. Herein is found another root of much administrative malfunctioning. The ability to delegate responsibility is essential to the success of any complex organization. Yet in many colleges the board of trustees does not know how to view the functions of the president or of the faculty, the president or dean does not know how to relinquish control over operational details, the faculty does not know how to assign work meaningfully to support staff. These deficiencies are especially conspicuous in the small Christian colleges. Many have failed to reach clear and firm agreements which permit an effective division of labor in the administration of institutional affairs. Too frequently the board of trustees intrudes its non-professional judgment into operational matters which should be left in the hands of professionals. Too often presidents and deans try to keep control of more details than they can possibly manage. There is too little understanding of the difference between issues which are worth a conference and those which are not, and there is too little willingness to accept the risk of instituting another way of doing things. A specialized talent is required to divide up the labor of running a complex institution in a way that gives individuals the freedom required for creative and independent action, and at the same time preserves the established line of responsibility. This talent is too rare in the Christian colleges.

Again, many of the smaller colleges, as Mayhew has stressed, are imitatively following irrelevant patterns of administrative organization. Bent on keeping abreast of the current trends or on satisfying the (presumed) standards which determine the extent of their educational recognition, smaller institutions copy patterns of administrative organization which, though appropriate in other institutions, are not functional in their own. Charts of administrative reorganization move from seminars on educational administration to the agenda of boards of trustees without being subjected to a rigorous scrutiny in the light of the circumstances and needs of the individual college.

Originality in administrative organization is not one of the strengths of the small colleges, despite the fact that in their case so much depends upon it. In recent years there have been some useful contributions to the literature on the administration of the small liberal arts college, but the models remain less systematic than is needed.[5] What can usually be observed in the small colleges is a quite unimaginative and uncritical persistence of administrative and office procedures which can only be described, in the light of recent technological improvements, as wasteful. For all their devotion to the ideals of Christian stewardship, the Christian colleges allow an incredible amount of sacrificially contributed money to go down the drain because of the inefficiency and wastefulness of their procedures.

The great sin of administration in the small Christian colleges, however, is pedantry. Too many college administrators consume their days in preoccupation with the mechanics and the routine of college operations, and they fail to focus attention on ultimate goals. Few administrators take time for significant reading, and the creeping indiscipline of their thought and the poverty of their imagination reflect the fact. The result is that the president or the dean is no longer looked up to as an intellectual leader for the campus. Administrative work has been permitted to distract a powerful mind from its engagement with fundamental questions. Yet in a Christian college, whose very life depends on the vitality and viability of its ideological commitment, the pedantic distraction of the people at the organizational core is fatal.

THE FUNCTIONS OF ADMINISTRATION

The main reason for having an administration is to facilitate teaching. The administrative function is a self-giving function and must be based on a highly developed altruism. The administrator must think of himself as existing for the purpose of enabling his colleagues to fulfill the basic aim of the institution, which is instruction. Lip service is generally paid to this idea. But even among Christian administrators one only rarely observes the self-effacing disposition of the one who considers himself the servant of all. Institutional procedures are all too

[5]In recent years a number of Christian colleges have benefited from the administrative improvement services of the Council for the Advancement of Small Colleges, now called the Council for Independent Colleges.

frequently established with a view to the convenience of the bureaucracy and with too little regard for the advantage of the teacher and of the student. Administrators, too, generally seek to perform their tasks in a way which is in accord with their own interests.

Another function of educational administration is to protect the college's personnel. Here, too, there is ample room for the exercise of the distinctive Christian virtues. The college which is Christian will exist as a means to the good of the individuals who comprise the college community and clientele. In many colleges, however, the means/end relation is reversed. Colleges use individuals as means for institutional ends. The tendency is by no means confined to the administrative branch of the college. Musical directors, athletic coaches, classroom teachers, and even students themselves are capable of exploiting individuals for the purpose of achieving a greater degree of success in performance. A major function of administration is to protect individuals from this tendency of an institution and its representatives to place institutional success ahead of individual welfare.

There are a number of respects in which the protective function is called for. The younger members of the college community, of course, require a broader kind of protection. Their physical and mental health must be safeguarded; their living accommodations must be made secure; their meals must be kept in proper balance. But the list of needed protections is much longer than this. There is a whole battery of student personnel services which are necessary for the protection of student welfare. The college program will have to strike a balance which combines protecting the student, even from his own mistakes in some cases, with allowing the student to exercise his own judgment and to mature by learning from his errors.

But the adult members of the college community require protection as well. With special reference to the academic staff, the administrative function includes the protection of the instructor in his freedom to teach conscientiously and to pursue truth wherever it leads. The administrator should be prepared to protect his colleagues from uninformed and prejudiced criticism, from that kind of external pressure which an academician can only interpret as intimidation. Of course, an instructor can be expected to be mature, and when criticism is deserved he should be made to bear it; but a major function of the administrator is to shield his academic colleagues from that kind of irresponsible attack which interferes with the freedom of thought and instruction.

Here, too, the administrator is primarily the protector of others.

A third function of administration is to introduce the element of universality into college planning. Departmentalization is a basic fact of American higher education. For the most part the communication of ideas on a fundamental level takes place only within departments. This condition poses a serious obstacle to integrative educational planning. The integration of disparate fields and conflicting interests is difficult on any basis, much less, given the present religious situation, on a religious basis. A Christian college, however, must be so organized that departmental concerns are constrained by a more universal commitment. The structure and operation of college administration have much to do with the ability of a college to organize its program of learning systematically and purposefully. For the most part, however, the administrations of the Christian colleges operate simply as another department of the college. Administration too often fails to represent the element of universality which it is supposed to imbue into college planning. Precisely because it is so difficult, the task of integrating the various parts of the college into a coherent organizational unity is seldom even begun in many colleges.

A fourth function of educational administration is to care for the external relationships of the institution. The performance of this role is centered in the president and the corps of assistants clustered around him. In most of the Christian colleges these functions are generally carried out with skill and tact. College presidents and their aides tend to be appointed on the basis of their public relations abilities, and their institutions' financial stakes in the success of their endeavors provide a ready motivation for giving the highest priority to the achievement of effectiveness in their work.

There are two respects, however, in which the public relations performance of the presidents of the Christian colleges is subject to severe criticism. The first is their handling of the external pressures which seek an adjustment of institutional policy or instructional method. Public information programs involve a two-way street. The college has information which it wants to distribute to the public, but the college's constituency also has opinions and information which it wants to communicate to the college. The president and the field representatives of the college inevitably must lend their ears to the criticism and the demands of dissatisfied or irate constituents, especially the more affluent ones. They must then make the decision whether to ignore the public demand or bring it home with them to faculty and administrative policy-making sessions. The decision reached is often an unfortunate one.

In college after college, policy debates are conducted against the background of pronouncements concerning what the college's constituency demands. Often these pronouncements are derived from the highly subjective impressions of the people who have direct contact with the field; sometimes they are stimulated by a letter or two. Actually there are few colleges in America which are in a position to make reliable generalizations about their constituencies. Yet faculty after faculty is thwarted in its desire for educational advance by the declaration that the proposed change is "not suited to the demands of the constituency." Few educational dogmas have done more to suppress educational innovation in American higher education than the myth about constituencies. Imagined or circumstantial public pressure has taken the place of principle in determining educational policy. Educational administrators must carry the major share of blame for allowing this condition to exist.

A second major weakness in the administrative care for external relationships of the Christian colleges is the inadequacy of presidential efforts for enhancing the effectiveness of their boards of trustees. In one sense, of course, the board is not external to the institution. But there are more respects than one in which the president's treatment of the board involves him in the exercise of his best public relations skills. Practically every board member in the Christian colleges begins by being woefully ignorant of educational practice in general and of the affairs of his own institution in particular. Yet in spite of this illiteracy, there are practically no arrangements for instructing the trustees of the Christian colleges in even the elementary principles of education.

The trustees are allowed to assume that fiscal planning can be detached from educational planning. In the name of the exercise of fiscal responsibility, the discharge of which they regard as within their competence, they establish control over educational processes which they admit, sometimes with pride, that they do not understand. Occasionally one finds a trustee who is fully informed and astute. Most college presidents have at least one such. But for the most part the trustees of the Christian colleges are educationally unprepared for their responsibilities. E. Fay Campbell's experience will be regarded as typical by those who are able to view Christian higher education candidly. "It has been my experience," he wrote, "in almost every case where there has been trouble in a college that the board of trustees was not prepared or qualified for the job in hand."[6] The fact that they are unprepared and unqualified is generally due to the failure of presidents to surround themselves with college trustees worthy of the name.

THE CULT OF EFFICIENCY

"The management of a university faculty has no analogy to that of a business corporation," Whitehead once wrote, and his view is echoed all through the ranks of education. "The modern university system in the great democratic countries will only be successful if the ultimate authorities exercise singular restraint so as to remember that universities cannot be dealt with according to the rules and policies which apply to the familiar business corporation."[7] In a number of respects, the point is well taken. A college is not a business enterprise; professors are not employees. Yet there are a number of respects in which a college has to be operated on the same principles as apply in the economic world. There is enough similarity between a college and a business for either to be forced to close or retrench for economic causes. And in an age of educational competition it is undeniable that the Christian colleges, struggling with their larger and more affluent competitors, will have to achieve a peak of business efficiency in order to maintain themselves.

Most of the Christian colleges operate with a student body of less than optimum size from an economic point of view. A larger student body enables a college to diversify and enrich its services and thus to compete more favorably with other institutions. The economic advantages tend to run towards the larger schools; the smaller institutions feel the pinch of economic competition the most keenly. It is therefore incumbent on the administrators of the smaller colleges to discover ways to counter-balance the competitive disadvantage associated with their size. For the smaller institutions the demand for operating efficiency has a special urgency.

It will not do, however, for the Christian colleges to seek to achieve savings by cutting back their services. For the most part this is the only

---

[6]E. Fay Campbell, "The Challenge," *The Christian Scholar* 41: Special Issue (Autumn 1958): 268.

[7]Whitehead, *The Aims of Education,* pp. 99, 100.

approach which is being tried among these colleges at present. Yet the attempt to economize through retrenchment is guaranteed to weaken the position of the Christian colleges still further. What is required by the competitiveness of the times is that the smaller colleges must find a way to provide better educational services than they have yet been able to manage at a cost lower than they have been paying heretofore. The challenge to their administrative inventiveness is an imposing one.

Fortunately, the wastefulness of the rest of the educational system brings the performance of this assignment within the realm of possibility. Practically any educational institution could have served Parkinson as well as the British navy when he was looking for illustrations of his now famous law. In view of this wastefulness, a tremendous competitive advantage accrues to the college which can overcome Parkinson's law and preserve the simplicity of its organization. If it shows the necessary courage, a college administration can create an organization which is both simple (and therefore inexpensive) and functional.

Most educational institutions are frightfully wasteful in their use of their resources. The daily schedule, the weekly schedule, and the annual calendar which habit has allowed to become entrenched in the American educational system cause buildings, equipment, and other resources to go unused for major periods of time. The college which can find a way to break the hammerlock which the scheduling pattern has placed on the collegiate system will gain a tremendous economic advantage over its competitors.

Another way in which alert and opportunistic small colleges might recoup some of the disadvantages which come from smallness is through establishing broad programs of inter-institutional cooperation. A number of new departures for cooperation have been indicated in recent years. These ventures, however, have as yet scarcely reached the colleges which need them most. The most dramatic demonstrations of cooperation among private colleges have been such associations as the Associated Colleges of the Midwest, the Claremont Group, the Great Lakes College Association, and the Mount Holyoke-Smith-Amherst-Massachusetts complex, but these have involved the more prestigious and affluent of the private liberal arts colleges. The Christian College Consortium and the Christian College Coalition have recently been established, but their promise as agencies of broad interinstitutional cooperation and sharing of resources has been only partially realized.

One would think that the weaker colleges would be leaders in the movement towards interinstitutional cooperation, and one would think that the Christian colleges, with their common purposes, would long ago have produced some meaningful agencies for cooperation. But the fact is just the reverse of what one would expect. Nowhere is it more difficult to get institutions to work together than in the evangelical branch of Christendom. Much warmth and friendliness passes, naturally, among the representatives of the evangelical colleges, but their philosophy of college administration is isolationist. The evangelicals are more anxious to preserve control over their enterprises than to realize the strength which cooperation might afford. Even within the same denomination, close interinstitutional cooperation is difficult to effect.

A whole range of patterns of evangelical cooperation in higher education is conceivable. Most of them stand little chance of being effected. There might be cooperative sponsorship of a single strong college by several denominations unable to maintain an educational program of quality on their own. There might be arrangements for sharing faculty, library, and other educational resources, for joint sponsorship of ambitious or innovative educational ventures and for joint ownership of expensive scientific equipment. There might be telephone or television hookups among the colleges, allowing immediate interinstitutional communication for a wide variety of purposes. There might be more intimate organizational structures at a single location, modeled after the "federation" idea or the "cluster-college" idea.

None of these exists on a large scale in Christian higher education, and one of the most disheartening and disillusioning of experiences is to discover the nature of the resistance which such perfectly reasonable and expedient ideas for interinstitutional cooperation meet when they are proposed to Christian educators. After one has disposed of all the explanations as to why such ideas are impractical and unworkable, it becomes clear that the real obstacles to cooperation are the protectionism and provincialism of the evangelical groups. Even modest programs of cooperation are eschewed because they pose the risk of a loss of institutional identity, an erosion of autonomous control, or a compromise of doctrinal or behavioral standards. The Christian colleges are failing to work together because they value control more highly than excellence.

Educational administration places high demands on personnel. The work is arduous and taxes the energy and stamina of even the strong and robust. Even more exacting are the demands on a person's virtue. To qualify as a leader of a college, an individual must first possess that kind of superior intellect which is the mark of the producing scholar. But in addition he requires special talent in the analysis of issues, in the imaginative consideration of possible solutions to problems, and in the synthesizing interpretation of data. For the administration of a Christian college he will need also a touch of the philosopher and the theologian. But most of all the administrator requires courage, combined with humility; determination, combined with tact; and firmness, combined with grace. He must be a person of dignity, patience, and self-control at the same time that he shows confidence and fearlessness in his pursuit of what he thinks is right. Above all, he must have humility and regard for the worth of others—the indispensable marks of Christian discipleship—combined with a strong sense of vocation as leader of his institution. Such combinations are rare, and the individuals who possess them quite naturally tend to gravitate towards the institutions of the greatest quality and size. It is, indeed, a fortunate Christian college which has leaders who are equal to their task.

THE COLLEGE AS INSTITUTION AND IDEA

John Dewey was fond of emphasizing that the moral purpose is universal and dominant in education—whatever the topic. To be sure, he recognized, an instructor must remain most directly concerned with intellectual matters; yet both the form and the content of an educational program must be determined on the basis of a moral understanding of what is needed to render conduct more enlightened and more consistent. For the business of an educator is not merely to teach subjects or to develop the psychological "faculties," but also to help the young acquire ideas in such a vital way that these ideas become motive-forces in the guidance of conduct. The structure and workings of an educational institution must be continually appraised, therefore, from the standpoint of the moral position and function of the school in relation to society.

Education must always be thought of as a moral function, as having aims which must be qualified by moral considerations. Educational theory must make clear the conditions under which education may have a viable basis in morality. The institutional form as well as the intellectual content of a program of education must be determined by reference to judgments as to what type of person is demanded by morality and what conditions will optimize the utility of education as a means for creating such persons. From the moral point of view, the problem of education is to identify the values which the educational process is to serve and to describe that type of organization for education which will best fit it into the good life.

Modern life is the life of institutions; so ethical inquiry must address itself to the functions and structure of institutions. Under modern conditions of life the objective means of action have been institutionalized and are no longer there for the taking. The institutional structure has become a limit on every individual's freedom to act. The structure of institutions may thus serve either as a vehicle of action or as an obstacle to action. If the structure of institutions makes it impossible for individuals to obtain the means to act morally, the moral life becomes impossible. Hence it is a part of the moral task to organize the material and institutional means of action to suit the demands of morality and to control the functioning of institutions as means for realizing moral ends.

Kant offered the categorical dictum that one ought always to act so as to treat humanity, whether in one's own person or in that of another, always as an end and never only as a means. The corollary of the Kantian imperative is the following: Act so as to treat institutions always as means and never as ends. From the moral point of view no institution can ever be regarded as having anything but instrumental value. Institutions may be valued only as the means for personal good. Institutions are always on trial for their lives.

To return, now, to the college as an institution, a moral assessment of the processes of the college must be assayed if the present educational controversy is to lead to constructive and beneficial results. The frame of reference for such an evaluation of the college as institution must be established, of course, by a concept of the college as an ideal. The components of the collegiate ideal are such as the following: implementation of a method of rational inquiry in the pursuit of truth and the correction of error; inter-personal relationships based on collegiality and freedom; coherence in both programs and organization, based on belief in the unity of science and the wholeness of truth;

aspiration for excellence and tolerance of the radicalism which is the expression of genius; flexibility and adaptability to the changing conditions of scholarship and human life.

Anyone who lives in academia experiences the tension between such ideals and the realities of institutional life. An adequate theory of the nature of the college must achieve a reconciliation of this tension and establish a norm affecting the institutional reality.

The idea of the Christian college must be defined in terms of the recognition that the college is an institution, and the operations of the institution must be evaluated in the light of standards derived from the ideal. Without a firm basis in the ideal, the college as institution is profane; on the other hand, until expressed in institutional terms the collegiate ideal is vacuous. The task of educational planning is to achieve institutional forms which give effective expression to the idea of the college as an ideal possibility.

Although necessary to the effective realization of the idea of the college, institutionalization often implicates the collegiate ideal in dubious compromises. The ideal of an intellectual community based on collegiality and freedom may take institutional form as a social arrangement which sanctifies special privilege and gives power to a few. The search for truth through the application of a rational methodology may be institutionalized in the form of a pattern of instruction which presumes to prescribe what is important or valid. The idea of a unified body of knowledge may be lost in an avalanche of instructional activities, broken into bits and pieces by a departmental provincialism. Open discussion and dialectical investigation may be subverted into vying for forensic advantage and rationalizing special interests.

Colleges as institutions tend to become ends in themselves, rather than means for the realization of more ultimate human purposes. Ideally the college exists for the service of individuals, but actually it tends, like other institutions, to use individuals as means. Colleges as institutions tend to become intractable, entrenched in established forms, unresponsive to individual efforts at control or reform. The college idealizes excellence, genius, and creativity, but as institution the college cultivates the mediocrity which fosters the ends of the organization and suppresses the genius whose potential radicalism threatens the stability of organizational processes. The college joins other institutions in a silent solidarity against excellence. Institutional conventions and bureaucratic routines rise up to sidetrack innovations. Or alternatively, the functioning of the college as organization leads to efforts to effect through artificial and mechanical contrivances changes which can only come about through organic development.

The institutionalization of the college is inevitably attended by some compromise of the ideal. But by no means are all of the compromises presently tolerated in American higher education inevitable. In the evaluation of possible institutional forms for the educational enterprise, the distinction between "better" and "worse" is more important then absolutistic distinctions to which idealists tend to resort. What is currently needed is an examination and an exposition of the circumstances under which the institutionalization of the ideal may, in spite of compromises of incidental importance, become the means for realizing the purposes of education. What is needed is a return to the ideal of the college to determine what institutional forms most adequately serve the ideal.

The basic requirement of the academy as institution is that it must be capable of being put to human uses. The college as institution must always be subjected to an evaluation which measures its utility as a means for the realization of the purposes of human beings. The college both exists for and depends upon persons. The merit of a college is its utility for bringing out the best in persons. The college passes the point of utility as a means for the service of persons when it begins to use persons as means for its own ends, when institutional control of individuals ceases to be justified as a means to the good of the persons controlled, when bureaucratic convenience and adherence to policy become more important than the welfare of persons.

The college as institution is a community of persons. But the freedom, openness, and deliberateness of the college as ideal render the institution one of the most fragile of human communities. More than most other institutional structures, the college as institution must depend on the integrity, self-control, and good will of its individual members. The college cannot approximate the ideal unless it can count on the exhibition of certain moral qualities on the part of the individuals who participate in its processes.

The character traits required for effective operation of the academy are too often lacking in its membership. The academic community is too often disrupted by the high-handedness of the arrogant or thwarted by the lame excuses of the defensive. University people exhibit a penchant for appearing stronger than they really are. Their attempt to create the illusion of strength easily turns into a ridiculous bravado. Young academic idealists begin to hope naively that they will be able to reconstitute the world by decree; they expect society to turn just, harmonious, and humane at their beckoning. Instead of learning self-discipline and concentrating on the cultivation of human growth, they rush out, in obedience to what they call an "idea," to make impossible "demands," to declare uncompromising "positions," and to issue threatening ultimatums. The weakness underlying all this unintelligent flailing about is not intellectual, however, but moral.

Institutions are mechanisms created to facilitate the transaction of business and the pursuit of human goals in safety and security. In the present moment the faith that institutions may be made to serve individual ends is greeted with derision and disbelief in many quarters. That faith, however, is essential to the life of the Christian college. The stability of the college as institution is an essential condition of intellectual work. The examination of the foundation of the college's order and the implementation of steps to preserve that foundation have never been more necessary.

The present threat is not to the continuance of the colleges as institutions. Recent experience has shown that it is easy to close even a strong university temporarily, almost impossible to close even a weak one permanently. Educational institutions will most certainly survive the heat of this day. What is in doubt is whether the conditions under which the colleges now operate will cause them as institutions to drift so far from their ideal moorings that they will cease to be of use to culture and to intellect. Despite their fragility, the colleges as institutions will doubtless survive. The question is whether they will manage to preserve their virtue.

"What we need in education more than anything else," said Dewey, "is a genuine, not merely nominal, faith in the existence of moral principles which are capable of effective application." The faith of an educator must include belief in the existence of such principles. The search for the moral basis of educational institutions must go on, despite the frustrations which beset that search at the moment. Faith in the relevance of morals for the restructuring of the college as institution does not automatically solve the complex planning problems facing higher education today. But it does direct the attention of planners to the right problems and to possible actions which intelligence may address to the solution of those problems. Faith in the applicability of morals to the task of institutional organization does not, as Dewey said, assure us against failure, but it might help us to learn from our failures.

The attempt to describe the good life and to create the conditions which make it possible is an adventure the outcome of which is not at all certain. But in times of stress it is doubly important to be clear as to what one is about. It is time to emphasize that after the smoke of the present controversies has cleared from academe, the basic task will remain what it was before, namely to organize the college as an institution in such a way that it serves the purposes of the college as idea. There is no simplistic solution to that planning problem, nor any guarantee that patient and painstaking effort will produce the solution. But the pursuit of the possibility remains worthy of the highest human devotion.

Chapter 9

THE CHRISTIAN COLLEGE AND PUBLIC SUPPORT

Christian colleges operate within the private sector and depend primarily on the churches for support. However, excellence in a program of higher education requires development of broadly based financial resources, including those which are now available for both public and private institutions through various agencies of government.

Since the late 1950s the American society has been depending more and more upon government as a means of channeling financial support to colleges and universities. Although the momentum of recent growth seems to be slowing, the basic forms of such support are by now well established.

The federal interest in higher education is historic. There have been several stages in the growth, culminating in the comprehensive programs established under the Eisenhower, Kennedy, and Johnson administrations. The landmarks in the emergence of the new federal interest in higher education were the GI Bill, the National Defense Education Act of 1958, the Higher Education Facilities Act of 1963, and the Higher Education Act of 1965, together with subsequent amendments.

In the states the support of higher education has focused on the establishment of a comprehensive system of educational institutions to assure the accessibility of educational opportunity. The development of networks of public institutions of higher education has been one of the more extraordinary phenomena of the postwar period. State support of private institutions has also grown remarkably, especially in the last two decades, through scholarships and grants in aid to state residents to assist them in attending the colleges of their choice. The size of such scholarship programs varies widely from state to state, but everywhere the student recruitment strategies of private colleges and universities have become heavily dependent on state supported student aid. It is hard now to imagine any college, even the most sectarian, continuing without the forms of federal and state assistance which have come to be accepted as a way of life in the economics of higher education.

The recent expansion of federal programs in higher education can be traced in the remarkable increase of the U. S. Office of Education budget and the emergence of the Department of Education in the executive hierarchy. But the education related expenditures of other federal agencies, like the National Science Foundation, the Atomic Energy Commission, the National Institute of Health, the National Endowment for the Humanities, and the Departments of Defense and of State, more than match those listed under the Department of Education. The proportions of present federal programs and the theoretical justification which has been developed for them through legislative and judicial processes go far beyond even the most radical proposals of the prewar era.

THE FEDERAL INTEREST IN HIGHER EDUCATION

Private institutions have always benefitted from the federal interest in higher education. In most of its programs affecting higher education the federal government has made a special effort to treat public and private institutions in a more or less even-handed way. Surplus government property has been distributed to private colleges; housing loans on favorable terms have been made available to private institutions; research grants have been made without regard to the nature of institutional control. And in the more comprehensive student aid programs of the past three decades, the federal system has taken special pains to include provision for private and even church-related colleges and universities, along with those controlled by state and local governments. Even the most sectarian of colleges have generally participated in whatever federal programs they could qualify for.

The federal interest in higher education has several bases. For one thing, the government is interested as consumer and purchaser of the educational and research services of the colleges and universities. The government is naturally concerned to protect and enhance the strength of these institutions in so far as it depends upon them as a consumer. The supportive programs by which the federal agencies express this kind of concern tend to be selective and mission-oriented, and they have tended to be concentrated in the natural sciences, and to a lesser extent in the social sciences, where the consumer-demands of the government have been the greatest.

But the federal interest also grows out of the importance of trained manpower to national defense and welfare. During the 1950s the importance of education for national defense was emphasized; in the 1960s the government began to act on the premise that a generally educated public is necessary to the national welfare. "Knowledge," as Clark Kerr has said, "is now central to society. It is wanted, even demanded, by more people and more institutions than ever before. The university as producer, wholesaler, and retailer of knowledge, cannot escape service. Knowledge, today, is for everybody's sake."[1] Education, whether conducted under public or private auspices, is a public act and hence a proper concern of government. Knowledge has come to be regarded as a national resource, and the federal government has undertaken to take steps to conserve it.

Furthermore, the federal government has a proper interest in the standards under which educational institutions operate. Accreditation of educational institutions is a private function, of course, but government at all levels has an interest in the quality of the educational services being offered to the American people. Beyond accreditation, the government must take steps to assure the educational consumer of the quality of the product. Government cannot ignore the question of the quality of the schools, whether public or private, secular or parochial. Nor can it forget the fact that the schools are an important means of education in the ideals of American democracy. Nondiscrimination in

[1]Clark Kerr, *The Uses of the University* (New York: Harper Torchbooks, 1966), p. 114.

the schools, for example, is a national necessity not merely as a right guaranteed under the constitution, but also as a means of nationwide education in one of the cardinal principles of democracy.

Federal spending is justified, presumably, in terms of the national interest. It is now an established premise of all discussion, both inside and outside the government, that there is a pressing national interest in the entire system of education. Kerr says that

> So many of the hopes and fears of the American people are now related to our educational system and particularly to our universities—the hope for longer life, for getting into outer space, for a higher standard of living; our fears of Russian or Chinese supremacy, of the bomb and annihilation, of individual loss of purpose in the changing world. For all these reasons and others, *the university has become a prime instrument of national purpose*. This is new. This is the essence of the transformation now engulfing our universities.[2]

The early 1960s witnessed a quite unexpected blossoming of federal programs and a flurry of Congressional and Presidential activity. The NDEA programs were individual oriented, and their support of fields was selective. In 1958 Congress had no concept of comprehensive and flexible aid to educational institutions as such. And the focus of attention was on the most pressing needs of national defense. By 1963, however, a broader concept of support was emerging. It was becoming plain that Congress could not aid individuals to obtain an education without guaranteeing that there would be sound educational institutions to serve them. The aid provided under The Higher Education Facilities Act of 1963 was still selective, and the foundation of the program was still the recognized necessity of providing educational opportunity to individuals. But the point of reference of the Congressional concern was not merely the national security but also the national welfare, and assistance was offered not only to individuals but also to institutions. Furthermore the needs with which Congress sought to cope were not only the immediate ones presented by the "present educational emergency" but also those which would be presented by "future generations of American youth." Here was a new point of departure, which led eventually to the educational legislation of 1965.

In 1965 Congress was caught up in the momentum created by President Johnson, who had urged the law-makers in his education

---

[2]Ibid., p. 87; italics added.

message to "push ahead with the No. 1 business of the American people—the education of our youth." President Johnson proposed that "we declare a national goal of full educational opportunity," and Congress's willingness caught most educators by surprise. Congress responded by creating a series of comprehensive, flexible, and across-the-board supports, the simple and direct aim of which was to strengthen the educational resources of the nation. For example, in Title III of the Higher Education Act of 1965, a title which a number of church-related colleges have exploited as "developing institutions" under the definition of the act, Congress declared:

> The purpose of this title is to assist in raising the academic quality of colleges which have the desire and potential to make a substantial contribution to the higher education resources of our Nation but which for financial and other reasons are struggling for survival or are isolated from the main currents of academic life.

Title III was adopted in response to Mr. Johnson's appeal in his education message for aid to the smaller, weaker, and more isolated colleges. The legislation was particularly targeted for colleges serving minority students and colleges in Appalachia. Congress agreed to the strategy of seeking a wider distribution of educational resources through strengthening these "developing institutions," and it passed the administration's proposal with scarcely any debate.

We are now fully established in a period when the federal government has resolved to provide direct support to institutions of higher education, including the small and struggling ones, on the ground that the national welfare requires it. It is in the light of the public commitment to subsidize institutions of higher education out of tax funds that colleges and universities, both public and private, must now lay their fiscal plans for the coming decades.

In the last twenty years both federal and state governments have heavily emphasized student aid programs as a means of channeling public revenues to colleges and universities. As much as eighty-five percent of the higher education budget of the U. S. Department of Education is now directed to student aid, and the direct support of facilities construction has become a much lower priority. In both federal and state legislation the student aid programs have been specifically designed to encourage enrollment in private as well as public institutions. Indeed, many advocates of these forms of public support have emphasized the preferability of directing funds to students rather than to institutions, since such aid is less likely to provoke questions of constitutionality and the public interest. The legislative and judicial processes of the last two decades, however, have established ample precedent for direct aid to institutions as well as for the student aid programs on which colleges and universities have now become so dependent.

SECTARIANISM AND TAX SUPPORT

The federal interest in higher education unavoidably affects private as well as public enterprise. The recent legislation has been carefully couched in a manner which includes the private colleges in the programs of support. Indeed, the current trends in the financing of higher education through student aid have reduced the significance of a classification of institutions by type of control. The provision of public funds for private institutions and the increasing dependence of public institutions on private contributions have tended to make the difference between the private and the public sectors one of degree rather than of kind. The rapprochement of these traditionally distinct sectors of American higher education is a sign of the times.

Not that the drift of policy has not been hotly contested. It can be expected, furthermore, that the debate over the issue of federal aid to education will continue for some time to come. It is significant, however, that President Johnson's education message, which is a kind of manifesto of the new social policy, blandly ignored all the theoretical problems and counter-arguments and proceeded in the name of welfare to inform the American people what had to be done. The private colleges, no less than the public ones, needed help, he said. The speech was not as astonishing as the response which it received. With scarcely a gesture to the philosophical debate, the Congress proceeded to do what it agreed had to be done. During the House debate on the Higher Education Facilities Act in 1963 an amendment was submitted which would have limited the appropriations to public institutions, but it was defeated two to one. The issue seems to have been a dead one, as far as Congress is concerned, ever since.

The language of the recent educational legislation provides for certain limitations against the use of tax money for sectarian religious purposes. The Higher Education Facilities Act, for example, specifically provides that federal funds may not be used to assist in the construction of

> any facility used or to be used for sectarian instruction or as a place for religious worship or any facility which (although not a facility described in the preceding clause) is used or to be used primarily in connection with any part of the program of a school or department of divinity. . . . For purposes of this subparagraph, the term "school or department of divinity" means an institution, or a department or branch of an institution, whose program is specifically for the education of students to prepare them to become ministers of religion or to enter upon some other religious vocation or to prepare them to teach theological subjects.

Almost identical language appears in the Higher Education Act of 1965. The general intention of these sentences is discernible, perhaps, but the language leaves unresolved a number of questions which arise in the minds of those who are acquainted with the operations of the sectarian colleges. The definitions are not altogether precise. What is "sectarian instruction" and what is a "theological subject"? When does the classroom of a sectarian college cease to be merely a classroom and become a "place for religious worship"? There remains also the question whether it is really possible to support a part of an institution without supporting another part or the institution as a whole. How can a department of divinity be isolated from the rest of the institution in a sectarian college? Federal money used to support a college's program in its nonsectarian aspects releases some of the college's other funds for unrestricted use in connection with its sectarian programs. There remains a substantial element of doubt in many minds, therefore, as to whether or not a sectarian institution is interdicted by the establishment clause of the federal constitution from participating in the new program of public aid to education.

President Kennedy campaigned on the position that it was unconstitutional to aid a parochial school through tax funds, although it was not unconstitutional to aid a student enrolled at a parochial school. No doubt, the principle was a matter of conscience with him, but it was also politically expedient, especially in the light of much Protestant apprehension over the prospect of a Catholic president. Mr. Kennedy also had the apparent backing of the Supreme Court opinion in the Everson case. The Kennedy recommendations to Congress were made against the background of this assumption—aid to sectarian institutions was unconstitutional; aid to individuals attending sectarian institutions was not.

But then the national interest intervened. "The national interest," Mr. Kennedy said in 1961, "requires an educational system on the college level sufficiency financed and equipped to provide every student with adequate physical facilities to meet his instructional, research, and residential needs." He urged Congress, therefore, (without much success during his tragically abbreviated term of office) to pass extensive legislation in support of higher education, both public and private, both secular and parochial—loans and grants for the construction of academic facilities; scholarships, supplemented by cost-of-education allowances to the colleges which scholarship recipients chose to attend; an expanded program of loans for college housing.

The proposals made by the Kennedy administration for aid to *higher* education went far beyond its proposals for *elementary* and *secondary* education. As some observers put it, the Kennedy position on federal aid to educational institutions was, "Higher education, yes; elementary and secondary education, no."

This point of view was elaborated at length and with considerable brilliance in the famous HEW *Memorandum on the Impact of the First Amendment to the Constitution Upon Federal Aid to Education*, prepared by Alanson W. Willcox, General Counsel for the Department of Health, Education, and Welfare, and sent to Congress in March 1961. The HEW view, based on such Supreme Court opinions as *Everson* and *McCollum*, was that the use of public funds to support religious institutions or to finance religious groups was unconstitutional, but that "laws designed to further the education and welfare of youth may not be unconstitutional if they afford only incidental benefits to church schools." The line between "direct support" and "incidental benefits" was admittedly vague, and the HEW memorandum expressed the opinion that it could be drawn only through the exercise of "judgment" in particular cases. Nevertheless, the distinction was fundamental to the administration's position, opposing legislation which would have made general educational grants to private, nonprofit (parochial) elementary and secondary schools, and even opposing general educational loans for the construction of facilities at such schools, but endorsing certain kinds of special-purpose grants.

When it came to higher education, however, HEW reached a

startlingly different conclusion. The constitutional principles are identical, said the memorandum, whether the institution in question is at the elementary/secondary level or at the higher level, but the "factual circumstances" in which the constitutional principles are to be applied are "dramatically different" in the two cases. This difference is a matter not of principle but of historical accident. For example, it is a matter of historical accident, the memorandum argued, that elementary education, and to a growing extent secondary education, are compulsory in the United States, whereas higher education is voluntary; that eighty-five percent of American school children attend public schools, whereas forty-one percent of American college students attend nonpublic institutions (of course, that proportion was substantially lower in 1980); that when the national interest requires Congress to encourage the expansion of college and university facilities, it has no alternative but to build upon what already exists, namely a complex of private and public institutions. Because of such differences in the "factual circumstances" HEW recommended programs of assistance for private colleges and universities which it at the same time opposed for parochial elementary and secondary schools; and it did not even boggle at the proposal that tax funds should be used to construct and expand academic facilities at church-related colleges. Mr. Willcox expressed the belief that there was nothing inconsistent in this policy, explaining that "if the public purpose is to be achieved at all, it can only be achieved by a general expansion of private as well as public colleges, of sectarian as well as secular ones."

Despite the constitutional complexities, the requirements of policy for higher education during the sixties seemed clear to the Kennedy administration. The HEW *Memorandum* sought to rationalize a policy which seemed inescapable in the light of the national interest. What the Kennedy administration attempted with hesitancy and scholarly judiciousness, the Johnson administration executed with dispatch and political adeptness. Under President Johnson Washington thrust aside the theoretical and constitutional questions and moved with abandon toward a national policy on higher education. Mr. Johnson said, upon signing the Higher Education Act of 1965:

> Too many people, for too many years, argued that education and health and human welfare were not the government's concern. And while they spoke, our schools fell behind, our sick people went unattended, and our poor fell deeper into despair. But now, at last, in the

> year of our Lord 1965, we have quit talking and started acting: the roots of change and reform are spreading, not just throughout Washington but throughout every community in every state of this great Nation.

Not only is the style of these remarks typical for Mr. Johnson, but the political philosophy expressed in them is also paradigmatic for our times.

For two decades, Washington has seemed determined to find ways to contribute to the well-being and strength of colleges and universities, whether small or large, church related or state supported, sectarian or secular. In Washington it is no longer a constitutional issue; it is a question of policy, and the national interest seems clear and paramount.

Problems of a philosophical nature remain. There are definitions in the recent legislation which are not sufficiently precise to remove the doubts of the sectarian colleges. Nor is it easy to obtain unambiguous answers from the federal agencies to specific questions about eligibility. An agency representative is understandably reluctant to offer a clarification or a definition which Congress has been unable or unwilling to give. But there seems little doubt that Washington will resolve such questions (if it is forced to) on the side of facilitating its established policy, which is to help every college that it can. The federal government can be expected to continue to lean over backwards to include the sectarian colleges in its benevolence.

The judicial branch moves more ponderously and, perhaps, less predictably in this case where new precedents are required. It would be a mistake, however, to think of the constitutional issue in static terms. The decisions of the courts cannot ignore the present state of the union, the drift of public opinion, and the requirements of the national defense and welfare. The Supreme Court can be expected to seek constitutional definitions which will serve the public interest.

The problem of judicial decision is complicated by the duality of the First Amendment itself, which not only prohibits the establishment of religion but also guarantees the free exercise thereof. A court could choose to emphasize one or the other aspect of the constitutional provision, as it felt constrained by its own estimate of the national interest. The point is, however, that the momentum of the recent movement towards the tax support of private colleges has generally resulted, whenever the issue has been brought before the Supreme

Court, in definitions which (in the language of *Everson*) would permit church colleges to "receive the benefits of public welfare legislation."

In *Tilton v. Richardson* in 1971 the Supreme Court explicitly confirmed the dualistic position articulated in the HEW *Memorandum*. In applying the limits of the establishment clause in federal and state programs affecting higher education, the Court accepted the principle that colleges are fundamentally different from elementary and secondary schools. The *Tilton* case challenged the operations of the Higher Education Facilities Act which, according to the plaintiff, involved direct federal support of religious institutions, which is forbidden by the First Amendment. By a narrow majority of five to four the Supreme Court decided in favor of the program of federal support on the grounds that, as operated through the particular private and church-related colleges in question, these programs did not involve a state establishment of religion.

College education, said the Court, is less religious in its impact on students than parochial education at the elementary and secondary levels. College students are less subject to indoctrination. College programs are less concerned with the propagation of faith. The professionalism, academic freedom, and voluntarism of programs of higher learning assure that the primary effects of public grants even for church-related colleges, operating within the limits of the legislation in question, would not be the establishment of religious belief or practice. The Court found that the primary purposes and impact of the federally subsidized facilities was secular rather than religious, and that a one-time program of aid carried no significant risk of a federal entanglement in religious affairs.

The Court's decision was significantly based on a finding of fact. The decision did not go so far as to say that no college could have a religious orientation so pronounced and controlling that federal aid for facilities should be denied it on grounds of the First Amendment. It found, however, that the Connecticut colleges in question in this case, even though church-related, did not follow so sectarian a pattern that the primary effect of federal aid would be religious. Rather, the court said, the secular dimension of their purpose and mission was so clear as to eliminate any question of an establishment of religion.

The foundations of this decision have been confirmed by subsequent actions of the Court. In *Hurst v. McNair* in 1973 the Court confirmed the constitutional authority of the State of Maryland to issue bonds to assist church-related colleges to construct buildings used for secular purposes on their campuses. A similar program in Minnesota was more recently confirmed as constitutional by the state supreme court. In *Roemer v. Board of Public Works* in 1976 the Supreme Court upheld a comprehensive program of annual grants by the State of Maryland which could be used by church-related colleges for the support of their secular educational programs.

The presuppositions underlying this sequence of judicial decisions are clear and consistent and there is no longer any serious doubt about the direction of public support of private higher education. The constitutional foundations of both institutional and student support programs have been confirmed. The only issue that remains concerns the priority which should be assigned to public support of higher education in the rough and tumble of state and federal politics and the growing crisis in public finance. A national policy for higher education has emerged, albeit a crude and fragmentary one. It is a policy which assures the authority of governmental agencies to dedicate tax funds for the support of church-related colleges. The sectarian colleges must now find a basis for accommodating this new social policy.

A GUIDE FOR THE SECTARIAN CONSCIENCE

Questions about the appropriateness of public support of sectarian colleges continue to disturb the educational leaders of the churches. Many of these questions are inspired by political views concerning the most effective form of government in the American democracy. Of course, conflicting opinions regarding the federal system are long standing in this country and are not necessarily based on a theological persuasion. The conscience which has led the leaders of some Christian colleges to reject public assistance has often had a political as well as a theological base.

More widespread has been the recent concern in higher education concerning the growth of government regulation. This concern, too, is far broader than sectarianism. The higher education community as a whole has been struggling recently to find mechanisms which would permit proper governmental monitoring of educational programs touching the public interest while assuring the autonomy which is essential for quality education. Warnings about the growing threat of federal regulation have beome commonplace in higher education conferences of late, and some colleges and universities have become particularly apprehensive about accepting certain forms of public assistance on grounds that doing so might compromise the integrity of their educational missions.

Some of the sectarian colleges, especially those of a Baptistic persuasion, have at times decided to abstain in conscience from participating in the new federal programs. The basis on which this decision has been justified varies considerably from case to case, but two kinds of apprehension seem to predominate. On the one hand, these colleges have apprehensions about the constitutional question. They think that accepting federal aid for their institutions would compromise their stand on the separation of church and state. On the other hand, these colleges—or their supporting churches and constituencies—are apprehensive about the risk of an increase of federal control and a decrease of ecclesiastical control over educational policy. Frequently the two kinds of apprehension are intermingled with politically derived fears of the centralization of government and dislike of the federal bureaucracy.

In some cases the evangelical rejection of federal aid under the educational legislation of 1963 and 1965 is based, ostensibly at least, on the principle of church-state separation. In fact, however, the evangelical churches do not apply the separationist principle with equal rigor throughout the entire range of church-state relationships. The appeal to principle is thereby deprived of much of its force. An absolutist position against federal support of sectarian institutions is extremely difficult to justify from the theoretical standpoint; nor are the evangelical groups which currently prohibit their colleges from accepting federal aid able, practically speaking, to follow the logic of an absolutist position in all their dealings with government.

In the present state of the law it is simply impossible to make any absolutistic pronouncements on the constitutional eligibility of church-related institutions to receive aid from tax sources. The system of interdependence between ecclesiastical institutions and state agencies is a continuum, along which lines of demarcation between legitimate and illegitimate aid have never been drawn with precision. Under these circumstances the only way to achieve total consistency in adopting a position of nonassistance to church-related institutions out of public funds would be to eradicate the whole system of relationships between church and state. But none of the groups which now renounce federal aid to Christian higher education are prepared to go that far—nor is it socially desirable or practically possible for them to do so.

Church programs presently receive financial aid from tax funds in many forms. The tax laws themselves include provisions which benefit the churches in a manner which can easily be interpreted as a kind of subsidy of church programs out of tax funds. The state accords a number of financially significant privileges and monopolies to the churches and their representatives. There are a number of ways in which church-state cooperation in programs of social service results in mutual assistance, adding considerable strength to the ecclesiastical agency or institution. The state gives aid to individuals to enable them to benefit from the educational and welfare services of the churches, and it is undeniable that these aids contribute substantially to the success of the church programs themselves, to the extent that without the subsidy the programs often could not be sustained. Surplus government property is distributed to church institutions, and government agencies purchase services from the churches, thereby enabling them to survive and prosper. Federal and state support of church-related hospitals and other institutions of medical assistance has reached astounding proportions. These forms of federal assistance seem to be fully endorsed by the ecclesiastical conscience and seem to involve no compromise of constitutionality. Of course, one might insist that there is a difference between these forms of assistance and direct subsidy or outright grants for the construction of educational buildings, but a disinterested observer would say that these are differences of degree and not of kind.

An absolutist position on the separation of church and state would, if consistent, lead to the rejection of all forms of aid. But an absolutist position is simply impossible. As Professor Mark DeWolfe Howe of Harvard has said,

> Not only in education but in many other areas, we find aid being given to religion in ways that we tolerate and permit. Some people, including Justice Douglas, would say that all these aids must go. But they are not politically likely to go; and while they continue, it is hard to pretend that there are absolute barriers to any kind of aid.[3]

---

[3]Seymour E. Harris, *Education and Public Policy* (Berkeley, CA: McCutchan Publishing Corporation, 1965), p. 53.

Another consideration which has led some evangelical colleges to reject federal aid is the apprehension that federal aid will bring federal control. But as Sidney Hook has said, the issue of federal control as a substantive issue in the debate about federal aid to education is a red herring.[4] The threat of federal control over the affairs of educational institutions which accept federal aid can easily be exaggerated. Nor is there any evidence that the forms of federal regulation of education that have emerged in the last fifteen years are at all directed against sectarianism as such. Under present conditions federal suspension of the principle of local control of public education, federal violation of the principle of the autonomy of private corporations, and federal interference with the free exercise of religion are both politically and constitutionally impossible. Both Congress and the president, indeed, have taken special pains to reassure the American people that federal support does not entail federal control, with respect to either public or private institutions, and the whole history of federal involvement in education confirms their promises.

Under present conditions federal control of education in the private colleges cannot be regarded as an important threat. Even if closer regulation of educational institutions were enacted by law, there is scarcely any possibility that it could be administered with stringency. On the contrary, there is ample evidence that public officials tend to be reluctant and careless in administering present statutory controls over private schools. The whole history of federal aid to higher education during the last century bears witness that federal support comes with fewer strings attached and with less threat to institutional autonomy than the typical contributions of private philanthropy. A private citizen or a corporation executive may assume that a dollar entitles him to a voice in the formulation and administration of educational policy, but there is no evidence that the federal government systematically acts on that assumption.

It is possible, of course, that all this might change. It is true that the government might some day begin to intervene directly in the affairs of private and sectarian educational institutions and establish closer controls over their policies and curriculums. But if the federal government ever decided to exercise direct control over private and sectarian

---

[4]Cited by Kerr, *The Uses of the University*, p. 57.

colleges, it would not require a system of federal supports to find an excuse to do so. It has that authority without the subsidies. The only question is whether it will ever be exercised. And the answer to that question is simply that the authority will not be exercised except in a national emergency or unless the American democracy gives way to another political form. Such exigencies are possible, of course, but the possibility is not one for which present policy must provide. The evangelical colleges simply have no basis for fearing that accepting a federal grant for a building or a science laboratory will bring any significant increase of the risk of federal control. As one persuasive writer has expressed it,

> Federal coercion is neither a certainty, a probability, nor a trend. It is simply a problem, nay more a challenge. Does anyone suppose that if our democratic state falls prey to tyranny, it will need the fact of tax support of schools to justify an invasion of educational integrity? On the contrary, the best antidote to tyranny is a flourishing panoply of Christian schools, feeding into American life graduates who *know* why they, and all men, are entitled to liberty. And such a panoply will never flourish more than if nourished by adequate funds, in generous measure from federal aid.[5]

There is one respect, however, in which federal control has been exerted over educational policies in recent years, and it is to be expected that this attempt at regulation will continue in the future. It is a control, however, which is not consequent upon the use of tax funds in education, although the existence of the support programs does afford an economic sanction through which the federal will may be enforced. We refer to the recent efforts of the federal government to secure a policy of non-discrimination in the schools, as in other organizations within the American society.

Here, too, there are definitions which are not sufficiently determinate to classify certain operations and policies in the evangelical colleges. The *Code of Federal Regulations* incorporates two documents on civil rights which, although having the same basic intention, employ language in a manner which produces ambiguity. The earlier document is Executive Order No. 11063, issued by President Kennedy on 10

---

[5]Lester DeKoster, "Federal Aid to Christian Education: Yes," *Christianity Today* 8 (28 February 1964): 486. Cf. the contrary view as expressed by V. Raymond Edman, then president of Wheaton College, in the same issue.

November 1962. The other is the Civil Rights Act of 1964.

Mr. Kennedy's order directed

> all departments and agencies in the executive branch of the Federal Government, insofar as their functions relate to the provision, rehabilitation, or operation of housing and related facilities, to take all action necessary and appropriate to prevent discrimination because of *race, color, creed,* or *national origin* (my italics) in the sale, leasing, rental, or other disposition of residential property and related facilities (including land to be developed for residential use), or in the use or occupancy thereof, if such property and related facilities are. . . . ii) provided in whole or in part with the aid of loans, advances, grants, or contributions hereafter agreed to be made by the Federal Government or iii) provided in whole or in part by loans hereafter insured, guaranteed, or otherwise secured by the credit of the Federal Government.

Title IV of the Civil Rights Act of 1964 (P.L. 88-352) followed a similar formula in requiring desegregation in public education. "Desegregation" was defined as "the assignment of students to public schools and within such schools without regard to their race, color, *religion*, or national origin."[6] Public institutions (but not private ones) are required to follow a nondiscriminatory policy in admissions, where "nondiscriminatory" is defined as including nondiscrimination on the basis of religion.

In Title VII, which deals with equal employment opportunity, a nondiscriminatory policy is imposed on all employers, including sectarian colleges. But in that title specific exemptions are provided to allow religious institutions to preserve their distinctive religious character. For example, the act provides in Section 703(e) that,

> Notwithstanding any other provision of this title, (1) it shall not be an unlawful employment practice for an employer to hire and employ employees on the basis . . . of his religion, sex, or national origin in those certain instances where religion, sex, or national origin is a bona fide occupational qualification reasonably necessary to the normal occupation of that particular business or enterprise, and (2) it shall not be an unlawful employment practice for a school, college, university, or other educational institution or institution of learning to hire and

---

[6]Italics added. It is interesting to note that the act defines a "public college" as one which is operated by some unit of government "or operated wholly or predominantly from or through the use of governmental funds or property, or funds or property derived from a governmental source." Under this definition a private college could become a public college, at least for purposes of this act, without any basic organizational or constitutional change, if it reached the point where it was operated with funds or property drawn *predominantly* from governmental sources.

> employ employees of a particular religion if such school, college, university, or other educational institution or institution of learning is, in whole or in substantial part, owned, supported, controlled, or managed by a particular religion or by a religious corporation, association, or society, or if the curriculum of such college, university, or other educational institution or institution of learning is directed toward the propagation of a particular religion.

Such exemptions are clearly designed to protect sectarian institutions in their right to employ persons on the basis of religious faith. It is perhaps not entirely clear whether, in certain positions of a religiously nonsensitive sort, a college might not be accused of an unlawful employment practice if it discriminated on the basis of religion, but the exemptions provided under Section 703(e) for sectarian institutions would probably permit a religious test even for maintenance personnel if that were essential for the character of the campus community. Sectarian organizations are required to follow an employment policy which is nondiscriminatory with respect to race, but they may follow a policy which is discriminatory with respect to creed.

A similar exemption has been incorporated into the omnibus provision under Title VI of the Act, which provides that "no person in the United States shall, on the ground of *race, color*, or *national origin* be excluded from participation in, be denied the benefits of, or be subject to discrimination under any program or activity receiving Federal assistance." (Italics added). Any reference to religion or creed has been deliberately omitted from this formula. Its effect is to render ineligible for federal assistance any college or university which discriminates in the admission of students on the basis of race, color, or national origin, although it does not make ineligible an institution which discriminates on the basis of religion. Since the passage of the Civil Rights Act the Office of Education, like all other federal agencies, has required an affidavit indicating compliance with this provision on the part of any institution applying for aid.

Mr. Kennedy's earlier executive order, with its particular variant on the nondiscriminatory formula, was directed especially at the Housing and Home Finance Agency, whose duties include administration of the college housing loan program. The Federal Housing Administration immediately implemented the order in all its regulations and has been enforcing a policy of nondiscrimination on the basis of *race or creed* ever since. The policy covers college dormitories and dining facilities financed under HHFA. The Department of Housing and

Urban Development has added a series of regulations to implement the Civil Rights Act, but the regulations issued under the earlier Executive Order have never been rescinded. In fact, after adding its summary of new procedures to implement the Civil Rights Act, HUD said that nothing in the new regulations should be deemed to supersede "Executive Order 11063 and regulations issued thereunder, insofar as such Order, regulations, or instructions prohibit discrimination on the ground of race, color, or national origin in any program or activity or situation to which this part is inapplicable *or prohibit discrimination on any other ground*" (italics added). HUD, in short, stands by its earlier regulations prohibiting it from supporting any housing program the use of which would involve any discrimination on the basis of religion.

Depending upon how stringently these regulations are enforced, many church-related colleges are thus ineligible for college housing loans. Many of these colleges admit only students who profess to be Christians, and many others give preferential treatment to applicants from their supporting churches and constituencies. HHFA has not formulated a determinate policy to establish the lengths to which it would go in enforcing its non-discriminatory regulations, but it would probably attempt to differentiate between the case of a sectarian college which required a particular religious profession for admission and the case of a nominally church-related college which merely showed preference for members of its supporting church. Evidently at least some of the sectarian colleges would be judged ineligible to participate in the college housing program on the basis of these regulations.

The case of civil rights, therefore, affords an instance where an institution might be prohibited from accepting federal aid without submitting to federal regulation. The Civil Rights Act, however, reflects a national policy which would be enforced in education even without the economic sanctions which are available as a result of the federal support programs. It is especially significant, furthermore, that in its regulations on civil rights the federal government has taken special pains to protect the autonomy and freedom of sectarian institutions, even in the face of strong pressures against sectarianism in many segments of the society. Selective admission and employment policies are the recognized right of the Christian colleges, and there is no sign of any modification of the federal government's historic will to protect that right.

As with the other federal programs affecting Christian higher education, the federal regulations on nondiscrimination are in need of a more precise formulation. It is not yet sufficiently clear which institutional policies in the sectarian colleges are discriminatory under the law and the constitution and which are not. But the way for the evangelical colleges to obtain the needed clarification is not to withdraw from the scene on the assumption that they have nothing to do with the government, nor will it help for them to debate the matter among themselves. The way to obtain clarification is by pressing the matter in Washington. It is entirely fitting that the federal government should have the burden of deciding whether a sectarian college, following a clearly understood set of educational policies, is eligible for benefits under the federal programs or not. Once Washington has clarified the national policy vis-a-vis the sectarian colleges, the issue should be resolved.

The evangelical conscience, which has led some of the sectarian colleges to renounce federal aid a priori, presumes to be superior to the conscience of the nation's leaders in judging the constitutionality of recent legislation. Aside from a certain arrogance which is exhibited in that presumption, it is based on a gross misunderstanding of the nature of the issue. In some matters the evangelical conscience is doubtless superior; but in this case what makes a person's judgment sound is his competence in the law, and that competence has nothing to do with evangelical theology. The question whether or not the sectarian colleges are constitutionally eligible for federal benefits should be decided not by these colleges or their constituencies through unilateral action, but by the legislators, by the administrative agencies of the executive branch, and by the courts on the basis of complete information concerning the policies and purposes of the sectarian colleges.

The conscientious thing for a college to do in the matter of federal aid is not to make general pronouncements about what is legal or constitutional or American, but to take every precaution to guarantee that at every stage where it deals with the government, the agency in question clearly understands what the college's program, purposes, and policies are and enters into an agreement with the college only in full knowledge of its character and goals. To take the other course—to refuse to take advantage of aid for which the college is declared, in light of a clear understanding of its character, to be eligible—would place the college in the untenable position of having to say that the government's determination of eligibility is either incompetent or unreliable.

But perhaps the real basis of the evangelical prohibition against federal aid is not conscience, after all, but expedience. Perhaps what motivates the evangelical constituencies which prohibit their colleges from accepting federal aid is not the principle of church-state separation but an estimate of the consequences which are likely to result from acceptance of federal aid. Perhaps it is thought that accepting federal aid will result in a loss of ideological independence in the life of learning or a reduction of denominational or individual contributions for educational ministries. Such arguments, indeed, may have a certain force. But if it is, after all, a utilitarian consideration which leads an evangelical group to renounce federal support, then the waters should not be muddied by the pretense that it is a matter of conscience or a question of constitutionality.

There is a special point, these days, to the warning that American education may be losing its autonomy in consequence of the conditions under which it is supported. Education requires freedom and social criticism requires independence, and both are hard to come by. The principle has even greater force in the context of Christian thought. But we live in a time when educational institutions are being strongly tempted to compromise their independence for the sake of a position of security within the society. Institutions of higher education have allowed themselves to become "prime instruments of national policy," in Kerr's pregnant phrase, and it is appropriate to ask whether they have not gained this position of national influence at the price of losing their integrity as educational institutions.

Among the Christian colleges, too, there is ground for fear that they may be drifting into patterns of support which can only eventuate in a change in their fundamental character. Certainly there is no dearth of educators and informed observers who point out the danger that large-scale federal support of the private colleges may set in motion economic forces which will irresistibly change the nature of these colleges. Furthermore, it is both theological and organizational good sense to teach that the basis of the effectiveness of the church's ministries in education is ultimately the stewardship of its own people. The churches are ill-advised to accept civic support for their programs if doing so will weaken that stewardship.

Such points are well taken, and vigilance in these matters has never been more necessary. But there is room for debate as to what is implied for institutional policy. The threats to the autonomy of a Christian college are legion; it may well be that a college which has sought to maintain its purity by rejecting aid from the government will only prove to be the house all swept and garnished which is taken over by a new set of adversaries of freedom.

It is by no means certain that a college will increase its autonomy as an educational institution by rejecting federal aid and relying only on ecclesiastical sources of support. Federal aid to education is a fact of life, but so are the vocationalization of learning and the mercantilization of knowledge which are destroying the critical powers of our educational centers. A Christian college which is concerned about the protection of its own independence and autonomy as an educational institution might well consider what price it is willing to pay to obtain a few dollars from its supporting church or constituency. Vigilance is no less necessary here. The economic intimidation of educators by Christian groups and individuals—threats to withdraw support unless some faculty member is dismissed, some instructional program installed, or some pattern of student social life prohibited—is also a threat to the autonomy of a college. As a matter of fact, there is no more risk of loss of honor in accepting the aid of a governmental agency than in accepting the benevolence of a quasi-public foundation.

Vigilance is certainly required, but what protects the honor and freedom of an educational institution is its conscientiousness, that is, its ability to justify its deeds by reference to principles. And conscientiousness is preserved if a college insists that it will receive money from no source whatever, public or private, unless that source knows, understands, and respects the purposes, ideals, and policies by which the college operates. Without such an understanding money obtained from any source carries with it the risk that the institution's ability to take a stand on principle will be weakened. Few colleges, however, have the nerve to follow such a rule in fund raising. J. Kenneth Little's warning, issued just before the boom in federal support, is still in order, only it should be applied more broadly to all efforts in institutional fund raising:

> Without discounting the crucial problem of finding the financial means to maintain strong colleges and universities or the helpful supplemental role the Federal Government is playing, I would urge

> educators and the public alike to *keep a steady eye upon the central purposes and objectives of their colleges and universities.* Universities and colleges are changing in important ways under the impact of forces, governmental and other, which are strong and pervasive.[7]

Conscientiousness requires that a sectarian college always make its character fully known when it asks for money. If a federal agency makes a grant to a college in full knowledge of its sectarian purposes and character, the college incurs no obligation whatever, either legal or moral, which it would not have freely accepted under a prior definition of its mission and function. Therein lies the path to integrity in institutional finance. The challenge to actually carry out the college's mission in the world remains to be met, of course, but the support of the federal government may well be one of the most important means of reaching that end.

Logan Wilson is entirely correct: "Politics and education are becoming inseparable, and it is up to us to make the most of this fact of modern life."[8] It has been established that there is a national interest in the welfare of the colleges, both public and private, both secular and sectarian. A national policy on higher education has emerged, at least in outline form, and there is no point in attempting by unilateral action or continuing argument to prevent that policy from being followed. There are a time and place for national policy to be debated, of course, and in a democracy any public policy may be called up for review. But there is also a time for accommodation to the conditions created by a policy which has been established by at least a provisional national consensus.

A Christian college can hardly expect foundations and corporations to make up what it has rejected in federal funds on the basis of a confused and inconsistent conscience. Nor will a college which has been judged ineligible for aid under a tax-supported program be likely to succeed in an application for aid from one of the major purveyors of private philanthropy. Private philanthropy tends to think of its contributions as supplemental to those which are available through public funds, just as government thinks of its support as supplemental to that

---

[7]J. Kenneth Little, "Higher Education and the Federal Government," *Higher Education* (October 1963): 23; italics added.

[8]Logan Wilson, "The Federal Government and Higher Education," in Harris, *Education and Public Policy*, p. 65.

provided by the private sector. And private philanthropy grants major financial assistance, for the most part, on very much the same ideological basis as do tax-supported agencies. The more conservative foundations and corporations, which show a certain eagerness to resist the intrusion of the federal government into new dimensions of American life, might provide a needed alternative for some colleges, but in accepting large contributions from such sources an institution may also have to accept a large measure of control by a conservative ideology.

If it is recognized, however, as an important instrument of social service, a Christian college has a clear basis of principle for approaching either public or quasi-public sources of financial support. The public can be expected to support an institution if that institution provides a service which meets a recognized social need and makes an important contribution to the general welfare. The Christian colleges have been slow to project an image of public service, however. They have given insufficient publicity to the broad social utility of their existing educational programs, and they have given insufficient attention to ways in which their service to the general public might be further enhanced, within the limits of their sectarian purposes and character. Many are isolated from the communities in which they are located. As a result the public tends to think of the Christian colleges as agents of denominational purposes, primarily engaged in the preparation of ministers, rather than as agents of public service, serving very broad public functions at the same time that they promote the cause of religious education. Isolation from the general public has caused many of the evangelical colleges to have an image which is several decades out of date. A stronger emphasis on public service would provide the sectarian institution with a firm basis on which to approach the public for aid.

It is a mistake to assume that a college can accept the function of public service only at the price of compromising its function as an arm of the church. The two emphases are by no means incompatible. Indeed, whether sectarian or not, any college worthy of its name must be engaged in an endeavor to meet public needs, both in its surrounding community and region and in the nation at large. The church's decision to conduct a college implicates it in social service, in both instruction and research, in both on-campus and off-campus programs, for both its immediate constituency and the general public. A college, like a hospital, performs a public function, and either institution, properly conducted, will be recognized by the public as being of value and as being worthy of support, even if it has a clear sectarian character. Public service and sectarian purposes can be combined with integrity, and any college which has effected the combination should be proud to expose itself to the public view. The public can then decide whether it is a combination which merits its support. The decision is likely to be that an institution engaged in important social service is entitled to the support of the society, even if that service has a sectarian motivation.

The Christian colleges are likely to find in federal support an important means—in most cases an indispensable means—for achieving excellence and independence. The reluctance of the evangelical colleges to tap this source is both dangerous and incomprehensible. Misplaced fears and misguided principles may be causing the churches to place in jeopardy what is left of their witness in Christian higher education. The competitive challenge today will not permit a mistake here.

Chapter 10

IDEOLOGY IN AN AGE OF PLURALISM

In its earliest development Western philosophy was stimulated by the debate concerning the one and the many. The early Greek philosophers were concerned with a series of questions about the world—questions like, What is there really? Why is there anything anyway? Why do things appear as they do? What explains the various changes that things undergo? There were pluralistic answers to such questions as well as monistic answers.

Coordinate with the consideration of such metaphysical issues in ancient philosophy was the search for a methodology which would reduce the range of differences in matters of belief or of value. Although the scope and complexity of Greek society do not compare with the conditions we confront in the twentieth century, thoughtful people in that day confronted the same kinds of conflicts about values, purposes, and ideals as we confront today. There were people then, too, who held that the rules or laws by which human behavior is governed had no more than a conventional basis and could not be justified on rational grounds. The same was said of religious beliefs. And there were educators who were prepared to teach any person (that is, anyone who was able and willing to pay) the skills of persuasion and of verbal self-defense, so that he might be able to protect and achieve his own interest in a society of persons often working at cross-purposes with one another.

The classical Greek philosophy of Socrates, Plato, and Aristotle was primarily addressed to the problem of whether or not it was possible to eliminate, or at least to reduce, differences in values and opinion among people by the application of a rational method. The questions which concerned these philosophers were: Is knowledge possible in the areas of morality and of religion? Or are we reduced to acknowledging that all opinions which individuals may happen to hold in these areas of human experience are equally valid? And how is knowledge possible anyway? These are the questions which inspired that extraordinary philosophical construction of the fourth and fifth centuries before Christ, to which much of the rest of the history of philosophy has been a succession of footnotes.

The philosophical attempt to bring unity out of difference has had an extraordinary history. And the appropriation of this history is an important key to the mission of the Christian college in the present age. Can we hope for a coherent system of belief, in which the antinomies of scholarship will be reconciled? Or must we accept the inevitability of a condition of irreducible difference in beliefs and values? Is there any way to combine ideological assurance with enlightened thought?

The theological crisis of the Christian college centers in the pluralization of institutional structures and belief systems in the modern world. Two developments are involved in the modern growth of pluralism. One is the rapid multiplication of the belief systems of which an individual may be aware and from which he might choose. The other is the loss of the coherence and correspondingly of the credibility of any specific belief system. The result of these developments is a widening of choice for individual belief and the enlargement of subjective factors in the determination of belief. Modernity, says Peter Berger, is an all but inconceivable expansion of the area of human life open to choices.[1]

What has been happening, then, as pluralism has expanded its scope in the modern world is that ideological viewpoints have been multiplying, while confidence in the reasonableness of any particular ideology has been weakening. The rate of change has been particularly rapid in the past two decades. Until recently there was an alliance—

---

[1]Peter Berger, *The Heretical Imperative: Contemporary Possibilities of Religious Affirmation* (New York: Anchor/Doubleday, 1979), p. 3.

often an uneasy alliance—between reason and moral-religious faith; but this alliance has been breaking down as the present generation has come to maturity. It is now common for young people to assume "that there is no single final truth in questions of morality, religion, art, politics, and the like."[2] Pluralism has thus come to mean relativism or subjectivism in matters of moral or religious belief. Most people assume that the method of rational inquiry can be expected to lead to the discovery of truth in mathematics and science; but in matters of morality and religion, in the humanities, and in the social sciences it is being assumed more and more that opinions are a matter of free choice and private judgment. In these areas it is often said that every individual chooses what is "true" for him; and even if by his own persuasiveness he is able to convince others that they should respect or adopt his viewpoint, it is thought that objective, rational conclusions are not to be expected in these areas. The effect is to turn morality and religion into matters of subjective preference and to deprive them of rational credibility or intellectual seriousness.

THE INSTABILITY OF PLURALISM

Most Americans like pluralism. For one thing it makes it unnecessary to struggle for satisfactory answers to the very difficult and complex issues which arise in the deepest areas of our experience. Moreover, it fosters that spirit of toleration which is so indispensable in the American democracy.

Yet pluralism is an unstable condition in the presence of reason. Reason cannot be satisfied with pluralism in belief. Reason assumes the possibility of reconciling conflicts among opinions and of developing a cogent interpretation which will be acceptable to all rational minds. The indefatigable work of reason is to seek to overcome pluralism. So the progress of thought is always in the direction of a rejection of pluralism; it is a movement out of pluralism and into ideology.

An ideology is a coherent system of beliefs, values, or explanatory theories by reference to which individual choices, interpretations, or evaluations may be judged (rationalized). An ideology is the product of reason's search for unity in experience.

The conflict among ideologies is a patently obvious fact of the

---

[2]Don Cupitt, *The Leap of Reason* (Philadelphia: Westminster, 1976), p. 3

modern world. We live in a society in which the search for explanatory theories, basic values, and fundamental beliefs fails to bring individuals and groups to identical conclusions. The result is pluralism in the life of mind, a multiplication of ideologies. Our question is, what can reason do when confronted by the conflict of ideologies?

One way of responding is that of rational acceptance of difference. This would be the rational response if it were really the case that there is no other foundation for ideology than personal or private choice. In the face of the arbitrariness of conflicting opinions, reason would say that every individual, group, or nation has the right to its own opinions. When every belief is ultimately arbitrary, we display our reasonableness by refusing to allow one arbitrarily derived ideology (either our own or that of someone else) to be given recognition as favored or preferred.

But the reasonableness of that response to the conflict of ideologies depends on whether or not the only basis for ideology is arbitrary choice. And that is precisely the question at issue. If there is, after all, a rational basis for choosing among conflicting ideologies, reason will not be satisfied with mere toleration of differences. It will pursue the course of reconciliation and will seek to escape the antithesis of conflicting ideologies through the discovery of a more comprehensive synthesis.

The struggle to attain a state of faith is inspired, as Peirce says, by the irritation of doubt. The purpose of inquiry is to resolve doubt and to settle opinion. But an opinion cannot finally be founded on the shifting sands of personal habit, on the limited perspective of one's own group, on the authority of some individual, group, or state, or on private intuition. Only one foundation will be finally satisfactory, and that is the foundation of comprehensive rational investigation of the warrantability of belief.

So reason searches endlessly for a basis of belief which will put an end to pluralism. We have all experienced the strangeness of another person's credo. The task of reason is to eliminate such strangeness and to establish a basis for ideological agreement among human beings.

The doctrine that pluralism is the last word in matters of morality and religion has become the new orthodoxy. It has become heretical to suggest the alternative which assumes that moral decision and religious belief might have a basis in rational thought. The new heresy is the doctrine that reason might be competent to discriminate among beliefs even in matters of morality and religion.

For many people the only basis of firm and unambiguous pronouncements in morality and religion is dogmatism. But in a pluralistic society we try to avoid a reputation for being dogmatic. Indeed, we have come to view dogmatism as one of the worst forms of heresy. The dogmatic affirmation of an ideology is a cardinal sin in the ethics of modernity. Adherence to an ideology is widely thought to be the essence of sectarianism and the major cause of fragmentation in our pluralistic society.

Paul Munz defines a schism as a community built upon a unified ideology.[3] Ideology, he says, breeds factionalism. In Christendom there have been two types of creeds—those which sought to include within the definition all those who were members of the household of faith, and those which sought to exclude all but the adherents of one's own sect. The general verdict on Protestantism has been that its history illustrates the tendency for ideology to create schism. And that verdict has led many people in our time to shy away from any appearance of determinacy in theological outlook, lest a new form of arbitrariness should appear to heighten the alienations of an already fractionated church.

So we are presented with our problem: How is ideology possible, particularly in an age when we are intensely conscious of the conflicts of ideology? Michael Novak has concluded that we have reached the end of ideology—that any form of ideology will now only serve to further increase the pluralism which has already reached unmanageable proportions. Other writers have taken to recommending that we make the most of the virtues of pluralism. For example, Clark Kerr wishes to replace the idea of a university, with its assumptions of the unity of truth and scholarship, with the idea of the multiversity, in which diversity and decentralization are the controlling institutional principles. And John Gardner, whose Common Cause is directed against the growing centralization of public power at the expense of the creativity of individuals and groups, warns against a national Establishment in which authority is vested for the management of an ideologically controlled society. Such writers are representatives of a

---

[3]Paul Munz, *Problems of Religious Knowledge*, (London: SCM Press, 1959), p. 177.

growing school of advocates of pluralism, who say that now our best recourse is to work consciously and deliberately in the direction of enhancing and preserving diversity in our social and intellectual life.

THE RECOVERY OF CONFIDENCE

The recovery of confidence requires demonstration of the applicability of a rational method in the consideration of moral and religious questions. Herein lies the crisis of our culture. The crudeness and profaneness of much of American life are related, either as symptoms or as cause, to the loss of confidence in the ideals of duty and of faith. Until there is a general recovery of the sense of the warrantability of these ideals, our individual and social experience will continue to drift in the direction of unrestrained pluralism.

The recovery of confidence will call for a kind of coming to oneself. There must be what Ortega y Gasset calls a "reform of intelligence." Our culture, says Ortega, must rediscover the true relations between action and contemplation so that our choices (of which we have so many in our complex world) may be guided by intelligence. Man must learn how to "stand inside himself," so that he may learn again how to control his world rather than be controlled by it. What is needed, as David Riesman has put it, is an increase of inner-directedness and a decrease of other-directedness. Ortega says:

> Few are the peoples who in these latter days still enjoy that tranquillity which permits one to choose the truth, to abstract oneself in meditations. Almost all the world is in tumult, and when man is beside himself he loses his most essential attribute: the possibility of meditating, or withdrawing into himself in order to come to terms with himself and define what it is he believes, what he truly esteems, and what he truly detests.
>
> In the world today a great thing is dying: it is truth, Why is it dying? For want of meditation. Without a certain margin of tranquillity, truth succumbs. Without a strategic retreat into the self, without vigilant thought, human life is impossible.[4]

The process of ideological clarification, as Plato emphasized, is dialectical. The movement of reason toward the fixation of belief is always in response to scepticism. Hence the alternation of doubt and

---

[4]José Ortega y Gasset, tr. William R. Trask, *Man and People* (New York: Norton, 1957), pp. 16, 35.

the resolution of doubt comprises the essential rhythm of the life of reason. Only we must not be misled by this rhythm into supposing that all the conclusions of rational inquiry are equally tenuous and unstable or that there is no progress in the dialectics of thought. As our knowledge expands and the coherence of our experience widens, we may become increasingly confident of the reliability of what we have found thus far. If then, new doubts arise at a new level of inquiry, that is only what we would expect as the point of departure for formation of a more adequate and more inclusive understanding. The dialectics of reason do not imply the relativity of opinion. Rather, as Plato says, dialectics are the process by which all knowledge is acquired.

The path to a recovery of confidence in ideology in matters of religious faith leads by way of an adequate theological understanding. The escape from pluralism is possible through a theological reconstruction which is based on the following principles:

- The propositions which comprise the essential content of Christian belief are not, in the ultimate sense, demonstrable by means of reason.
- The content of Christian belief, though not demonstrable by means of rational proof, is fully reconcilable with enlightened thought.
- The Christian faith is understandable; the message proclaimed by the Christian church has a determinate meaning, which can be comprehended by ordinary people and can be made the object of systematic study.
- The disagreements which arise among theologians in their attempts to analyze the meaning and implications of the Christian faith are, in principle, reconcilable by the application of a rational method of inquiry and criticism.

(1) An extraordinary scholarship has gone into the search for a rational confirmation of religious belief. The talent of the philosophers has developed assorted proofs for the existence of God and a profound scholarship, both scholastic and existentialist, has gone into the related attempt to integrate philosophy and theology. There are also the remarkable attempts of scholars, particularly within the last century, to reduce the range of pluralism in religion by the strategy, as it has been put, of finding religion among the religions, and to establish the universality of religiosity not only in the sense of its commonness amidst a variety of applications in belief and practice, but also in the sense of its derivation from an essential aspect of human nature. This

scholarship, too, is enviable in terms of its rigor, scope, and imaginativeness. One can respect, also, the scholarship which has sought to recast the traditional formulations of religion in the categories of scientific (rational) thought, to reduce religious beliefs to terms that permit rational verification of what is believed—to give us religion without revelation (as Huxley puts it) or religion without myth (as Bultmann puts it).

No one can be disparaging of this scholarship. The conclusion to which it leads, however, is negative. There is no way, by means of either inductive or deductive proof, to establish the truth of the essential propositions of the Christian religion. The ultimate issues of life as they are presented in the major religious and irreligious ideologies are simply not accessible to rational determination. In these matters persons of equal good will and equal reasonableness are simply going to continue to disagree.

(2) So the first presupposition of an adequate theological construction is the recognition that there are no adequate proofs which demonstrate the truth of the basic content of Christian faith. But if this was all that could be said pluralism would be the last word in religion. A second presupposition for theological reconstruction is that there is no inherent inconsistency between Christian faith and enlightened thought. I do not deny that there are apparent inconsistencies or that there are those who claim that there are irreducible and fundamental inconsistencies. But I believe that all such apparent inconsistencies and announced inconsistencies will disappear on closer and more comprehensive analysis.

I believe, for example, that there is no contradiction between any fairly interpreted statement of the Bible and any established principle of social or natural science. Any contradictoriness that might appear is explainable, I believe, as due either to misinterpretation of the biblical statement or to the incompleteness or unreliability of the scientific principle. Neither is there any contradictoriness within the system of biblical truth itself. Truth is one, and no one who adopts the Christian faith is required to compartmentalize his mind or to accept "two truths." The content of Christian faith is not inconsistent with any finding of rational inquiry in any area of human experience. Hence, even though reason may fail to produce the proofs which provide the sufficient condition for Christian belief, a Christian scholar can still achieve a coherent system of thought, one free of contradiction, which combines his faith and his scholarship.

(3) And there is a third presupposition which must be added: Although the Christian faith is indemonstrable, it is not incomprehensible. The communication of divine truth is not an ecstatic utterance, which cannot be understood by ordinary people. The gospel is not jibberish, nor is it a vague and unclear exposition, nor is it a chain of contradictory affirmations. The message which the Christian faith proclaims is an understandable message—that is, it is comprehensible to the human mind.

Wittgenstein says in the *Investigations* that even though the sense of a sentence may "leave this or that open, the sentence must nevertheless have *a* definite sense." When he says a sentence may "leave this or that open," I think he means that the question of the truth of the sentence may be open to question. But every meaningful sentence, he says, has a definite or determinate meaning. "An indefinite sense—that would really not be any sense *at all.*" Suppose one wanted to hold that a given sentence had a meaning, although its meaning was not quite clear. That, says Wittgenstein, would be like saying that a boundary was a boundary even though it was an indefinite boundary. It would be like saying: "I have locked him up tight in the room—only one door is left open." With that added qualification, it is no longer true, of course, that the man has really been locked in. So it is with any so-called meaningful utterance, the meaning of which is not specifiable.[5] Or as Wittgenstein puts it in the *Tractatus*: "Anything that can be thought can be thought clearly. Anything that can be said can be said clearly."[6]

There may be some poetic souls who will want to challenge such a requirement as narrow and dogmatic. But I am prepared to argue that Wittgenstein's logical requirement of the clarity and understandableness of meaningful expressions is applicable to the church's proclamation of its faith as well as to any other form of verbal communication. The medium of religious communication, too, is language; and if language is to be a vehicle of communication it must be understandable. "Faith comes from what is heard, and what is heard comes by the preaching of Christ." (Rom. 10:17)

---

[5]Ludwig Wittgenstein, tr. G. E. M. Anscombe, *Philosophical Investigations*, 3rd ed. (New York: Macmillan, 1958), para. 99.

[6]Ludwig Wittgenstein, trs. D. F. Pears and B. F. McGuinness, *Tractatus logico-philosophicus* (New York: Humanities Press, 1961), 4.112.

We must distinguish here between two senses of understanding, as that term may be applied to the proclamation of the Christian church. When I say "I do not understand what you are saying," I might mean either, "I do not grasp the meaning of your words" or "I do not find what you are saying acceptable or credible." These senses are often confused in complex discourse. Thus Descartes, for example, meant by a "clear and distinct perception," or a clear understanding, an intuitive apprehension of truth which was certain and undeniable. Similarly, some contemporary theologians have sought to *clarify* the meaning of the Christian proclamation in a mode which would make it *credible* to modern readers. But I wish to stress the importance of maintaining the distinction between understanding a declaration in the sense of grasping its *meaning*, on the one hand, and accepting its *truth*, on the other. I have said that I think reason is not competent to establish, by means of sufficient proof, the truth or credibility of what is said in the church's proclamation. On the other hand, however, I want now to declare that reason is fully competent to clarify the *meaning* and the *implications* of what is said. Indeed, I hold that the service of reason in the analysis and clarification of this meaning is indispensable for the effective communication of the gospel. This distinction, between understanding the *meaning* of a proposition and accepting (perhaps for good reasons) the *truth* of a proposition, is of the utmost importance in appreciating what reason can and cannot do in its analysis of the church's proclamation.

The recent attempts to make the preaching of the gospel credible to modern man by demythologizing it are, like earlier attempts to make Christianity more acceptable to the "scientific mind" by eliminating its supernatural elements, simply misplaced attempts. They stem in part from a failure to maintain the distinction between meaning and truth. In the case of the de-mythologizers the approach assumes that the function of the preacher of the gospel is not only that of making the gospel clear to modern readers, but also that of rendering it credible to modern readers. This assumption is further specified by reference to the assumed opposition between the first century world view, in terms of which the biblical message was originally constituted, and the scientific world view, in terms of which it is expected to be read in the twentieth century. Because of the contrast between these world views, it is assumed, the twentieth century reader needs an interpretation of the New Testament which frees it of its primitive and distracting categories. The demythologization of the New Testament is presumed to be the means by which it may come to terms with the conceptual scheme and belief system of modern man and so be made "understandable" in the sense of credible.

This new strategy of apologetics is no different, in terms of its inner logic, from those which have been tried (I believe without success) in preceding generations. The strategy assumes that all understanding occurs within a conceptual framework—what Bultmann calls a preunderstanding—a kind of screen, whose structure limits what can get through to our understanding and belief. The contention is that since the scientific world view is the one in which any contemporary reader will unavoidably have to construe the New Testament, only those aspects of the New Testament which are compatible with that scientific world view can be retained in the twentieth century proclamation of the church. When stated in these terms the whole enterprise is patently relativistic. The changing conceptual frameworks by which people determine the credibility of what they hear is made the norm by reference to which we determine both the meaning and the truth of what is said. The approach assumes the validity, or at least the unavoidability, of the conceptual framework which happens to prevail in contemporary culture and scholarship—as though that framework had anything whatever to do with the validity of the proclamation of the church as that is found in the New Testament. It is not thus that reason would ordinarily proceed in trying to make clear what the New Testament says—even though it might be a strategy to which some people might want to resort in seeking to rationalize what the New Testament says.

(4) This confusion of matters in the current literature of hermeneutics is illustrative of a deeper crisis confronted by theology. From the perspective of reason the situation in contemporary theology is a scandal. Two things about theological scholarship are scandalous. The first scandal is the exaggeration of its claims, as if it had to do with confirmation and verification of faith. From the point of view of the rational recognition of the limits of proof, the pretensions of Christian apologetics (which have their existentialist and liberal, as well as their fundamentalist forms) are an affront both to the ideals of reason and to the autonomy of the Word of God. Paul Holmer calls it a "slander upon the actual life of Christian belief."

But a second scandalous thing about theology is its pluralism. Radical disagreement among theologians with no recognized method for resolving their differences is a scandalous denial of the very possibility of theology as a science, as systematic inquiry guided by rational methods. The competition among theological partisans reminds Holmer of the kind of teaching he assimilated when he was a student of philosophy, "where reigning systems were thought to be irreducible and options were loosely paraded in the textbook culture we all imbibed and even taught. Much of the fecundity of theology looks like speculation, some like senseless system-mongering, an awful lot like talking without even doing the hard job of ascertaining the relevant criteria."[7]

That is a harsh indictment. Other observers would like to present the pluralism of theology as a virtue, and in any case as unavoidable. For example, Edward Schillebeeckx, the Dutch Catholic theologian has said of theological pluralism that it is only a sign of the limitations of all human knowledge:

> A theologian, or even a group of theologians working together, has no more than a limited and one-sided view of the totality of the reality of faith, both qualitatively and quantitatively. Because of this, no theologian can say that what he does not see is theologically irrelevant, or even less important than what he has himself discovered. In this way, theological pluralism is bound to develop more and more, and theologians are bound to realize that, on the basis of the factors I have mentioned, pluralism is simply inevitable and, in this sense, impossible to overcome.[8]

Differences of viewpoint from which to construe the rich meaning and varied implications of the Christian faith may be enriching and edifying. Nor would reason be offended by a complex and many-faceted investigation of a complex problem in which thought proceeds dialectically through a series of antinomies which eventuate, through the application of a rational method, in a coherent synthesis. What is scandalous is not disagreement among scholars, but the inadequacy of a method for resolving scholarly disagreement. It is the crisis of method which is at the heart of the present scandal of theological pluralism.

---

[7]Paul L. Holmer, *The Grammar of Faith* (San Francisco: Harper, 1978), p. x.

[8]Edward Schillebeeckx, tr. N. D. Smith, *The Understanding of Faith* (New York: Seabury, 1974), p. 51.

The outlines of an adequate method which will permit theology to escape from pluralism have been developed by the school of theologians who worked during the second quarter of the twentieth century at the University of Lund (Sweden). This development was associated with the names of Ragnar Bring, Gustaf Aulen, and Anders Nygren. Their work needs to be adapted to the context of theological research in the English-speaking world, which is somewhat different from that of Scandinavian scholarship. But the main features of their theological method are indispensable for placing theology on a firm rational basis. One of these features is rigorous attention to the traditon of Christian faith and thought, centering on the essential elements of the gospel as proclaimed in the Christian church. The consideration of this tradition, including analysis of both its main themes or motifs and its logical implications, involves the application of a rational method of historical research. The other main feature of the Lundensian method involves the separation of theology from speculative philosophy or metaphysics—or, to put the matter positively, the application of a *critical* philosophical method, the method of linguistic analysis, in the study of the meaning and implications of the Christian faith. It is, I believe, through the application of such a method, with these two major elements, that the scandal of theological pluralism may be ended.

THE FAITH OF A CHRISTIAN SCHOLAR

The concern of this exploration of the idea of a Christian college has been to consider the extent to which rational inquiry and a coherent view of educational processes can be combined with Christian belief. The book springs from a deep faith in the possibility of overcoming pluralism and achieving unity in one's understanding of basic values.

In the midst of an age of pluralism, we must persist in the search for ideology, yet without dogmatism. In this search the Christian college must insist on the freedom and openness of inquiry. There can be no arbitrary restrictions on the mind, no prohibition of doubt, no sacred authority. At the same time the Christian college must reject the notion of the relativity of truth and value, lest the whole search be rendered vain and fruitless. We must believe that truth is so if we are to have any reason to struggle, through the rigors of honest inquiry, to possess it. The possibility of ideology, I have argued, presupposes the instability of pluralism; but the avoidance of dogmatism, on the other hand, presupposes a dialectical progression in the direction of unity in thought by way of an open, free, and uninhibited consideration of alternatives. The problem of ideology in an age of pluralism is, then, another form of the classic problem of freedom in human life and thought.

What I have been recommending is the recovery of confidence in the power of reason to bring unity to thought; and I have been urging scholarship not to despair too quickly when it finds itself in the midst of pluralism. Call it a hope, call it the faith of a scholar—call it a pious wish, if you like—but I am prepared to declare my conviction that out of the deepest dialectical confrontation with a plurality of intellectual options can arise coherence in the total system of beliefs.

The dialectics of ideology versus pluralism lie at the center of the idea of a Christian college, in its practical as well as its philosophical expression. The idea of the Christian college is inherently an ideology. The idea is dominated by the ideal of *reason*, on the one hand, and by an ideal conception of *Christian faith*, on the other. In respect to both sets of controlling ideals, the Christian college must refuse to allow pluralism to be the last word about human culture. Yet the idea of freedom is no less essential to the idea of a Christian college. Ideology without freedom is not only a philosophical monstrosity, but also an educational self-contradiction.

My purpose in this book has been to declare my belief that the Christian colleges can meet the challenge presented by the fragmentization and pluralization of thought. Ideology without dogmatism, rational persuasion without indoctrination, orthodoxy without obscurantism—these are the presuppositions of a program of education which is Christian and yet free. There are two kinds of restraints on the freedom of the human mind: either the tyranny of ignorance or restrictions on the right to inquire. Both forms of restraint are opposed to the idea of a Christian college. The Christian college seeks the freedom which comes from possession of the truth; at the same time it understands that the pursuit of truth can never be limited by arbitrary or dogmatic authority. The aim of Christian higher education is freedom in the highest sense of that term. And there is no higher calling or responsibility than to be united to work in the direction of implementing a program of education which is both resolutely Christian and free.

BIBLIOGRAPHY

Astin, Alexander W.; and Lee, Calvin T. *The Invisible Colleges: A Profile of Small Private Colleges with Limited Resources.* New York: McGraw Hill, 1971.

Averill, Lloyd. *A Strategy for the Protestant College.* Philadelphia: Westminister Press, 1966.

Baly, Denis. *Academic Illusions.* Greenwich, CT: Seabury Press, 1961.

Bender, Richard, ed. *The Church Related College Today: Anachronism or Opportunity?.* United Methodist Church, General Board of Education, 1971.

Brown, Kenneth. *Not Minds Alone: Some Frontiers of Christian Education.* New York: Harper, 1954.

Buttrick, George A. *Biblical Thought and the Secular University.* Baton Rouge: Louisiana State University Press, 1960.

Buttrick, George A. *Faith and Education.* New York: Abingdon-Cokesbury Press, 1952.

Calvin College Curriculum Study Committee. *Christian Liberal Arts Education.* Grand Rapids: Eerdmans Publishing Co., 1970.

Coleman, Albert John. *The Task of the Christian in the University.* New York: Association Press, 1947.

Ditmanson; Hong; and Quanbeck. *Christian Faith and the Liberal Arts.* Minneapolis; Augsburg Publishing House, 1960.

Doescher, Waldemar. *The Church College in Today's Culture.* Minneapolis: Augsburg Publishing House, 1963.

Faculty Christian Fellowship. *Faith-Learning Studies: A Series Examining the Academic Disciplines.* Published by the Faculty Christian Fellowship, 1964.

I. Charles S. McCoy, *The Meaning of Theological Reflection.*
II. W. Taylor Stevenson, *History.*
III. Joseph W. Havens, *Psychology.*

IV. Thomas F. Green, *Education.*
V. Dante Germino, *Political Science.*
VI. Philip N. Joranson, *Conservation.*
VII. John W. Dixon, Jr., *Criticism.*
VIII. Earl A. Holmer, *Business Administration.*
IX. Cameron P. Hall, *Economics.*
X. Arnold S. Nash, *Sociology.*

Fairchild, Hoxie N. *Religious Perspectives in College Teaching.* New York: Ronald Press, 1952.

Ferré, Nels F. S. *Christian Faith and Higher Education.* New York: Harper, 1954.

Fisher, Ben C., ed. *New Pathways: A Dialogue in Christian Higher Education.* Macon, GA: Mercer University Press, 1980.

Fuller, Edmund, ed. *The Christian Idea of Education.* Yale University Press, 1957.

Gaebelein, Frank E. *Christian Education in a Democracy: The Report of the NAE Committee.* New York: Oxford University Press, 1951.

Gauss, Christian, ed. *The Teaching of Religion in American Higher Education.* New York: Ronald Press, 1951.

Greeley, Andrew. *From Backwater to Mainstream: A Profile of Catholic Higher Education.* New York: McGraw-Hill, 1969.

Grueningen, J. P. von, ed. *Towards a Christian Philosophy of Higher Education.* Philadelphia: Westminister Press, 1957.

Hartt, Julian. *Theology and the Church in the University.* Philadelphia: Westminster Press, 1969.

Holmes, Arthur F. *The Idea of a Christian College.* Grand Rapids: Eerdmans Publishing Co., 1975.

Keeton, Morris; and Hilberry, Conrad. *Struggle and Promise: A Future for Colleges.* New York: McGraw-Hill, 1969.

Kraemer, Hendrik. *The Communication of the Christian Faith.* Philadelphia: Westminster Press, 1956.

LeFevre, Perry. *The Christian Teacher.* New York: Abingdon Press, 1958.

Limbert, Paul M., ed. *College Teaching and Christian Values.* New York: Association Press, 1951.

Lowry, Harold. *The Mind's Adventure: Religion and Higher Education.* Philadelphia: Westminster Press, 1950.

Mayhew, Lewis B. *The Smaller Liberal Arts College.* Washington, D. C.: Center for Applied Research in Education, 1962.

Miller, Alexander. *Faith and Learning; Christian Faith and Higher Education in the Twentieth Century.* New York: Association Press, 1960.

Moberly, Walter H. *The Crisis in the University.* London: SCM Press, 1949.

Mundahl, Anne and Tom. *Vision and Revision: Old Roots and New Routes for Lutheran Higher Education.* American Lutheran Church, Division for College and University Services, 1977.

Pace, C. Robert. *Education and Evangelism: A Profile of Protestant Colleges.* Carnegie Commission on Higher Education; New York: McGraw-Hill, 1972.

Parsonage, Robert R. *Church Related Higher Education: Perceptions and Perspectives,* Valley Forge PA: Judson Press, 1978.

Pattillo, Manning; and MacKenzie, Donald. *Church-Sponsored Education.* Report of the Danforth Commission. American Council on Education, 1966.

Pelikan, Jaroslav. *The Christian Intellectual.* New York: Harper, 1965.

Pelikan, Jaroslav J., et. al. *Religion and the Universtiy.* University of Toronto Press, 1964.

Ramm, Bernard. *The Christian College in the Twentieth Century.* Grand Rapids: Eerdmans Publishing Co., 1963.

Saint Olaf College Self-Study Committee. *Integration in the Christian Liberal Arts College.* St. Olaf College Press, 1956.

Scaff, Marilee K., ed. *Perspectives on a College Church.* New York: Association Press, 1961.

Schilling, Harold K. *The New Consciousness in Science and Religion.* Philadelphia; United Church Press, 1973.

Schilling, Harold K. *Science and Religion: An Interpretation of Two Communities.* New York: Scribners, 1962.

Shuster, George N. *Catholic Education in a Changing World.* New York: Holt, Rinehart, and Winston, 1967.

Smith, Huston.*The Purposes of Higher Education.* New York: Harper, 1955.

Trueblood, D. Elton. *The Idea of a College.* New York: Harper, 1959.

Walsh, Chad. *Campus Gods on Trial.* New York: Macmillan, 1953.

Westerhoff, John H., ed. *The Church's Ministry in Higher education.* New York: United Ministries in Higher Education Communications Office, 1978.

Wilder, Amos N. *Liberal Learning and Religion.* New York: Harper, 1951.

Williams, George Hunston. *Wilderness and Paradise in Christian Thought: The Biblical Experience of the Desert in the History of Christianity and the Paradise Theme in the Theological Idea of the University.* New York: Harper, 1962.

Williams, George Hunston. *The Theological Idea of the University.* New York: National Council of Churches, Commission on Higher Education, 1958.

A Selection of Articles on Christian Faith in Higher Education from *The Christian Scholar*

(Published by the Department of Higher Education of the National Council of Churches)

Two Special Issues

1. "The Christian College and Its Responsibilities in American Life Today," First Quadrennial Convocation of Christian Colleges (1954), Volume 37, Autumn 1954.

2. "The Vocation of the Christian College," Second Quadrennial Convocation of Christian Colleges (1958), Volume 41, Autumn 1958.

Volume 36 (1953)

No. 1, March 1953
Daniel D. Williams, "Christian Freedom and Academic Freedom."
Kenneth I. Brown, "The Terrible Responsibility of the Teacher."

No. 2, June 1953
Chad Walsh, "Flat Minds, Kind Hearts, and Fine Arts."
William G. Pollard, "The Place of Science in Religion."
Kirtley F. Mather, "The Natural Sciences and the Christian Faith."

No. 3, September 1953
Theodore M. Greene, "Christianity, Culture, and Academic Integrity."
E. Harris Harbison, "Christian Belief and Intellectual Freedom."
Howard Hong, "Toward a Christian Objectivity."
Rene de Visme Williamson, "The Christian in the Social Sciences."

No. 4, December 1953
Will Herberg, "Toward a Biblical Theology of Education."

Volume 37 (1954)

No. 1, March 1954
Walter E. Wiest, "Education for Freedom: An Interpretation of the Christian College."
William H. Poteat, John Dillenberger, Roger L. Shinn, and Charles E. Sheedy, "Symposium: Can and Should a College Be Christian?"
Howard B. Jefferson, "Concerning a Theology of Education."

No. 2, June 1954
J. V. Langmead Casserley, "The Theology of Education."
A. John Coleman, "The Christian Task in the University."

No. 3, September 1954
John A. Hutchison, "Theology and Education."
Seward Hiltner, "The Christian as Psychologist."
L. Charles Birch, "Interpreting the Lower in Terms of the Higher."
Willis B. Glover, "The Vocation of a Christian Scholar."
John W. Dixon, Jr., "Basic Education in a Christian College."

No. 4, December 1954
Roland M. Frye, "A Christian Approach to Literature."
Edward J. McShane, "The Modern Conception of the Universe and Christian Faith."
Philip N. Joranson, "Biological Development and the Christian Doctrine of Man."

Volume 38 (1955)

No. 1, March 1955
Curtis W. R. Larson, "The Intellectual Crisis of the Colleges."

No. 4, December 1955
Robert E. Fitch, "Christian Faith and the Inquiring Mind."
John H. Hallowell, "Christian Apologetics and the College Campus."

Volume 39 (1956)

No. 2, June 1956
John E. Smith, "The Task of the Christian in Philosophy."

No. 3, September 1956
William L. Kolb, "Religion and Values in Sociological Theory."

No. 4, December 1956
Gordon D. Kaufman, "Theological Dogma and Historical Work."
Harold P. Ford, "Religious Commitment and Foreign Policy Decision."

Volume 40 (1957)

No. 1, March 1957
James D. Bryden, "Specialization and Secularism in Higher Education."

No. 2, June 1957
Richard N. Bender, "On Being a Christian Professor."

No. 3, September 1957
Wilber G. Katz, "Law, Christianity, and the University."
Samuel Enoch Stumpf, "Theology and Jurisprudence."
E. Benjamin MacKinnon, "The Effect of Religious Principles on Lawyers' Ethical Problems."

No. 4, December 1957
Amos N. Wilder, "Christianity and the Arts."
Geddes MacGregor, "Christian Discrimination in the Realm of Aesthetic Judgment."
John W. Dixon, Jr., "On the Possibility of a Christian Criticism of the Arts."
Tom F. Driver, "The Arts and the Christian Evangel."

Volume 41 (1958)

No. 2, June 1958
Richard N. Bender, "'Illumined' Liberal Education."
Nels F. S. Ferré, "Contemporary Theology and Higher Education."

No. 3, September 1958
Harold K. Schilling, "On Relating Science and Religion."
John H. Robertson, "Christian Faith and Science" (Review article).

Volume 42 (1959)

No. 2, June 1959
Ordway, Tead, "Value Emphasis in College Teaching."
Ralph W. Condee, "Preaching or Teaching: The Professor's Ethics and the Student's Values."
D. Elton Trueblood, "The Encounter With Excellence."
Theodore D. Lockwood, "The Role of Christianity in Modern History."
Jacques Ellul, "Concerning the Christian Attitude Toward Law."

No. 3, September 1959

J. Donald Butler, "The Church, the College, and Human Values."

No. 4, December 1959

Harry R. Garvin, "Religion and the Arts."

Volume 43 (1960)

No. 1, March 1960
Sydney E. Ahlstrom, "Toward the Idea of a Church College."

No. 2, Summer 1960
Wiliam R. Mueller, "Invitation to Theological Learning."

No. 4, Winter 1960
Charles S. McCoy, "Theological Tensions in Academic Life."

Volume 44 (1961)

No. 2, Summer 1961
Warren Ashby, "The Christian Teacher."

No. 3, Fall 1961
Joseph D. Havens, "Psychology, the Problematic Science."

Volume 45 (1962)

No. 1, Spring 1962
Jaroslav Pelikan, "The Christian as an Intellectual."
John Wild, "The Christian and Contemporary Philosophy."
Jeffrey Russell, "Religious Commitment and Historical Writing."
Christopher Dawson, "On the Place of Religious Study in Education."

No. 2, Summer 1962
George A. Buttrick, et. al., "Toward a Philosophy of the Church-Related University."

Volume 50 (1967)—last issue of the journal

No. 1, Spring 1967
Philip H. Phenix, "Liberal Learning and the Practice of Freedom."
J. A. Martin, Jr., "Christians and the University: Retrospect and Prospect."

No. 2, Summer 1967
Hubert C. Noble, "Reappraising the Role and Responsibility of the Church-Related College."

INDEX

Academic Freedom, 35-41
Access to Education, 163, 164
Accreditation, 193
Accuracy, 141, 142
Adelson, Joseph, 130
Administration, 20, 38, 171-84
Admission Policies, 153-60, 209, 210
Aesthetic Experience, 68, 99, 100
Affective Goals, 67-72, 118, 119
American Association of University Professors, 39
Analytical Method, 64
Apologetics, 65
Application of Ideas, 55
Aquinas, St. Thomas, 64
Arendt, Hannah, 44
Aristotle, 218
Arnold, Matthew, 132, 143
Articulateness, 142
Art, 97-101
Assurance 77, 142, 143
Astin, Alexander W., 6
Augustine, St., 32
Aulén, Gustaf, 34, 35, 229
Axelrod, Joseph, 130, 131, 135

Baly, Denis, 10, 124
Barzun, Jacques, 88, 124-26
Becker, Howard, 149
Berger, Peter, 218
Biblical Studies, 103, 104
Biblicism, 22, 23, 33
Bloom, Benjamin, 140
Bonhoeffer, Dietrich, 147
Brauer, Jerald C., 8, 113
Bring, Ragnar, 229
Bultmann, Rudolf, 224

Calvin, John, 26, 100
Campbell, E. Fay, 180, 181
Carlyle, Thomas, 11
Catholicism, 3, 34, 228
Certification, 140
Character, 71, 72
Chickering, Arthur, 72-77
Christian College Consortium, 182
Church and State, 203, 204
Civil Rights Act of 1964, 207-209
Clarity of Religious Propositions, 65, 225, 226
Cognitive Goals, 64-67, 118, 119
Coleridge, Samuel, 86
Communications, 87-89
Community in College, 148-55
Competence, 105, 106, 173
Competitive Challenge, 7
Concentration in Learning, 137
Conformity, 70, 153, 162, 163
Core Curriculum, 85, 115
Council for Independent Colleges, 177
Cox, Harvey, 158, 159
Creation, 33
Credit System, 50, 102
Creedalism, 33, 34, 36
Critical Thinking, 86, 87
Criticism, Literary, 97
Culture, 44, 45, 96
Cupitt, Don, 219

Curriculum, 79-82, 105-21

Danforth Commission, 2, 17, 18, 129, 172, 174
Data, 53, 54
Decision Making, 71, 119, 126
Decisiveness in Teaching, 142, 143
DeKoster, Lester, 206
Demythologizing, 226, 227
Departmentalization, 179
Descartes, René, 226
Dewey, John, 48-57, 73, 131, 132, 184, 188, 189
Dialectical Instruction, 127, 151, 155-57
Didactic Teaching, 135
Discipline, 46, 61, 125, 126, 141, 153
Discrimination, 158, 207-10
Dogmatism, 61, 62, 104, 127, 128, 230
Dodds, Harold W., 174
Doubt, 39, 40
Durant, Will and Ariel, 11
Dynamic Faith, 8

Ecumenism, 27, 34, 35
Edman, V. Raymond, 206
Education and Experience, 51, 53, 124, 125, 138
Education and Growth, 48-50
Education Without Instruction, 123-30
Efficiency, 181-84
Elective System, 112, 115
Elliott, George R., 80
Eurich, Alvin, 131
Ethical Neutrality, 67
Evaluation, 121, 139-43
Everson v. McCollum, 198
Evidence, 57, 58
Evocative Teaching, 135, 136
Excellence, 9, 10
Existentialism, 31, 65

Faculty Competence, 5, 6
Failure of Nerve, 10, 79, 80
Faith, Flexibility of, 35, 36, 40
Federal Interest in Higher Education, 191-96, 205-10
Ferré, Nels F. S., 8, 10, 16, 35, 36, 37, 68, 160, 161
Fine Arts, 97-101
First Amendment, 200-204
Fragmentation, 19, 20, 48, 58, 230
Frankel, Charles, 62
Freedom of Inquiry, 31, 35-41, 56, 61, 63
Fundamentals of Christian Belief, 25-33

Gardner, John, 221
Geer, Blanche, 149
General Education, 79-104, 109
God,
  Doctrine of, 29, 30, 32
  Knowledge of, 64
Grading, 139-43
Greeley, Andrew, 6
Growth, 48-50, 67, 68

Harris, Seymour, 204
Harvard Report on General Education, 16
Higher Education Act of 1965, 191, 195, 197, 199
Higher Education Facilities Act of 1963, 191, 194, 201
Highet, Gilbert, 138, 144, 145
Historical Studies, 83, 89-91
Holmer, Paul L., 226, 227
Holmes, Oliver Wendell, 62
Hook, Sidney, 205
Howe, Mark De Wolfe, 204
Human Behavior, 91, 92
Humanistic Studies, 83, 84, 95
Hunt, Everett Lee, 155, 156
Hurst v. McNair, 201
Hutchins, Robert M., 48
Huxley, Thomas, 224

Ideas, 54-58
Ideology, 218-30
Imagination, 61, 62, 95
Inerrancy, Biblical, 22,33
Individuality, 73, 119, 120, 161, 162
Institution, College as, 184-89
Instructional Methods, 56, 120, 121
Integration, 41, 47, 63, 64, 81, 86, 97, 105-10, 118
Intellect, 36, 46, 87
Interinstitutional Cooperation, 182, 183

Jacobi, Friedrich H., 41
Johnson, Lyndon B., 194-96, 199, 200

Kant, Immanuel, 185
Kennedy, John F., 197-99, 206-208
Kerr, Clark, 193, 194, 205, 211, 221

Kierkegaard, Soren, 144, 145
Klapper, Paul, 133
Knowledge, 61-67, 69, 105

Language, 34, 87-89
Lee, Calvin T., 6
Liberal Education, 45-47, 49, 54, 59-62, 82-85, 107-10
Library Holdings, 5
Lijon, Ernest M., 71
Literature, 95-97
Little, Clarence Cook, 156
Little, J. Kenneth, 212, 213
Loomer, Bernard, 9, 17, 150
Lowry, Harold, 15
Luthardt, Christopher Ernest, 28, 41
Luther, Martin, 26, 28, 33, 99, 100

MacIver, Robert M., 39
MacKenzie, Donald, 3, 17, 18, 129, 172, 174
Major/Minor, 106
Man, Nature of, 29, 32, 90, 91
Maturity, 72-77, 165, 166
Mayhew, Lewis B., 6, 160, 162, 171, 172, 176
McCoy, Presley C., 150
McGrath, Earl, 2
Meaning, 226
Metaphysics, 229
Methods of Teaching, 56, 120, 121, 132, 135-37
Moral Education, 69-72
Moral Function of Education, 184-89
Motivation of Learning, 137-39
Munz, Paul, 221

Naturalism, 93, 94
Natural Science, 92-95
Necessary Doctrines, 26
Newman, John Henry, 16, 45-48, 149
Novak, Michael, 221
Nygren, Anders, 229

Objectives, 133, 134, 140, 141
Ontological Method, 64
Organization of Learning, 132-34
Ortega y Gasset, José, 89, 90, 112, 122

Pace, C. Robert, 6
Pattillo, Manning M., Jr., 3, 17, 18, 129, 172, 174
Parsimony, 110-15
Paterson, W. P., 22, 23, 26, 28, 29
Peirce, Charles Sanders, 220
Persuasion, 88
Philanthropy, 126, 143, 213, 214
Philosophical Studies, 84
Philosophy, 95-97
Physical Education, 101, 102
Plato, 110, 218, 222, 223
Pluralism, 218-30
Problem Solving, 52
Professionalism, 47, 61, 80, 103
Private Colleges and Federal Aid, 192, 196-202
Protestantism, 22, 24, 34, 90, 103, 128, 221
Public Relations, 179, 180
Public Service, 214, 215
Purpose in Education, 43

Quality, 2-6

Reason and Religion, 86, 87, 219-30
Redemption, 30-32, 91, 147
Reformers, 22, 99
Relativism, 217-22
Religion, 17, 18, 102-104, 166, 167
Remnant, 7, 8
Rhythm of Education, 60, 119
Riesman, David, 44, 222
Roemer v. Board of Public Works, 202
Rule of Faith, 21-25

St. Olaf College, 114
Salvation, 30-32, 91
Schillebeeckx, Edward, 228
Schilling, S. Paul, 27
Schleiermacher, Friedrich, 23, 29
Scholasticism, 65
Schweitzer, Albert, 18, 86
Science and Religion, 25, 94, 224
Sectarianism, and Federal Aid, 196-215
Secularism, 12
Selection in Education, 112, 134
Self-Discipline, 71, 134
Shillito, E., 99
Social Sciences, 91, 92
Socrates, 55, 83, 125, 127, 128, 130, 218
Solbert, Richard W., 90
Sophists, 57, 217,
Specialization, 59, 81, 105-10
Structure in Curriculum, 105, 134
Student-Centered Teaching, 131, 136

Student Culture, 149, 150
Student Participation in Governance, 167, 168
Student Personnel Administration, 160-63
Student Rights, 163-65
Subjectivism, 23-25
Survival of Christian Colleges, 8

Teacher
    as Artist, 136
    as Learner, 55
    as Model, 130, 131
Teacher, Christian, 144-145
Teacher, Functions of, 130-43
Technology, 93
Terminal Education, 144, 145
Theological Basis of Christian Higher Education, 21
Theological Studies, 84, 85
Theological Method, 33, 34, 229
Thinking, 52-56, 116
Tillich, Paul, 24
Tilton v. Richardson, 201
Tradition of College, 138
Trueblood, D. Elton, 15, 16
Truth, 87
Tuition at Christian Colleges, 5
Types of Christian College, 2-4
Types of Scholarly Disciplines, 114

Universities, Dominance of, 111, 160, 176
Uses
    of Education, 47, 60, 138
    of Ideas, 58
    of Knowledge, 60, 69

Values and Education, 68, 69, 76, 77, 115-21
Van Doren, Mark, 113
Vocation and Education, 107-110
Vocation of Teacher, 143-45

Waste in Higher Education, 110-115, 182
Weber, Max, 90, 128
Wesley, John, 26-28
Whitehead, Alfred North, 57-61, 63, 68, 69, 82, 97, 98, 112, 113, 134, 135, 157, 168, 181
Whiting, Albert H., 148, 149, 153
Willcox, Alanson W., 198, 199
Wilson, John, 117, 118
Wilson, Logan, 213
Wittgenstein, Ludwig, 225
Worship, 99, 100, 151, 152

MUP THE SEARCH FOR EXCELLENCE

Composition was by Mercer Press Services, Macon, Georgia:
designed by Jane Denslow,
the text was "read" by a Hendrix Typereader II OCR Scanner
and formatted by Janet Middlebrooks on an Addressograph Multigraph Comp/Set 5404, then paginated on an A/M Comp/Set 4510.

Design and production specifications:
typeface—11/13 Times Roman;
text papers—60 pound Warrens Olde Style;
endpapers—Multicolor Antique, Bombay;
cover—3 piece, spine Roxite A 49245 (blue) vellum finished; boards Holliston Sail Cloth 15047 (blue)

Printing (offset lithography) was by Mercer Press Services, Macon, Georgia.